60

DONATED BY

META SIDDENS

Famous Writers Course

Famous Writers School Inc.
Westport Connecticut

Famous Writers Course

Principles
of good writing

Volume II

Contents

IV section

V section

Principles
of good writing

Volume II

Section IV

Lesson twelve

Principles of good writing

Four forms
of writing

As a writer begins to put words on paper, he is aware of a specific goal, a definite purpose. The intention varies considerably from writer to writer and from time to time.

One writer may wish to describe a character or the setting of a story. Another may wish to tell a tale of adventure. Another may want to explain certain facts or theories to his reader. A fourth plans to present arguments to settle a debate.

These four general purposes are basic to all writing. Usually the writer intends to accomplish more than one purpose—occasionally he has all four in mind. In writing, these four purposes take on names which may seem ponderous and awkward to you but which have come to be accepted labels for the basic forms of writing. They are:

1. *Description* (how to describe things)
2. *Narration* (how to tell about events)
3. *Exposition* (how to explain facts)
4. *Argument* (how to argue about ideas)

Take the word *Exposition,* for example. A far better name for it in most cases would be *explanation.* But traditionally this whole area of writing is labeled Exposition; for the sake of clarity we'll go along with it, as we did with some of the complicated but necessary labels in basic grammar.

In succeeding Lessons we shall go into greater detail on each of the four standard writing forms, one at a time. Here, however, our purpose is quickly to refresh your mind, to show what the general distinctions are and to give samples of each, with our comments.

Following the detailed Lessons on Description, Narration, Exposition and Argument, we shall also discuss Dialogue—a variety of writing which doesn't seem to fall precisely into any one of the four basic forms but encompasses them all and has its own peculiarities and problems.

When a writer seeks to give his reader a clear word-picture or background, scene or character, he uses the form known as Description. When he wishes to tell the reader of the movement of a story, he employs Narration. If the writer's object is to explain things to the reader, Exposition is used. If the intention is to persuade the reader, to make him change his attitude, then the form is called Argument.

Seldom is a piece of writing devoted to one intention only—in its pure form. Think back over some of the things you've read, fiction and non-fiction, and you'll readily understand that forms of writing are usually combined to create the finished product.

Forms of writing
are usually combined

For instance, one magazine article on polio vaccine used all four forms. It *described* the vaccine, its discoverer's background and physical appearance, the laboratory and the triumphant scene of the Ann Arbor announcement. The author *narrated* how Dr. Jonas Salk found the vaccine after agonizing years of trial and error. He *explained* the ways in which polio had been reduced through use of the vaccine, how the preventive measure was administered, the prospects for wide distribution. Finally, through sheer weight of evidence, the writer *argued* that everyone under the age of forty should be vaccinated against polio, basing his case on the facts presented throughout the article.

In fiction (and in articles, news or advertising copy) all four forms are sometimes employed, and Dialogue besides. Longer fiction allows the author room in which to describe over and over again, to narrate almost continuously, to explain ideas, situations and backgrounds, and to persuade the reader of the value of the story. In novels by great Russian writers—Dostoevski and Tolstoy—page after page is devoted to philosophical argument, usually at the end of the book. This sort of summing up isn't quite as popular nowadays, but the Argument, the persuasion of the novelist's main idea or theme, is made in all novels, however subtly.

In discussing the major forms of writing in this Lesson we will give you examples from the works of Faith Baldwin, Kenneth Roberts, Vincent Sheean, Mignon Eberhart and William Makepeace Thackeray. We're not assuming that you will equal the writing of these professionals. But that is not the purpose of the excerpts. We merely present the fiction and non-fiction samples, along with our comment, so you will be exposed to professional prose and see how successful authors use the different forms of writing.

As we have said before, reading is an excellent aid for the student writer—reading in all fields on all subjects. By reading, you learn, perhaps unconsciously, certain things about the craft of writing, for there's no better way to achieve success than to observe the work of successful people. The examples given in this Lesson, plus the marginal or parenthetical comments we have supplied, should help to guide you as you practice the major forms of writing in your own beginning efforts.

The descriptive form

The descriptive form in writing always involves the senses and what they do to stimulate the reader as he reacts to words. There are five general sources for descriptive writing and they are the things you

see . . . hear . . . smell . . . taste . . . touch.

Description stirs
the reader's senses

There is also the all-inclusive personal reaction to what you see, hear, smell, taste and touch, and this reaction is what we call our feelings or emotional reactions. In all cases of Description, our six general sources are the five human senses plus our general reactions, emotions and feelings. When we describe, we call in the physical world around us through our senses.

These sources of Description stimulate in the reader's mind a series of reactions. Because the reader has the same five senses, he should know what the writer is trying to say to him.

How well the writer's Description registers with the reader depends on how clearly the writer has translated to paper his own personal reaction or feelings to what he has seen, heard, smelled, tasted and touched, or imagined his characters to have seen, heard, smelled, tasted and touched.

Fiction writers must be especially *sensitive* (aware of the senses), since without sensitivity there is no possible way of bringing their imagination to the printed page. Creative writers must create Description so that their words stimulate in their readers an expression of the very sense reactions they themselves felt in their innermost imagination.

The descriptive form in fiction may be something like these paragraphs from *American Family* by Faith Baldwin. In this novel she is writing about David, the hero, who is beginning his medical training in a 19th-Century hospital. In a cleverly woven descriptive pattern, Miss Baldwin describes not only the place he works in but his reactions to it:

Use of familiar, simple words to describe simple, familiar things is highly effective:

(a) "striped uniforms rustling, stiff with starch, the round cap perched on hair that was brown or black or red.
(b) "in the torrid operating room with its odor of carbolic spray."

Note the reader's reaction to the senses: sight (color of the nurses' uniforms), sound (stiff rustling of the starch), smell (carbolic spray). At other points the senses of taste and touch are invoked.

The knife drawing "so quick, so sure a line" involves the sense of touch, the "feeling" of a sharp knife on the skin.

Description requires facts. And facts require observation.

As usual, and easily, David made friends. Men liked him, and women smiled at him. There were pretty women among the nurses, the big white aprons spotless, their grayish blue, striped uniforms rustling, stiff with starch, the round cap perched on hair that was brown or black or red. Social intercourse between the young internes and the nurses was not encouraged, but it flourished in secret, as must any sweet and forbidden fruit. Therefore, some of David's gayer colleagues laughed at him for his reluctance, and his professional manner.

But if he had no heroines at the time, he had heroes in plenty. He would follow the doctors on their rounds, listening, watching. He would stand almost breathless, as he had stood at the New Haven Hospital, in the torrid operating room with its odor of carbolic spray, and watch the surgeon moving deftly, with skill and precision. For the time would come when he could not watch but could only pray, in some remote part of his intelligence, for then it would be his hand that held the knife steadily and drew so quick, so sure a line upon the field of operation, and his eyes which, his life concentrated into their blazing blue, would watch and decide and send the message to brain and muscle.

Over the table the gaslight flickered. It was not enough. There were candles taped into bottles to augment the illumination; and it was the duty of one person to see that the fumes of the anesthetic did not rise and explode in the tapering flames.

The service was rotary: medicine, obstetrics, surgery. During his last six months he would be required to serve courses in erysipelas, obstetrics and acute alcoholism, and would during this time be resident within the hospital instead of, as now, boarding in the district.

The hours were long and tedious. At night the gas-lighted wards were eerie. Wails broke the silence, sobs, the voice of terror, the voice of pain. Oaths, prayers . . .

It was only recently, he learned from a graduate nurse, that the gas was permitted to burn all night. At a not very distant date in the past two candles were permitted each ward per week—other necessary candles must be supplied by the nurses themselves, out of their twelve dollars a month allowance. For the dimly burning gas had been turned off entirely by the captain of the night watch, at five A.M.

Senses of sight, smell and hearing are invoked.

The gas-lighted setting is well described, eerie, terrifying. The readers' own reactions, their personal feelings become a tool of Description.

In his non-fiction autobiography, *I Wanted to Write,* novelist Kenneth Roberts describes Newspaper Row in Boston as he saw it as a cub reporter:

Boston was fertile ground in those days for an inquiring and aspiring reporter, even though financial rewards were insignificant. The city was almost as small as the rewards, and a reporter could get around it nearly as easily as he could make a tour of Kennebunkport, Maine.

Newspaper Row, home of the *Globe, Post, Transcript, Record, Journal* and *Herald,* was contained within a few cozy, grimy blocks on lower Washington Street, a section decorated by tall newspaper blackboards on which employees wrote, in chalk and at considerable length, the news of the day.

Those chalk writers had a profound attraction for me, yet filled me with discomfort. They seemed symbolical of something I disliked to contemplate: scrawling, scrawling, scrawling, day after day after day after day after day, only to have their work destroyed every night, wiped from existence, washed out—never a word saved.

This portion is describing a city. This involves the senses of sight and touch, sound and smell.

The sense of sight and, probably, sound.

Now we are confronted with Description of human beings for the first time. The repeated word "scrawling" is effective here.

The narrative form

Narration is typical of fiction, yet non-fiction writers use the form constantly to move their explanation from one premise to another. Look at these paragraphs of non-fiction narration from *Between the Thunder and the Sun,* by the famous journalist Vincent Sheean:

The Windsors' dinner was very grand, and the guests consisted of assorted notables from up and down the coast, mostly English people of high rank who were holidaying in the South. My Lords Rothermere and Beaverbrook had been prevented from attending by colds. (Lord Beaverbrook's cold did not prevent his attendance at the

Narration's aim is storytelling

All newspaper writers use Narration because they are telling stories most of the time. Yet they are writing non-fiction, not fiction.

The essential difference between a man steeped in the royal tradition and one of the great realists of our time is cleverly made through narrative dialogue, though this isn't a piece of fiction. Narration is storytelling.

Exposition, Description, even Argument come into this paragraph, too. Just the same, this is basically narrative because Narration is "a connected succession of happenings."

Through narrative form, the author has described and explained, too. But the thread has been a story being spun, or Narration.

In Narration, movement is an essential element. The reader moves with the characters through the city.

Casino, where we saw him afterward.) When some of the more over-powering guests had departed, after the long and stately meal in the white-and-gold dining room, the Duke of Windsor and Mr. Churchill settled down to a prolonged argument with the rest of the party listening in silence.

The Duke had read with amazement Mr. Churchill's recent articles on Spain and his newest one (out that day, I believe) in which he appealed for an alliance with Soviet Russia. "You of all people, Winston," was the gist of his argument, "you cannot wish to make friends of these murderers and thieves." At one point Mr. Churchill, who was defending his point of view stubbornly and with undiplomatic vigor, said: "Sir, I would make a friend of the devil himself, if it would save England."

It resulted plainly from the statements on the two sides that the self-willed, pleasure-loving little Prince, filled to the fingertips with royal prejudice, had no conception of the deadly danger to England involved in his dalliance with Hitler, while Mr. Churchill, disliking the Bolshevik theory and practice as much as ever, was so thoroughly aware of England's peril that he would seek the alliance of Stalin at once.

We sat by the fireplace, Mr. Churchill frowning with intentness at the floor in front of him, mincing no words, reminding H.R.H. of the British Constitution, on occasion—"when our kings are in conflict with our Constitution we change our kings," he said—and declaring flatly that the nation stood in the gravest danger of its long history.

The kilted Duke in his Stuart tartan sat on the edge of the sofa, eagerly interrupting whenever he could, contesting every point, but receiving—in terms of the utmost politeness so far as the words went—an object lesson in political wisdom and public spirit. The rest of us sat fixed in silence; there was something dramatically final, irrevocable about this dispute.

Since the essential element of fiction is Narration or storytelling, the fiction writer is keenly aware of what makes a story move. In this regard few writers equal Mignon Eberhart. Here's an excerpt from one of her famous mystery novels, *Postmark Murder,* in which the chief characters are being followed as they stroll near their apartment in Chicago. This is simple, basic Narration—a movement of the story through the movement of its characters.

It was about three when Laura and Jonny went for their usual outing, a walk this time along the lake. They were followed probably from the moment they left the apartment house.

Laura was not aware of the pursuit for some time. They turned north along Lake Shore Drive, Jonny, a bright and happy figure in her little red coat and hat, trudging along beside Laura. It was foggy and cold. Laura turned up the collar of her coat, and the scarf Matt had given her seemed to provide a particularly gentle warmth around her throat.

The sidewalk was damp from the fog. At that time in the after-noon traffic was slower but still cars swished constantly over the wet pavements. Off at the right, across the Drive, the lake was only a blank gray, almost hidden in fog. They passed various pedestrians, the women bundled in furs, walking briskly along. Jonny stopped to speak to a black French poodle scampering gaily at the end of a yellow leash, and his owner smiled and talked to Jonny as Jonny fondled the dog.

> The words "swished constantly over the wet pavements" give the narrative movement, too.

Frequently they took one of the several subway passages, long tunnels for pedestrians, which went under Lake Shore Drive and its thudding traffic, and came out at the short strip of park and Oak Street Beach. This time, however, the steps going down into the crossing at Division Street looked dark and rather forbidding. Some-how Laura did not wish to enter the long tunnel with its echoes, its damp concrete walls, its few lights. They went on toward North Avenue, and the entrance to the park. It was as they stopped for a traffic light at Scott Street that she first saw a man trudging along through the fog about two blocks behind them. She glanced idly at him and away as the traffic light changed and they crossed the street. Perhaps halfway down the next block Laura thought suddenly, why, he reminded her of Conrad Stanislowski!

> At the very end of this rather moody paragraph (purposely forbidding in its Description) we, as readers, come to the fact that something isn't quite right, that a man's shadow is on the street, too. They stop for a traffic light, so the reader pictures them standing still as the narrative lets the reader see for the first time the man who is following them.

That was odd. In spite of herself she glanced back. The figure was still there, strolling along behind them, still about two blocks away, apparently paying no attention to them. But she then knew why he had reminded her of Conrad Stanislowski for, even at that distance, there was something vaguely foreign in his appearance. Perhaps it was his bulky black overcoat, or his wide-brimmed hat pulled in a straight line over his face. He was hunched up, his hands in his coat pockets. She couldn't see his face.

> In Narration this "flashback" to an event or person formerly involved draws one thread of the story up into the present and, in doing so, moves the story along.

But of course, that was it; merely a chance resemblance of cloth-ing had reminded her of the murdered man. They went on, crossed North Avenue and entered the park.

The benches were damp with fog and it was too cold to sit for long, anyway. They took a brisk pace along the winding pathways. Here, perhaps because of the foggy weather, there were not as many pedestrians as usual, fewer people exercising capering dogs, no neatly uniformed nursemaids pushing huge perambulators. Indeed the park itself began to seem oddly unpopulated. Unexpectedly, for no reason, Laura glanced back along the sloping, winding path. The man in the bulky overcoat had entered the park, too. She caught the barest glimpse of him through some bare, brown shrubbery.

> Now we are adding complication and conflict to the mere Narration of a walk in cold, foggy Chicago. The story is taking a new direction.

The Narration tells us that it's possible (for the first time) that the man in the bulky overcoat is following them—wherever they go, he goes. And suddenly . . ."Jonny, another target–"

Laura's mounting fears accentuate the story's intensity. So does the use of "curiously persistent . . . walker."

'Going where they went, pausing apparently when they paused . . ." intensifies the narrative suspense.

And suddenly she thought, Jonny, another target!

They would go over to Lake Shore Drive. They would take a taxi home. She hastened her footsteps and Jonny's. They reached Lake Shore Drive again. A taxi was drifting along the street. Laura signaled it. As she got in she glanced back through the glass. There was no sight of the curiously persistent, curiously ubiquitous walker in the fog.

Had he in fact followed them? They had met other people along the streets, but they passed and went on; they turned and took different ways. The figure in the dark coat had trudged on through the fog, going where they went, pausing apparently when they paused, always just far enough away so she could not see his face. Yet he had not approached them. He had not spoken to them.

It was a short ride back to her apartment house. As they drew up at the entrance, another taxi went slowly past them. Its single passenger was only a dark blur in the shadow of the back seat.

The expository form

As we have seen, both fiction and non-fiction writers use Description and Narration. Exposition, however, belongs largely to the non-fiction field. While it's true that storytellers explain facts to give the reader a clearer background, Exposition and non-fiction are practically synonymous.

An enormous proportion of all writing done anywhere is expository. Exposition includes articles for magazines, auditors' reports, biography, history, criticism, the business letter, reference books, classroom lectures, sermons, advertisements and news stories. Political speeches are expository; so are textbooks. Specifications for a new highway bridge are also expository. So are laboratory directions—and the results of an experiment. A compilation of statistics is in this form. Instruction sheets are pure Exposition.

As we defined Exposition in the beginning, its purpose is to instruct the reader and explain ideas to him, not to stimulate him emotionally (as in fiction) nor to stir his imagination. Since Exposition is universally used every hour of every day, samples of it are all about us. Here's the purest Exposition of all—and one of the most widely used—a cooking recipe. This is for a New England boiled dinner:

Put a 6–7 pound fine-grained corned brisket of beef into a large

Exposition means explaining things

kettle. Cover with cold water. Bring water to a boil, then drain and rinse beef. Repeat 3 times. Once more cover the corned beef with cold water. Add a piece of salt pork, 6 peppercorns, and a stalk of celery. Simmer beef 3 to 4 hours or until fork-tender.

Peel 8 to 10 small white potatoes and 5 carrots. Cut the carrots into chunks 1½ to 2 inches long. Add the potatoes and carrots to the broth. Cook until tender. About 15 minutes before serving, add 2 packages frozen Brussels sprouts to the broth.

Cook until crisp-tender. Serve corned brisket on a platter garnished with potatoes, Brussels sprouts and carrots. Makes 8–10 servings.

Exposition is essentially instructive and interpretive. It explains and teaches. Let's look at an average sample of expository writing from a book of detailed instructions on operating a newly-installed air conditioner in a small factory or office building. A diagram and illustration accompanied it in the original:

The reader learns from Exposition

To remove filters

1. Press down on hinged support at bottom of left-hand filter, pull bottom edge of filter forward and drop filter enough to clear top of filter support. (On some units the hinged filter retains the right-hand filter as well.)
2. Slide the other filter horizontally until it occupies the position formerly taken by the one just removed and remove it in the same manner as the first filter.
3. *Note:* Filters can be removed without opening the two front side panels.

In typical instruction writing, three things are characteristic:

1. It's usually in the present tense, since you're asking your reader to take one step after another. You may not have realized it, but it's true. Think back to the mystifying instructions which came with your child's Christmas toy. They said "then place bolt X inside opening Y, turn until secure and tighten with wrench provided." Cooking recipes are likewise in the present tense. So are the instructions in your Study Guide for the Course.

2. Words like "the," "an," "a" (called *definite* and *indefinite articles*) frequently are omitted in the telegraphic style of instruction writing, as: "Set coffee urn in safe place, add water, turn on switch and let coffee percolate for 8–10 minutes." No "the," "an" or "a" words in that sentence, which is typical of instruction writing.

3. Almost every instruction sheet has titles, subtitles and numbered steps, as well as constant references to figures, illustrations and diagrams, usually numbered. Figures, illustrations, diagrams and titles do help instruct when done logically and clearly, but they can

also defeat the purpose of Exposition if the writer's thinking is muddy and his expression inconclusive.

One "how to" in writing instructions is a truism: it helps if you not only tell the reader *how* to do something but also tell *why* it should be done. When you can give a reason, the instruction goes deeper and is remembered longer. For example, you've sold a television set to a housewife and installed the aerial. There's a certain plug which hangs down from the back of the set with an instruction tag explaining *how* it connects to the TV aerial outlet. Not only must you tell the new television set owner *how* it's to be connected but *why*—that if she doesn't plug it in she won't get TV reception. This may seem elementary to you because it's your business, but by adding the *why* to any instruction sheet your explanation goes deeper, is remembered longer, leaves fewer readers baffled.

You've got to tell
the TV set owner

Some of the best expository writing is put out by the public utility companies, which must make themselves clear to stay in business. The telephone book, for instance, does a wonderful job in its prefatory pages. Take its instructions on how to dial an out-of-state call:

To place a call to any telephone outside of Connecticut, first dial "112," then dial the area code, followed by the two letters and five figures of the telephone number you wish to reach. (For list of out-of-state places you can dial and their area code numbers, see pages I–IV of this Directory.)

For example, if you wish to call RIchmond 2-9991 in Boston, Mass., first dial "112," then the Boston area code 617, then RIchmond 2-9991.

Expository writing, including pure "how to" instructions such as assembling a child's toy, boils down to a very simple formula:

(a) The mental act of analysis of the job at hand,
(b) After breaking down the job into the logical steps, using foolproof English clear enough to be understood.

The argument form

The fourth of the forms, Argument, essentially seeks to persuade someone of something. In the larger sense, of course, all storytelling is persuasion; the writer wants to evoke sympathy or condemnation for certain characters and what they stand for, for a way of life or a philosophy which the author reveres or detests. Through story line and character, the writer of significant fiction is forever arguing certain truths, trying to persuade the reader to accept an opinion of great value to the writer.

Some writers, especially Victorian, liked to end their novels with a sort of sermon—a summary of the persuasive points made through the story and its characters. Perhaps you remember Thackeray's concluding paragraph in *Vanity Fair:*

Ah! Vanity of vanities! Which of us is happy in this world? Which of us has his desire? or, having it, is satisfied?—Come, children, let us shut up the box and the puppets, for our play is played out.

Essentially, however, Argument belongs to non-fiction. Like Exposition, the very natures of subject matter and purpose fall into the non-fiction category. Brooks and Warren in *Fundamentals of Good Writing* say that "Argument is used to make the audience (reader or listener) think or act as the arguer desires. Often, the purpose of Argument is not only to persuade but to lead the reader or listener to act."

For example, *The Saturday Evening Post* editorial page quoted below is arguing that it takes a daredevil racetrack driver to teach safe driving to teen-agers. The Argument first tells a story (Narration), then gives the boys' reaction (Description and Exposition), and sends up *arguing* for more of this effective high school lecturing by racetrack heroes:

A couple of years ago the Champion Spark Plug Company, of Toledo, Ohio, had a good idea: It hired half a dozen speed kings from the Indianapolis 500-mile race to tour the nation to lecture high-school pupils on safe driving.

Narrative opening.

A nippy, crew-cut young fellow named Jimmy Daywalt, who has been through the Indianapolis ordeal four times, recently brought the current version of this program to a New Jersey high school. The auditorium was full of 800-odd teen-age hero-worshipers. Jimmy first showed them a movie of hair-raising episodes from recent races; then gave them forty minutes of personal lowdown on race drivers' habits and skills, each item applied to safety-conscious highway driving. For he and his colleagues are more than daredevil racers. What with the racing circuit and their speaking season, they drive their own standard cars from 35,000 to 50,000 miles a year under normal highway conditions.

Still Narration. Actually, this is a blend of Narration and Description, as is quite often the case in editorials.

The kids lapped it up. To judge by enthusiastic letters from high-school principals all over, the five other drivers on the same assign-

Description and Exposition.

ment get over just about as well. And the special beauty of it is that these pop-eyed audiences consist of all the kids in the school, including the show-off tire screamers who will listen to Daywalt as they wouldn't to anybody else.

Conclusion: An Argument for more of these missions.

The only thing wrong with this program is that these six missionaries can't possibly cover more than a minority of the thousands of secondary schools that need them.

The Argument form which seeks to persuade people is most commonly used in advertising. As Mark Wiseman says, copywriters use Argument every day of their lives. He adds:

Newspapers, billboards, television commercials, radio station-breaks brim with this form of writing and have a common purpose: to persuade the reader or listener to buy something. They not only *explain* and *argue:* they seek to *stir action,* through words.

Here's a good example of Argument as used by an advertising copywriter:

"Warmth from the sparkling sun . . . from the friendly people . . . the nice warm feeling you have when beauty surrounds you—that's Spain!

"Visit exciting cities . . . quaint villages . . . magnificent art galleries . . . museums . . . cathedrals . . . world-famous shrines . . . brilliant seaside resorts.

"You can actually *live* in a Castle in Spain . . . a castle converted to a modern Parador . . . with all the comforts you like . . . at very modest prices.

"You can do such thrilling things . . . have such a good time . . . and it costs much less than you'd expect! Go to Spain by ship or plane . . . but *go* . . . for the vacation of a lifetime!

"See Your Travel Agent"

The copywriter has used Description, Narration and Exposition to persuade readers of this ad that they should go to Spain. His basic *purpose,* however, is Argument: his job is to persuade the readers of his ad to go to Spain, not simply to read the ad and wish they were going. He is arguing the rightness of certain ideas, in this case traveling to Spain. His copy is typical of advertising's constant use of Argument.

Summing up

We have briefly viewed in this Lesson the four generally accepted basic forms—Description, Narration, Exposition and Argument—from which all writing derives. We have seen that the forms overlap, that all four may come into play in differing proportions, whether it be fiction or non-fiction, novel or magazine article, short story or editorial, recipe or business report.

There is no such thing as a whole piece of writing which is purely descriptive, purely narrative, purely expository or purely argumentative, any more than a single day is composed of only one element of weather. Always there is some wind, however slight, or sun or cloud or precipitation or heat or cold, and they will be mixed together in varying proportions into what we humans call weather. Writing is equally complex.

But this much we can say with certainty: Description is the most elemental tool of a writer because it supplies a basic framework for all writing, sets a stage and erects a background for what a writer is trying to express to a reader, regardless of content or purpose.

A simple rule for getting started

How do you get started on a piece of writing? The best answer I know is: sit down and write. I love to write but I hate to get to work. I answer phones, write letters, pull down shades, empty ashtrays and, when all else fails, I work. I sit down and reread what I have written the day before. Very often I tear it up. Sometimes I revise or rewrite it. But if I have an idea, even a skeleton for, say, a short story, I start it.

It doesn't make any difference if I tear that up and begin again. I must put something down on paper. If I achieve a thousand or a hundred words, I've made a start. I'll probably rewrite them several times, but it's a beginning.

Books are different, naturally, but I try to set myself a stint of so many words a day. Sometimes I exceed this, sometimes I don't. The point is: start now—preferably at the beginning—and keep going. Next working period you have something to start *from,* even if you destroy the original.—Faith Baldwin

Lesson thirteen

Principles of good writing

Writing description

Description is essentially the kind of writing that has to do with the way places, people and things present themselves to our senses—the physical appearance of the world about us.

When we write, "The banana is yellow," we refer to the sense of sight. If we write, "The banana is fragrant," the sense of smell is involved. If we say, "The banana is smooth," we're using the sense of touch. When we describe a banana as "sweet," it's the sense of taste. Or we may say that the leaves of the banana tree move in the wind "with a brittle sound"—the sense of hearing.

This is direct, forthright Description. But a good writer won't usually be content with such general phrases. The addition of a word or two will help: "The banana was butter-yellow" or "The banana was smooth as kidskin" gives a clearer picture.

Then there is suggestive Description. For example, under-statement says more than a hundred words in this phrase describing a blind man's feelings of uselessness in the tough, wild West: "Us blind fellows ain't kept too busy."

You might also describe something through overpowering detail. Read Robert Carse's description of tropical Nassau, in his Civil War book *Blockade*. Italicized are descriptive words and phrases which add up to the sense of realism good writers are able to convey. On the left are comments on what Carse has done to invoke the senses through Description:

There were many colors. Use of the *ands* strings these colors together like Chinese lanterns. The sense of sight .s first involved.

Taylor was ready for shore. This was the first foreign port *and the low, verdant island, the pink and white and pale blue and green houses in their gardens under the palm trees* greatly attracted him. He reported as he should to his company's agents on Bay Street and learned that the bark which had been sent with a load of coal for the *Despatch* was in the harbor, but then he gave his mind to other things.

He walked slowly through the *white sunlight glare* on Market Street between Bay Street and the harbor and he was *far from the Mersey fog, the clinging, bitter soot of Liverpool.* Here, heaped in piles and sold by the *laughing, chattering, yelling Negro women* whose English he barely understood, were heaps of fruits he had never before seen and only vaguely imagined.

As he remembers tawdry smells and sights back home, tropical Nassau leaps out in contrast.

It doesn't matter that the reader is unfamiliar with all the names. Notice his use of "turtle" as the plural. All five senses are invoked in this paragraph—sight, sound, smell, taste and touch.

Those, he was told, the *brown ones,* were *sapodillas,* and the *green ones sugar apples;* over beyond were *scarlet plums and yellow jujubes, and tamarinds and mangoes, and sea grapes and pawpaws and mammees and soursops.* The rest were *ochra, and akees, yams, guavas, pigeon peas.* He bought *bananas no thicker than his thumb* and stared at fish that were called *grouper and gogoleye and passing jacket and grunt. Turtle lay sprawled beside them.*

Heat and fragrance ... and tall pink flamingos. The first sentence is typical of good Description: "fragrance ... sharp to his nostrils ... the dust ... stung his eyes ... sun glare made his head hurt." All of these things are sensory reactions in writer and reader. Detail after detail ... color, movement, sound, even a hint of the taste and smell of supper being cooked aboard colorful fishing sloops.

The street bore a *fragrance* that was *sharp to his nostrils;* the dust kicked up by the *bare Negro feet stung his eyes,* and the *sun glare* made his head hurt. He turned away towards the Royal Victoria Hotel. It was time he talked with some of the veteran blockade-runner captains and pilots about the degree of success the *Despatch* would have in the trade. Still, he stopped to stare back at the *tall pink flamingos* along the curve of the beach.

There were *red hibiscus, scarlet poinciana* in bloom above a *yellow wall* he passed. *Hummingbirds swept around butterflies perched among the lavender of Pride of India trees. Cicadas cried in chorus as the dusk spread.* Out in the harbor, *anchor lights were swinging up on the halyards* of the ships. The sunset reflection touched the *brown, patched sails* of the fishermen's inward-bound sloops and the *supper fires glowed in the cabooses.*

By contrast, we're shocked to return to realistic fact.

Taylor kept on to the hotel. This was almost like a dream. A man could lose himself. But there were orders that he must obey. *He was here to make money.*

The senses are involved to some degree in almost every instance of descriptive writing. Fiction writers must be particularly susceptible and sensitive because they have no other means of translating descriptive imagination to the reality of the printed page. Writers of non-fiction, though not called upon as often to produce descriptive passages, usually invoke the senses when they describe, for Description is essentially of the senses.

Let's suppose you are a fiction writer and want to establish in the reader's mind a calm and peaceful countryside. You hope your reader will get your own feeling of the serenity of early evening. This is the feeling you have within yourself, and as you sit on your front porch looking out over the sweet-smelling hay fields and darkening hills, you wonder where to begin. There's so much to describe, so much to see, hear, smell, taste and touch.

So, being a writer, you begin to put what you're seeing, hearing, smelling, tasting and touching into words. The first words coming to your mind are, of course, *adjectives* because adjectives are sharp tools of Description. Through adjectives a writer can specify and differentiate, paint a special scene out of general nouns. So you marshal some of the adjectives that strike you at this particular time of day, sitting on your front porch in early evening:

Adjectives are
your sharpest tools

hazy	calm	serene
sleepy	muted	subdued
gentle	pale	beautiful
shadowy	peaceful	indistinct
dusky	restful	vague
gloomy	lovely	glimmering
misty	rosy	shaded

This is a pretty impressive list. These adjectives seem to fit the peaceful evening countryside you look out upon. Yet, brimming with feeling as they are, these adjectives by themselves won't tell your reader very much. They won't move him or re-create for him the scene you yourself are seeing, hearing, smelling, tasting and touching.

So, instead of using these words by themselves, you fit them into the basic elements of Description which come from six general sources, the five senses of sight, sound, smell, taste and touch, plus the over-all personal reaction known to human beings as "feelings." Taking these senses one at a time, you begin to express the terms of Description.

Sight

The cattle cluster around a shadowy tree . . . their dark silhouettes stand out against the hazy evening light . . . the warm dark red of the barn has patches of rosy light from the setting sun . . . the red flush of lovely sky . . . the glow of your pipe bowl in the muted light . . . a full moon beginning to rise out of the trees beyond your hay field, pale yellow at first, then deeper and deeper until it's the color of country butter . . . a layer of deep blue beginning in the sky above the departed sun . . . lights of a passing car.

Sound

Train whistle in the distance . . . muted clang of cowbells . . . the breathing of the dog at your feet . . . the sound of the rocking chair next to you . . . evening locusts beginning their singing rhythm . . . frogs in the lowlands beyond the pasture . . . a horse's gentle neigh . . . melodic thread of birds' song . . . clop-clop of a horse on pavement . . . a distant auto horn . . . the subdued rustling of apple branches in the fresh evening breeze.

Smell

Fresh-cut hay from the field . . . the barn smells, diluted by distance . . . spicy odor of baked apples from the kitchen . . . the hinted ozone of a shower in the fresh evening wind . . . a sudden, vague fragrance from a flowerbed . . . the pungent aroma of tobacco . . . the dog's woolly smell.

Taste

The aftertaste of a fine dinner . . . the chocolate mint you're nibbling on between puffs . . . the rich, fresh taste of a newly-lit pipe . . . a sudden bitterness at the tip of the pipe stem.

Touch

The dog's curly damp coat in your hand . . . warm pipe-bowl in the palm . . . kiss of evening wind . . . awareness of your tired muscles . . . clean feeling of fresh clothes after your shower . . . softness of the inside of your slippers on bare feet . . . comfortable support of the rocking chair against the small of your back . . . the uneven hardness of the wooden porch floor to the tip of your toes as they alternately touch and rise with the rocking chair.

These few sense impressions communicate immediately with your reader, who quickly puts himself in your place because what you've written has meaning to him. He's seen, heard, smelled, tasted and touched these familiar things with you, so you've established contact with him. You have done it by invoking the five senses, the essential sources of Description.

Over and above the specific senses there is, however, a sixth set of impressions of great value in Description. This sixth source is best described as your own personal reaction or feelings, your over-all perception or inner reaction to what you're experiencing or imagining and seek to put into words. It might be written something like this:

Feelings

It's been a good day . . . five tons of hay baled and hauled to the barn . . . that's enough for a whole month of winter feeding . . . five more tomorrow and the worst of it will be over . . . feel tired but happy . . . contented . . . satisfied with the day's work . . . feel relaxed, sense of well-being as I sit here smoking and rocking . . . what a sleepy, peaceful night it is! . . . serene is the word, better than just calm . . . restful, rocking here with dog and pipe in fresh clothes after a fine dinner . . . no roar of busses, no din of traffic, no raw fumes, no forbidding concrete, just my own farm land growing fragrant hay for my own cattle to eat . . . a night like this makes a man want to stretch his hands over his head and be glad he's alive.

These are raw materials of Description, words you can put on paper to communicate with your reader's own senses and feelings. Creative writers often are inspired by just such an evening stimulus, though they may also be able to imagine it in the dark depths of a winter morning in the city. The point is that something like this flow of word reactions to the five senses and the sixth sense of over-all personal feeling is the first act of a writer at work on the stuff of life. Combining phrases from the six sense groups above could give a descriptive scene like this:

Adjectives rouse reader's emotions

It's been a good day, he thought. Five tons of hay baled and hauled to the barn, fresh-cut hay whose smell filled the air. He saw his cattle clustered around a shadowy tree, their dark silhouettes standing out against the hazy evening light. Peace surrounded him. A lonesome train whistled in the distance and the weary dog at his feet breathed heavily. He lit his pipe, felt the warmth of the bowl in his hand and tasted the rich tobacco. A night like this made a man feel satisfied and glad he was alive.

Imaginative use of description

Good description often has movement as well as color, shape, size and form. Sometimes the use of sensuous words gives Description unity and power, at the same time evoking deepdown emotions in the reader. From the novel *Look Homeward, Angel,* we quote Thomas Wolfe, a master of Description:

Extraordinary impact on the senses of smell and touch.

He knew the inchoate sharp excitement of hot dandelions in young spring grass at noon; the smell of cellars, cobwebs, and built-on secret earth; in July, of watermelons bedded in sweet hay, inside a farmer's covered wagon; of cantaloupe and crated peaches; and the scent of orange rind, bittersweet, before a fire of coals.

In *South Wind* by Norman Douglas, the British novelist, we get a feeling of colorful activity from this Description of the sea. We have italicized those descriptive words or phrases which give the reader a better picture of this water scene through their impact upon our five senses and that sixth sense of inner feelings:

Leaning over the parapet he enjoyed, once more, the *strangely intimate companionship* of the sea. He glanced into the water *whose uneven floor was diapered with long weedy patches, fragments of fallen rock* and *brighter patches of sand;* he inhaled the *pungent odor of sea-wrack* and listened to the *breathings of the waves.* They *lapped softly* against the *rounded boulders* which strewed the shore like *a flock of nodding Behemoths.* He remembered his visits at daybreak to the beach—*those unspoken confidences* with the *sunlit element* to whose *friendly caresses* he had *abandoned his body.*

How calm it was, too, in this evening light. Near at hand, somewhere, lay a *sounding cave;* it *sang a melody of moist content.* Shadows lengthened; fishing boats, moving outward for the night-work, *steered darkly* across the *luminous river* at his feet. Those *jewel-like morning tints of blue and green* had faded from the water; the southern *cliff-scenery,* projections of it, caught a *fiery glare.*

Joseph Conrad's descriptions have tremendous movement. In *Typhoon* he has young Jukes, the ship's chief mate, log the beginning of a great storm. We can almost feel the exaggerated roll of the ship. The vivid Description is most impressive when we realize that Conrad, born in Poland, was writing in English, a foreign language he had mastered only after much struggle:

You must read this very slowly, savoring every word of a master of the descriptive form. All the way through, this paragraph is pure Conrad at his finest.

At its setting the sun had a diminished diameter and an expiring brown, rayless glow, as if millions of centuries elapsing since the morning had brought it near its end. A dense bank of cloud became visible to the northward; it had a sinister dark olive tint, and lay low and motionless upon the sea, resembling a solid obstacle in the path of the ship. She went floundering towards it like an exhausted creature driven to its death. The coppery twilight retired slowly, and the darkness brought out overhead a swarm of unsteady, big stars, that, as if blown upon, flickered exceedingly and seemed to hang very near the earth. At eight o'clock Jukes went into the chartroom to write up the ship's log.

He copied neatly out of the rough book the number of miles, the course of the ship, and in the column for "wind" scrawled the word "calm" from top to bottom of the eight hours since noon. He was exasperated by the continuous, monotonous rolling of the ship. The heavy inkstand would slide away in a manner that suggested perverse intelligence in dodging the pen. Having written in the large space under the head of "Remarks" "Heat very oppressive," he stuck the end of the penholder in his teeth, pipe fashion, and mopped his face carefully.

"Ship rolling heavily in a high cross swell," he began again, and commented to himself, "Heavily is no word for it." Then he wrote: "Sunset threatening, with a low bank of clouds to N. and E. Sky clear overhead."

Sprawling over the table with arrested pen, he glanced out of the door, and in that frame of his vision he saw all the stars flying upwards between the teakwood jambs on a black sky. The whole lot took flight together and disappeared, leaving only a blackness flecked with white flashes, for the sea was as black as the sky and speckled with foam afar. The stars that had flown to the roll came back on the return swing of the ship, rushing downwards in their glittering multitude, not of fiery points, but enlarged to tiny discs brilliant with a clear wet sheen.

Jukes watched the flying big stars for a moment, and then wrote: "8 P.M. Swell increasing. Ship labouring and taking water on her decks. Battened down the coolies for the night. Barometer still falling." He paused, and thought to himself, "Perhaps nothing whatever'll come of it." And then he closed resolutely his entries: "Every appearance of a typhoon coming on."

Let's pretend that you're taking an automobile trip through farm country. You're a writer and you wish to describe your experiences to someone back home. How do you find what to say?

Well, as you spin along the highway you see the landscape passing in review. When you stop at a filling station, you talk with the attendant and there's a reaction to *sound*. While driving you employ the *sense of touch*—the bumps, the curves, the wheel beneath your fingers.

As you drive on and on into the spring panorama, you notice that the woods are thinning out; now there are cultivated fields and farmhouses. After a while you observe that the rivers you

Conrad's description stops and the storytelling continues.

But not for long. Conrad the writer is one of the few with the genius to think of that word "exasperated" in the second sentence.

He lets the chief mate do his own describing by means of narrative entries in the log.

Conrad is withholding his own descriptive powers from the mate, who would not have them.

Seldom in literature will you find as great a passage as this one about the stars in a black, typhoon-heralding sky. 'Stars that had flown to the roll" is especially good writing.

Conrad's sensitivity is simply amazing. Tiny things that might escape most writers affect his five senses. Go back and pick them out.

cross are very low. You're getting into the drought area you've been reading about. All this involves the *sense of sight*.

Pretty soon the sky doesn't seem to be as bright. There's a haze over the dusty fields and roads. It seems to be a thin acrid cloud which soon stings your nose and eyes. You have to hold a handkerchief over your mouth and nose and close all the windows of your car. This brings into play your *sense of smell*.

Travel gives you
sensory impressions

Suddenly you realize you're in a dust storm. You've read about them in the newspapers. Now your senses tell you what they're really like. If you're a writer, you'll be making mental notes when the bits of stinging sand strike your face as you crank up your windows. At this point you are informed by your *sense of touch*.

After two hours of hard driving, your car begins to move out of the dust storm area and you stop at a gasoline station. You have it washed, but the moment you're back on the road you can hear the crunch of sand as it whirls and sprays around your wheels and strikes the underside of your fenders. You have invoked again the *sense of sound*.

By evening you're tired out. Four hundred miles is a long way to drive in a single day, especially through dust storms and unfamiliar country. After registering, you go up to your hotel room and take a shower, then change to fresh clothes and go down to dinner. There you'll become involved with the *sense of taste*.

When you return to your room you start to write a letter home about your first day's travels. How do you describe them? What will you write?

Well, you refer to the five senses. All day you've been seeing and hearing and smelling and tasting and touching and feeling. Put on paper what you've seen and heard, what you've smelled and tasted, what you've felt with your body. Through all five senses you have received countless impressions. Put these impressions on paper. Recall their effects on all your senses: the sight of dried-up streams, the smell of a dust storm, the touch of blowing sand, the sound of grit under your fenders, the taste of a welcome dinner.

In short, put down an account of the total effect of the day on your five senses and that over-all feeling or impression these things made on you. If you select sharp, telling details, words which will evoke in your reader the sensory experiences you went through, you will succeed in creating out of words what is technically called *Description*.

The use of description in non-fiction

So far, most of our examples of Description have come from fiction. But Description is invaluable in *non*-fiction too. Let's look at a *Life* magazine article by Phyllis McGinley on her hobby of gardening. The italicized words are particularly useful in describing her subject and summoning up in the reader the picture she wants to convey:

Gardening has compensations out of all proportion to its goals. It is *pure creation*. That *dungareed figure scrabbling in the earth,* with *dirt under his fingernails* and *thorn scratches* on his arms, is *no figure of fun but half a god.* The sun beats on him, the rain wets him, *arthritis lurks under his kneeling pad, ants run up and down his sleeves.* Still, it is the posture and the task he has chosen and loves.

To be able to walk around a border after dinner and *smell the fragrance of his mignonette,* to *speak a personal word to each painted daisy,* to *pull up a wild onion* or *congratulate the tuberous begonia* he has steered into *preposterous flowering*—those are pleasures past explaining.

In journalism, which is basic non-fiction, Description plays a powerful role. From *Time* magazine we quote three paragraphs from the description of Pope John XXIII's first papal Mass. The italicized descriptive words give special flavor and color to the reading. Notice how the five senses are all involved, despite the shortness of this excerpt:

Twelve silver trumpets sounded, and the procession entered the *vast* church. Behind representatives of the ancient orders—Franciscans, Dominicans, Benedictines, Cistercians—walked dignitaries of Rome's churches, *breastplated Swiss guardsmen, velvet-clad chamberlains* of honor, honorary privy chaplains, patriarchs, *mace bearers* and *scarlet-mantled* cardinals, *fan bearers* and Noble Guards. In the chapel of St. Gregory the cardinals made obeisance to the Pope, *kissing his right hand.* Then John XXIII was vested to celebrate his solemn papal Mass.

Three times during the procession to the main altar the Pope was halted by the master of ceremonies to receive a *small brazier of glowing coals* and a *handful of flax* that the Pope *threw upon the fire.* Then, as the *flax flared up* and *was gone in a puff of smoke,* the master of ceremonies looked into the Pontiff's eyes and intoned the

Senses of sight and sound.

Vivid pageantry affecting the sense of sight.

Sense of touch.

Senses of sight, sound and smell.

Sense of sound.

Senses of taste and touch.

Senses of sight and touch.

Over-all reaction to the
ceremony the reporter
is witnessing.

Description is vital
to sports writing

ancient warning: *"Pater sancte, sic transit gloria mundi (Holy
Father, thus passes the glory of the world)."* In the course of the
Mass, an assisting cardinal placed on the Pope's shoulders *the
pallium, a white wool band symbolizing his authority* as Bishop of
Rome, and the sacristan performed the grim ritual of *tasting the
wine* to be used, as reminder of the *days when Popes often died by
poison.* At the conclusion of the Mass a *silk purse* containing *25
ancient coins* was presented to the Pontiff, traditional payment for "a
Mass well done."

Outside St. Peter's *all Rome seemed to be assembled,* kneeling
and praying. Finally the new Pope appeared on the balcony and *the
papal tiara—the jewel-studded triple diadem* that symbolizes the
sanctifying, ruling and teaching powers of the church—was placed
on the *large, rugged peasant head* of Angelo Roncalli.

In sports writing, Description is so much a part of narrative
that the reader doesn't realize where one begins and the other
ends. Red Smith is famous for his colorful language. The following is from one of his columns entitled "The Strongest Lady."
Again, the italicized descriptive words give the reader an insight
that does not come from clichés and ordinary words.

For a few hours yesterday New York wore, *like an orchid in her
hair, a flower of femininity* named Miss Dorcas Lehman, who is the
strongest lady in the world. Miss Lehman is a *red-haired saloon-
keeper* of York, Pennsylvania, and a Dunkard—a member of one of
those Pennsylvania German sects whose members *paint hex marks
on the barn and wear somber black sunbonnets if they are women,
and spade whiskers and porkpie hats if they are men.* Miss Lehman,
however, is a nonconformist in costume and custom. Her clothes,
lips, and fingernails *have a good deal of red in them,* and *her hobby
is letting large gentlemen jump on her stomach.*

It amuses the lady to form a bridge by placing her feet on one
wooden bench and her head on another, whereupon a *230-pound
man sits on her abdomen and swings his feet.* York, which is a nest
of weight-lifters, has a 132-pound Hawaiian named Emerick Ishi-
kawa, national featherweight champion. When Dorcas is *making
like the Triborough Bridge,* she permits little Emerick to *leap upon
her diaphragm from a height of five or six feet.*

Dorcas was *trig as a trip-hammer* in a dress of soft gray with a
bow at the throat, a beige jacket, red shoes, a *rather frivolous hat* of
red and white, and *harlequin spectacles with red plastic frames.* She
had *diamonds on both brightly manicured hands. Turned out she
was in town to buy contact lenses.*

She weighs 160 pounds, is five feet six inches tall and comely in a
strapping, healthy sort of way. To a timid question she replied read-

ily that her age was thirty-two and smiled, adding, "Don't mind being asked; only *sometimes they think I'm forty, and that burns me up."*

Five years ago she weighed 210 pounds. She attended a weight-lifting demonstration and was *smitten with admiration for the physiques on display.* So she bought a fifty-pound dumbbell and went home and started lifting it.

She can *break a chain by expanding her chest.* She can *fit her feet into straps anchored to a wall, place a forty-pound dumbbell on each shoulder and bend backward until her head touches the floor, then straighten up.* She can *swing seventy-five pounds overhead eighteen times with one hand.* She can *lift 375 pounds of dead weight.* With a bar across her shoulders and *a man hanging on each end, she can support 600 pounds.* She can *do a deep knee-bend with a 216-pound man and a 100-pound barbell on her back.* She can *do a 1,000-pound* leg press—that is, *lie on her back and hoist that weight with her feet.*

When this recital was complete, the lady was ready to depart. Walking downstairs, she said she liked to visit New York, but *hankered for York* after about four days here. Said she *guessed she was just small-town.* She smiled good-by and strode *off, shoulders squared.*

Description in a technical article

Some specifications are almost pure Description. Here's a report from *Architectural Forum* on a new kind of laborer's scaffold that works on the scissors principle:

Useful for repair work and light construction, the 860-lb. Jim Dandy jr. scaffold pantographs up to 10 feet with a platform and 800-lb. pay load. Easily carried around in a small truck, the hydraulic unit is fitted with casters for mobility on the job. A workman controls the elevating and lowering from the 2½ foot by 8 foot platform and a one-third horsepower motor provides the power. The model sells for about $450.

Description of this scaffold necessarily involves what it can do when built. The writer of these specifications knows that his reader will be aware of certain facts from the way he's described the scaffold:

1. It can be used only for repair and light construction.
2. It can be used only for relatively low jobs.
3. It can carry only a limited number of men and equipment (800 pounds) in its scissors-action rise.

4. It's very mobile.
5. A small (⅓ horsepower) motor will drive it.
6. As scaffolds go, this one's inexpensive ($450).
7. Operated by one man from platform.

This descriptive information sets up pictures in the mind of a potential buyer. He can "see" the pantograph being raised and lowered, as applied to his own building problems. He can "hear" the small motor humming. He can probably "feel" the platform under his feet if he's a professional builder, and he can picture in his mind how high 10 feet is and how much a pay load of 800 pounds would be. All this is very useful to him—and the medium has largely been *Description*.

Fashion reporting is close to undiluted Description. When the Paris collections have their first showings in the fall and spring, women fashion writers, with a vocabulary all their own, are able to describe what they've seen as easily as a sports writer doing play-by-play at the World Series.

The audience is usually limited, but the technique is basic Description which, in these instances, overlaps to a large extent the field of Exposition or explanation.

Here's a paragraph from the *Ladies' Home Journal*, typical of women's fashion talk. The general subject is "Separates . . . night and day"—combinations of feminine costumes that may be used in a great variety of ways:

Senses of touch and sight are always acute in fashion Description.

Here we show you some of the delightful possibilities that the new fabrics offer you this autumn. We love the classic look of a *silk-linen shirt* with a *gray flannel button-front skirt,* but on the other hand, we can't resist the gaiety of *bright flowered challis* accompanied by *wool jersey.*

"Soft white crepe blouse" and "coziness" are words that connote touch.

We are partial to the look of a *bright braid-bound jacket,* wonderful over a *black sheath,* or with a *pleated jersey skirt* and a *soft white crepe blouse,* but can't overlook the *coziness* (not to mention its fashion news) of a *great blanket-plaid skirt.*

Colors and textures involving the senses of touch and sight.

Small details are important too. Take, for instance, the *small brass coin buttons, wool fringe dyed to match wool jersey,* or a *foulard Paisley cummerbund.*

The advertising writer uses Description constantly. Here's part of a famous advertisement about Rolls-Royce automobiles which appeared in the *New Yorker* magazine. The copy, written by David Ogilvy, is non-fiction Description which tells the reader why a Rolls-Royce is "the best car in the world."

What's Under the Bonnet of a Rolls-Royce?

What makes Rolls-Royce the best car in the world? "There is really no magic about it—it is merely patient attention to detail," says an eminent Rolls-Royce engineer . . .

For example, every engine is run for eight full hours on a test bed before it is placed in a car—thirty minutes idling, thirty minutes at normal revolutions, and *seven hours at full throttle.*

On removal from the test bed, one engine in twenty is stripped down to the last bolt, laid out on a table and examined with microscopes.

If any component has faltered, every engine in the entire batch of twenty is taken out of production, stripped down, and then individually examined . . .

The coachwork is first given *five* coats of primer paint, and hand rubbed between each coat, before nine coats of color paint go on.

The radiator shells are made entirely by hand—in burnished stainless steel. Not a single surface on the radiator is flat. Its surfaces are *bowed* to an infinitely slight degree, on the same theory whereby the ancient Greeks made the outer edges of their temple columns slightly convex. In this way the design, viewed as a whole, appears geometrically correct. This radiator has never changed, except that when Sir Henry Royce died in 1933, the famous monogram RR was changed from red to black.

The ad writer
uses description

In upholstering the seats, Rolls-Royce uses the same English leather used on the seats in the House of Commons.

Eight full hides—enough to make 128 pairs of shoes—are selected from thirty or more to obtain perfect matching for color, texture, thickness and grain.

Once the hides have been selected for your car, a label containing your serial number is attached to each. The complete process of stitching, filling and covering the seats, squabs and door panels is then handled by one team of craftsmen . . .

The silence in a Rolls-Royce is uncanny. "At 60 miles an hour the loudest noise comes from the electric clock," reports the Technical Editor of *The Motor.*

The car weighs 4780 pounds. But it is delicately maneuverable, and its reserves of power are instantly available in an emergency.

Acceleration is lively—a smooth, silent, inexorable surge that takes you from 0 to 60 m.p.h. in 11.6 seconds.

Although the Rolls-Royce advertisement is technical Description, Mr. Ogilvy's copy is far from routine, mechanical or telegraphic. There are several facts in every sentence, usually facts which evoke emotional response in the reader. This is the sort of copy that could be printed verbatim in a non-fiction magazine article—hard-hitting, factual and succinct.

To illustrate the difference between technical Description and ordinary Description, we first print a real estate advertisement, then a non-technical Description of the same house:

For Sale—Westport—one-year-old, two-story Colonial on one and a half acres of woodland; suitable for small family or couple, walk to town and school; large livingroom, glass wall on one side with Sound view; library with beamed ceiling, fireplace; two bedrooms, new refrigerator and stove; FHA mortgage available. Box HT 450.

As an example of non-technical Description which gives the reader an experience of the same subject, here is a letter from the young couple who answered this ad and bought the house. The wife is writing to her mother:

Dearest Mamma,

We've found it at last, our dream house! And you'd never guess in a thousand years where it is—your old stamping ground of Westport!

We saw an ad in the Sunday paper, answered it that afternoon and took the house Tuesday night. It's darling. Two floors, built about a year ago and sort of country Colonial, white with green shutters and the cutest garden you ever saw. It's just right for Tom and me, and when the baby is old enough for school (it won't be very long, either, the way she's growing) she won't have to go very far. I shop three blocks away and in the town proper I can get just about everything you'd expect to find in New York.

The two rooms we like best are the livingroom, which has a tremendous glass wall overlooking Long Island Sound, and a very bookish library with fireplace and oak beams where Tom can write. The kitchen and bedrooms are adorable. In fact, we've found our dream house at last. We can't wait for you to come for a visit, but that will have to be in October. The present owner can't get into his new place until October 1st.

Tom joins me in sending all love to you and Papa.

Sally

Technical Description is factual, statistical, businesslike, succinct. Non-technical Description adds emotion, feelings and sensuousness.

Advertising uses Description constantly. The ad copywriter would be hopelessly handicapped if he couldn't describe his product. Imagine how frustrated he'd have been if he'd had to delete the following from an ad for Rath's "Chop-ettes":

The writing style is necessarily staccato or telegraphic because of the usual space limitations in classified advertising.

Says it better than the newspaper ad said the same thing, because this appeals to the reader's senses to a greater degree than the cold, formal, technical ad. The greater the evocation of the senses in readers, the more powerful is Description.

If the classified ad had as much space as this letter, it could be as descriptively warm, too. These examples are given not only to show that Description can be a sort of technical cataloguing, but also non-technical, non-telegraphic and sensuous.

Do you like old-time, crispy, breaded pork chops? Fry up a skilletful of Chop-ettes! They're pure corn-fed pork—chopped, shaped and breaded with a delicious whole-egg and milk breading. All you have to do is sizzle them just six minutes. No work at all, and every bite is old-fashioned *good*.

For a change, make Chop-ettes, Southern Style: Cover fried Chop-ettes with swirls of mashed sweet potatoes, seasoned with orange juice and grated orange rind. Dot with butter and brown quickly in the broiler. Couldn't be easier—or taste more delicious!

The selling in this ad is done through the copywriter's skill with Description. He's given you all the technical details of the chops he wants you to buy, but he's added descriptive phrases like "pure, corn-fed," "delicious whole-egg and milk breading," "old-fashioned good," "couldn't . . . taste more delicious." Description, technical and non-technical, has helped him sell his client's product through words on a printed page.

Summing up

Having considered in this Lesson several kinds of *Description*, including statistical and technical Description, we're now ready for a simplified definition of the word, the essence of what we've been reading about.

The dictionary defines Description as "discourse, or an example of it, designed to describe a scene, person, emotion, etc." And the word *describe* is defined: "To represent by words, to give an account of. To trace or traverse the outline of." Better still, perhaps, Description can be said to evoke the senses in a reader as does no other writing form.

This first of the four basic forms is, then, intrinsic to all writing and overlaps the other three in most instances. Certainly, very little writing is possible without Description of some sort. Its usefulness as a tool for the writer, full or part-time, professional or novice, far surpasses that of Narration, Exposition or Argument.

Description comes first in writing

Lesson fourteen

Principles of good writing

Writing narration

By definition, Narration is writing "designed to represent a connected succession of happenings." Narration differs from Description in being essentially concerned with action, with moving the story along. Narration supplies the magic touch which transforms "stationary" information into prose with suspense, action and life.

While Description concentrates on the representation by words of people and things—the way they present themselves to our senses, the physical background or outline against which a story or an article is told—Narration goes the next logical step. Whether it's non-fiction facts written in story form or a fiction yarn of sheer imagination, the energy, pace and movement of all writing come from Narration.

Narration isn't limited to fiction; it gives to some non-fiction that bright change of pace which creates a memorable article. Just the same, Narration and fiction are practically synonymous because they both mean "storytelling," so when we discuss Narration we're examining the core of creative writing technique.

The typical narrative incident, whether amplified with many details or briefly related, has three distinct, classical parts:

1. *The opening sentences:* These must arouse interest without giving away the outcome. They should also throw some light on the theme of the story about to be told.
2. *The body of the incident:* Action progresses by presenting facts given life through Dialogue, chronological order, suspense, and other techniques.
3. *The climactic ending:* When the story nears its finish, the reader must perceive some point or meaning to it. This point is usually near the climax of the incident.

Whether your Narration is fiction or non-fiction, you'll find it's built along the above lines. Narration, as we said in the opening paragraph of this Lesson, is essentially concerned with action, with moving the story along. It doesn't matter what kind of narrative you're creating. The energy, pace and movement indigenous to Narration are vital to all storytelling.

Narration moves
the story along

Let's take an example.

You have a short story in mind. It's about a man who lives up in the hills, far from town. First you describe him and the rugged country he lives in. Through words that play on the senses, you make your reader feel as if this man were actually living and the setting real. But up to now he hasn't moved, he hasn't done anything, the story hasn't started.

Now the Narration begins. You start to tell your reader what this man's situation is, what happened to him before and what's happening right now. You move him about like a chessman on a board; you bring him into conflict with events and other human beings. You supply, through Narration, the magic touch which transforms this "stationary" person into active life.

It's as though you first snapped a still picture of the man and his surroundings, then began to take motion pictures which gave movement to the man, the elements of nature and the threads of action. This is the fundamental difference between the first two writing forms: Description is the snapshot—and Narration is the movie.

Narration is like
a movie strip

Here are some Narration techniques useful to know at this stage of your writing.

1. You don't have to narrate everything about the background of your story right away. You can tell the reader who, what, when, where and why, so gradually he's scarcely aware of the process. Probably the best way of explaining to your readers

what's gone on up to the time the story opens (*antecedent action*) will be through Dialogue, through the thoughts of your chief characters, and by formal memories called "flashbacks" in fiction. But do this gradually; don't swamp the reader all at once. Drop in bits of *antecedent action* here and there as the current story unfolds.

2. Quote actual talk verbatim instead of reporting indirectly (*paraphrasing*) what characters said. There's something wonderfully authentic about the verbatim talk writers call *Dialogue*.

3. Learn to *limit the incidents* in your narrative. Pick highlights, then enlarge with rich detail. By selecting highly dramatic peaks, you'll sustain the reader's interest and he'll fill in his own narrative gaps. Every event isn't of equal narrative importance. There are peaks in all narratives. Select them, then dramatize them.

4. Let the main characters struggle toward some definite goal, object or desire. Whatever *conflict* arises in your writing will be intensified by this moving toward a particular goal through struggle. That's what *narrative conflict* is—movement toward a prescribed goal in spite of barriers, handicaps, drawbacks and delays. Will Joe catch the pass that wins the game? Will he stumble, will he drop the ball, will he be the goat or the hero?

Create conflict
with characters

5. There's natural *suspense* in the main characters' hopes, fears and efforts. The greater the suspense the greater your reader's interest. But keep your camera focused on relatively few characters. By limiting the width of your stage and the number of characters to what you can handle easily, you create *unity* and intensify *suspense*.

These broad techniques, to which writers have given the terms used above, apply to all fiction and many types of non-fiction Narration. Let's look now at some examples of non-fiction Narration, observing the application of the techniques listed above.

Non-fiction narration

Since we think of narration as storytelling we often identify it with fiction. But *non*-fiction uses an enormous amount of Narration, and journalism would be badly off indeed without the narrative form.

Narrative news stories and articles are published in all newspapers and most magazines. In *Magazine Article Writing* by Ernest Brennecke, Jr., and Donald Lemen Clark, the authors point out that the non-fiction articles which thrill most readers are stories that stress danger, action, heroism and conflict.

The narrative article in its simplest form starts at the beginning of the story and follows the time order to the end. But narrative articles, like all other types of article, rarely exist in pure form. The steady flow of the narrative may be interrupted by a paragraph of necessary explanation or a passage of picturesque description.

Like the writer of fiction, the writer of narratives of fact may cut back one or more times to tell what had happened before the story began. Like the writer of detective stories, he may temporarily suppress certain information to add suspense to his narrative. But whatever departures the writer may make from an orderly account of what happened, the course of the narrative must be laid out and followed.

Most readers like
action articles

The opening paragraphs of a narrative article almost always break away from a strictly chronological arrangement of happenings. Very rarely does the first of a series of incidents possess enough intrinsic interest to grip the reader's attention and force him to read of the succeeding incidents in their natural order.

Unless the first incident does possess sufficient intrinsic interest, the writer must select from elsewhere in the story some scene, bit of dialogue or incident which possesses sufficient interest and tell it first. After the reader's interest has been seized, the writer may interrupt the narrative and cut back to the antecedent action.

A non-fiction narrative article thus follows the same pattern that applies to narrative fiction—the divisions of Beginning, Middle and Ending. The writer of a non-fiction narrative article employs the same techniques of created suspense, conflict, emotional tension, flashback or antecedent action, chronology of events, and Dialogue as does the author of a short story.

Openings should
arouse interest

These storytelling techniques show up clearly in the examples of narrative non-fiction which follow. Remember while reading them that a narrative article doesn't have to be limited to what the writer actually experienced, nor does the time element have to be consecutive.

In short, the non-fiction writer can use all of the short story writer's bag of tricks.

In *Time* magazine's classic account of Calvin Coolidge's death on January 5, 1933, the reader pictures through Dialogue, flashbacks, conflict and suspense, impression, contrast, descriptive pauses and straight chronology how the sudden end of a former President affects the United States Senate, the White House, a small New England town, a variety of important and unimportant citizens—all of this journalistic non-fiction using the writing form called Narration:

Early one afternoon last week Senator Glass was warmly expounding his bank reform bill on the Senate Floor when Senator Swanson, his Virginia colleague, nudged him, whispered something. For a moment Senator Glass looked dumbfounded. Then in a quavering voice he announced: "Mr. President, I have just been apprised of a fact very, very distressing to the nation generally and to me particularly. Former President Coolidge has just dropped dead. I think the Senate should immediately adjourn." Numb with shock, the Senate adjourned.

At the White House President Hoover was lunching with Secretary of State Stimson. Chief Usher Irwin Hood ("Ike") Hoover tiptoed into the dining room. Into the President's ear he whispered the news: "Mr. Coolidge has died of heart failure." After a stunned moment, the President pushed back his chair, laid down his napkin, strode to his office. There he hastily dispatched a special message to Congress, issued a proclamation for 30 days of public mourning. Within five minutes, down to half-staff came the White House flag. Down came the flags of Washington, of the nation.

The House, after it had heard the news by word of mouth, continued in session an hour to receive the President's message. It read: "It is my painful duty to inform you of the death today of Calvin Coolidge . . . There is no occasion for me to recount his eminent services . . . His entire lifetime has been one of single devotion to our country . . ." Then the House, too, adjourned.

At Plymouth, Vt., Miss Aurora Pierce, longtime Coolidge housekeeper, heard a tap on the homestead window. Allen Brown, a neighbor, was outside. She raised the sash to hear him say: "Calvin's dead, Aurora." She sat down in the room in which the 30th President of the U.S. had taken the oath from his father at 2:47 A.M., August 3, 1923, and let her tears run in silent grief.

In New York President-elect Roosevelt got word by telephone from a press association in the study of his home. He was "inexpressibly shocked" at the death of the man who had defeated him for the Vice-Presidency in 1920.

On the New York Stock Exchange, hundreds of brokers got the news simultaneously from their office tickers. They stared blankly, incredulously at each other. Trading slacked off uncertainly with falling prices. The day closed with a brief little rally—a farewell salute to the man whose name has been given to the greatest bull market in history.

Frank Billings Kellogg, his Secretary of State, heard about it at Des Moines on his way to California. Andrew William Mellon, his Secretary of the Treasury, found it hard to believe the news as the

Time is fixed through the narrative form. What were others doing at the moment? This is a dramatic, narrative device which gives the article its classic strong opening which immediately arouses interest in the reader.

The power of verbatim quotation rather than paraphrase.

These are limited incidents, highlights among thousands of reactions to the death of a President. But by dramatizing a few of the most important the writer enlivens his narrative.

What Hoover wrote is read immediately to the House. We now have setting in depth—through narrative form, though this is non-fiction.

The narrative continues, but moves closer to its true locale. These scenes are, of course, parallel in time.

Another view of contemporary reaction—by Narration. This highlighting of the various viewpoints is effective.

The Cabinet reacts to the ex-President's death.

And here, Calvin Coolidge's best friend. By now we have viewed the incident—the main fact of Coolidge's death—from several points and we have a full story.

Chronology of Coolidge's final day on earth. Narration need not be consecutive. The flashback can be done gradually as the narrative unfolds—but it *must be done.*

Again, the power of actual Dialogue, not just paraphrase, clearly advantageous to Narration.

This is chronological storytelling, step after step. In this case the trivia, the ex-President's fiddling with tiny unimportant things, tend to enhance the narrative's suspense.

The way it happened ... sheer narrative article writing. This climax of the narrative has been postponed by the various "reactions" to the ex-President's death. By putting off the actual telling of the moment of death, suspense is created.

Again, the power and felicity of verbatim Dialogue are demonstrated here.

S.S. *Majestic* carried him back to his ambassadorial post at London. Dwight Filley Davis, his Secretary of War, was at Tallahassee. John Garibaldi Sargent, his Attorney General, was recovering from influenza at his Ludlow, Vt., home. Frank Stearns, his closest personal friend, the man who picked him for President long before the Boston police strike, was so overcome with grief that he could say nothing for hours.

At "The Beeches," his Northampton home, Calvin Coolidge had gotten up that morning as usual at 7 A.M. At the breakfast table he grumbled over the lack of news in the papers. At 8:30 he was at his office (Coolidge & Hemenway) on Main Street, reading his mail, attending to minor personal business. What he thought was another attack of indigestion—he had been doctoring himself for it with soda for three weeks—made him feel uncomfortable. So about 10 o'clock he said to Harry Ross, his secretary: "Well, I guess we'll go up to the house."

As they entered, Mrs. Coolidge was just going out shopping. Said her husband: "Don't you want the car?" "No," she replied, "it's such a nice day I'd rather walk." She left. Mr. Coolidge sat talking with secretary Ross—about the Plymouth place, last year's pa'tridge shooting, hay fever. He strolled to the kitchen to get a drink of water. He put a stray book neatly back into the case. He evened up pens on the desk. He idly fingered a jigsaw puzzle with his name on it. He went "down cellar," watched the furnace man shovel coal. About noon he disappeared upstairs, presumably to shave, as so many New Englanders do about midday.

Returning a few minutes later, Mrs. Coolidge went upstairs to summon him for luncheon. In his dressing room she found him lying on the floor on his back in his shirtsleeves. To him Death had come 15 minutes before, swiftly, easily, without pain. For "cause" the official death certificate said: "coronary thrombosis."

That night the body of Calvin Coolidge lay on its own bed in its own room.

Outside the window a half moon played tricks with heavy night mists rising from the Mount Tom Meadows. Beyond the mist and the moonlight a people mourned the loss of its greatest private citizen, its only ex-President ... Smith College girls, just back from holidays, went to the Calvin Theatre as usual, saw "Under-Cover Man" on the screen. Northampton's Mayor Bliss announced that the city's merchants would draw their shades but keep their doors open during the funeral. Said he: "I'm not going to ask them to close because I don't think Calvin Coolidge would want that. He knew what they've been through. Every nickel counts with them. He wouldn't want them to lose a sale."

Next night a plain bronze casket stood before the fireplace of "The Beeches" living room. On it was engraved: "Calvin Coolidge—

1872–1933." Above it hung an oil painting of the onetime Presidential yacht *Mayflower,* one of Calvin Coolidge's few genuine diversions in office. Harry Ross stood close by. The only sound in the stillness of the house was the pitter-patter of Tiny Tim's claws as the Coolidge chow came and went on the hardwood floors. Far away through the same night with many a long whistle there roared a 13-car special bearing the great of Washington to Northampton.

After the climax, the narrative slowly declines to its natural end. It's amazing how all storytelling is similar, whether journalism or novel writing.

Narration keeps the story moving

The true function of Narration is storytelling and that means fiction to most readers. Let's look at the climax of the best-selling suspense novel, *The Desperate Hours,* by Joseph Hayes.

In this novel, Dan Hilliard's family is about to be freed after being held captive in their home by a band of cop-killers, hiding from the police. The Hilliards are an ordinary, average family in Indianapolis, to whom gang killings are something you see on TV or read about in a detective thriller. The people mentioned in this excerpt from the novel are: Glenn Griffin, one of the killers; Chuck Wright, a young man who loves Cindy, the Hilliards' daughter; Ralphie, the young Hilliard son who is being held as hostage; Robish, one of the killers who has just fled the house; and Webb, the armed deputy, waiting outside the Hilliard home for Griffin to emerge.

The scene is inside the house. We suggest you read the excerpt once straight through—then read it again with reference to the marginal notes.

Dan Hilliard mounted the stairs, his tread heavy and determined, hearing, instead of the police fusillade he had expected, the motor of his car grinding over outside. As he reached the head of the stairway, where Glenn Griffin had been lying a few moments before, he saw a streak of blood on the carpet and heard, outside, the spit of gravel and the mounting roar of motor that receded toward the street. He paused.

The climax approaches as Dan Hilliard mounts his own stairway, wary but determined. His small son is hostage upstairs.

But only briefly because, while he heard Griffin's voice on his right, behind the smashed door—"In here, Hilliard"—he saw something in the door of Cindy's room that drew him there instead. He looked down, with the ugly bleakness returning in him, into the gray face of Chuck Wright. His whirling mind took in the dark stain on the floor, the twisted and lifeless-looking body, the blood-spattered and odd-shaped gun.

In one fluid movement, Dan Hilliard stopped, picked up the auto-

The suspense in this bit of fiction is built up line by line. Watch the conflict develop between Dan and the cornered cop-killer.

matic, the blood warm against his hand, and turned to cross the hall. It flickered through his mind that Robish had taken Chuck Wright to be a policeman; this had brought him downstairs in terror. Dan Hilliard thanked Chuck Wright silently and stopped in front of the splintered door of his own bedroom.

He knew what he was going to do now. Before the police came in, before anything else, he was going to do it. It was simple, really. But the thought of Ralphie in that room made Dan Hilliard slip the gun into his coat pocket, with his hand closed over it. He would shoot through the coat. He would empty it into Glenn Griffin, and that then would be the end of it.

He stepped into the room. Ralphie was on the bed, huddled in one corner, and in the corner behind him stood Glenn Griffin. His dark, unnaturally bright eyes turned from the window and fixed glassily on Dan. But Dan was looking at the icy-white and frozen terror on the face of his son.

It would not be so easy. The boy's eyes returned at once, in sickened fascination, to the muzzle of the gun that Glenn Griffin kept fixed on him. The gun was empty, but still it was not going to be so simple.

"You got to get me out of here, Pop." But the insolence was gone; the attempt at arrogance thin and worn. "That copper over there nicked me. You got more of 'em outside?"

Dan saw, with a twist of pleasure that he did not like, the blood-edged furrow along the side of Glenn Griffin's scalp, and he realized that Chuck Wright's first shot had stunned but not seriously wounded the convict. Well, he'd finish the job, now. He, Dan Hilliard.

First, though, he had another job. One more. "Ralphie," he said quietly, his voice a dry whisper, "Ralphie, look at me. Listen!"

"No time now, no time!" Glenn Griffin cried, licking at his lips, and he moved his gun closer to the boy's head.

Dan Hilliard became aware of something else then, recorded it, worked around it. He couldn't startle Griffin into lifting that gun, bringing it down in desperate frustration on the boy's skull.

"Son," Dan said slowly, very low and definite, the word spreading a hypnotic effect over the quiet room, "listen to me. Nothing's going to happen to you. That man is not going to shoot you, Ralphie, and I'll tell you why, son. Believe me, because . . ."

"Lay off, Hilliard! You don't lay off, I'll get it over with. You got to get me out of here, see!" The frantic note was clear, and it was this that Dan feared.

Dan's hand was on the butt of the automatic, his finger looped over the trigger. Ralphie was between him and his target. "I wouldn't lie to you. Have I ever lied to you, Ralph?"

The boy's head shook, once.

The story is anticipated: we are told what the father is determined to do to the gang killers who have violated the sanctity of his home. This is conflict which intensifies the suspense.

We must pause in the narrative to describe what Dan Hilliard saw as he entered the room. The pause itself is suspenseful by contrast.

Suspense again in the phrase "in sickened fascination," etc.

Verbatim quotation: perhaps the most powerful single technique in Narration.

This heightens the conflict of the story: little boy in danger, father talking him to safety: killer getting nervous. Conflict in every line as the narrative unfolds.

The cross-current conflicts of the narrative now begin mounting until they burst into a climax.

Griffin screamed: "Will you stop it! Are there any more cops out there, Hilliard? Why didn't they knock off Robish? There ain't any more, are there? They'd be in here by now!"

Still, Dan ignored him, concentrating on his son. "Ralphie, that man's gun is not loaded. It doesn't have any bullets in it. Do you believe me?"

He was conscious of the start in Glenn Griffin, the quick grin of disbelief, but he was studying his son's face.

"Do you believe me?"

Then very slowly, the boy nodded his head.

"What's going on here?" Griffin shrilled. "Hilliard, you deaf? It's loaded, Hilliard. You wouldn't have brought it back with you if . . ."

Griffin stopped then, the eyes brightening into a glazed stare.

Dan said, as slowly as before: "Ralph, you're a very big boy. I want you to mind me, understand? I want you to do whatever I say now."

"Stop it!" Griffin yelled. "Stop the talk! My head hurts. I got to . . ." He broke off, and somewhere in his reeling mind a suspicion took root. He lowered his voice. "You wouldn't a-come in here with an empty . . ."

That moment of self-doubt was what Dan had been playing for. "Ralphie!" he barked suddenly. "Run!"

The shout brought the boy up off the bed in one bound before Griffin could move.

"Get downstairs and outside!" Dan Hilliard shouted.

And then he saw Glenn Griffin lifting the gun, swinging it after the boy. Dan had to break his first impulse with a great and terrible effort of will that cracked like pain through his body. He kept the automatic in his pocket even when he heard the empty gun clicking, but he was more certain, hearing those frantic fruitless clicks, what he was going to do now. He heard Ralphie on the stairs, skittering down. The boy was gone. He would not see this. Dan had made sure of that.

He watched the dazed bleak horror in the face across the room; he saw the white teeth bared; he heard the faint boylike cry in the back of the young man's throat as he brought the deputy sheriff's gun up to point directly at Dan Hilliard. Dan heard the clicks, over and over, and then, above this, a stranger sound than any: the short explosion of his own laughter.

It was then that he brought the automatic from his own coat pocket. The rage was cold in him now, and he continued to think of that gun muzzle pointed at his son's back. He could feel his grip on the automatic climb like a pain up to his shoulder. He was going to do it now.

Whatever Glenn Griffin saw on Dan Hilliard's face then—the pitiless eyes, the set of jaw, the purple swelling of the bruise that Griffin

---

This Dialogue is particularly effective—especially the cop-killer's whining fears and doubts as expressed in his characteristic speech.

The climax of the whole story. From here on, the killer is doomed and knows it himself. The suspense has become almost unbearable. The reader is now held captive—through sheer narrative technique.

Verbatim words, a powerful narrative weapon.

Cleverly, the author points out Dan Hilliard's new, tremendous decision—that he won't desecrate his own house by killing a man, by sinking to a killer's level.

Sheer, chronological narrative. Physical reactions help to punctuate it by holding back the action.

Holding back of normal, expected events, only enhances the climax.

himself had put along one cheek—whatever it was, it caused him to back into the corner, his tongue darting wetly from between his lips. His eyes dropped, but they appeared not to see, not quite to comprehend the meaning of that gun in the white-knuckled hand that moved closer.

Dan Hilliard had no control over what he was going to do now. They had put the people he loved through two days of nightmarish hell; they had beaten and threatened and terrified; they had brought violence and the smell of blood and filth into his home. There was only this now, this one final act, and then it would be over.

Glenn Griffin was sliding down against the wall, the saliva dribbling in little bubbles down his jumping chin. His mouth opened and closed and opened again, working loosely, but no sound came. He pleaded with those fluttering hands at his neck. The grotesque pantomime of frenzy did not touch Dan Hilliard's icy intention.

Now. Now. Why don't you pull the trigger? Why don't you get it over with? Why should anything hold you back? Why should you, Dan Hilliard, live by scruples these men never felt? Why should you hesitate when they . . .

But Dan Hilliard was not one of them. This was his room, the bedroom in which he and his wife slept. This was his home. And down below, his wife and daughter and son were waiting, wondering, not knowing any of this, still trembling with the fear this scum had brought into the house. Across the hall lay the young man who loved Cindy, who must love her deeply, and he, perhaps, was dead now. He needed help, and quick. In the electric brilliance of this moment, Dan Hilliard lowered the gun slowly until the muzzle pointed at the floor. He didn't have the right. He was not one of them.

The quivering mass of animal-being crumpled in the corner before him sickened Dan Hilliard.

"Get out," he said softly. He felt dirty all over, as though some of the slime had wiped off on him somehow. "Get out of my house," he said, but still quietly.

Then, staring out of the window, seeing in the distance a man on a ladder against the roof of the Wallings' house, he heard the scrabbling behind him, as Glenn Griffin, whimpering, clawed his way across the bed, staggered toward the hall; Dan heard the quick drum of steps on the stairway and the opening of the front door. Dan tossed the automatic to the floor. He had almost murdered a man; he had almost become one of them.

He threw open the window. "Webb!" he shouted, and a blade seemed to turn over in his throat. "Webb! Get a doctor and ambulance, fast!"

Then he whirled about and strode swiftly toward his daughter's bedroom where Chuck Wright still lay crumpled and unconscious.

Margin notes:

Flashback narrative. It helps delay the climax.

Marvelous Description of a cowering villain.

Narrative counterpoint once more: the vital decision—to do or not to do. Conflict greater than ever before—this time *within* Dan—is emotional tension at its best.

The decent man determines to stay decent. The inner conflict is being resolved and when the conflict resolves, all the suspense dies.

In Narration there is often simply no substitute for straight chronology.

Dan was bending down, kneeling in the blood, when he heard two shots outside. They seemed to come from a distance, with a whine in them.

Narration in a classic novel

The excerpt from Hayes' novel is modern fiction using the narrative form to keep the pace moving rapidly. But narrative writers of other times were also aware of the importance of contrast, dramatic suspense, conflict, verbatim Dialogue and emotional tension. These are not today's inventions.

Half a century before *The Desperate Hours,* Edith Wharton, one of America's great authors, wrote a classic novel called *Ethan Frome,* in which the climax is the attempt by Ethan and his invalid wife's cousin, Mattie, to kill themselves on a bobsled ride rather than lose each other.

Mattie is the one who suggests it, for to her Ethan Frome is the finest thing in her life, the only person who has ever loved her, and she simply cannot go back to her former lonely ways. Following is the Narration of the bobsled ride—a ride made even more poignant for the reader because neither Ethan nor Mattie dies in the crash but both are crippled for life:

He took his seat on the sled and Mattie instantly placed herself in front of him. Her hat had fallen into the snow and his lips were in her hair. He stretched out his legs, drove his heels into the road to keep the sled from slipping forward, and bent her head back between his hands. Then suddenly he sprang up.

"Get up!" he ordered her.

It was the tone she always heeded, but she cowered down in her seat, repeating vehemently:

"No, no, no!"

"Get up!"

"Why?"

"I want to sit in front."

"No, no! How can you steer in front?"

"I don't have to. We'll follow the track."

They spoke in smothered whispers, as though the night were listening.

"Get up! Get up!" he urged her; but she kept on repeating: "Why do you want to sit in front?"

"Because I . . . because I want to feel you holding me," he stammered, and dragged her to her feet.

You realize this is going to be no ordinary ride down a hill on a sled.

The "glassy slide" of ice—this is a dangerous hill and the peril at the foot of it is now all too clear. Conflict and suspense intensify the emotional tension in the reader.

The answer seemed to satisfy her, or else she yielded to the power of his voice. He bent down, feeling in the obscurity for the glassy slide worn by preceding coasters, and placed the runners carefully between the edges. She waited while he seated himself with crossed legs in the front of the sled; then she crouched quickly down at his back and clasped her arms about him. Her breath in his neck set him shuddering again, and he almost sprang from his seat. But in a flash he remembered the alternative. She was right: it was better than parting. He leaned back and drew her mouth to his . . .

The narrative flies down the hill as fast as the sled on the ice. There are many conflicts here—physical and mental.

Just as they started he heard the sorrel's whinny again, and the familiar wistful call, and all the confused images it brought with it, went with him down the first reach of the road. Half-way down there was a sudden drop, then a rise, and after that another delirious descent. As they took wing for this it seemed to him that they were flying indeed, flying far up into the cloudy night, with Starkfield immeasurably below them, falling away like a speck . . . space . . . Then the big elm shot up ahead, lying in wait for them at the bend of the road, and he said between his teeth: "We can fetch it; I know we can fetch it . . ."

As they flew toward the tree Mattie pressed her arms tighter, and her blood seemed to be in his veins. Once or twice the sled swerved a little under them. He slanted his body to keep it headed for the elm, repeating to himself again and again: "I know we can fetch it;" and little phrases danced before him on the air. The big tree loomed bigger and closer, and as they bore down on it he thought: "It's waiting for us: it seems to know."

Gathers momentum to a peak of suspense as the racing sled nears the tree.

Just at the moment of climax yet another conflict arises in the hero's situation.

But suddenly his wife's face, with twisted monstrous lineaments, thrust itself between him and his goal, and he made an instinctive movement to brush it aside. The sled swerved in response, but he righted it again, kept it straight, and drove down onto the black, projecting mass. There was a last instant when the air shot past him like millions of fiery wires; and then the elm . . . !

When two elements overlap

If narrative in fiction or non-fiction is involved with action or pace or movement, Narration and Description often overlap, sometimes to a remarkable degree. You may frequently say to yourself while reading: "Why this is Description *and* Narration, and I can't tell where one leaves off and the other commences." And you'll be perfectly right.

As always in the craft of writing, there are few clear-cut and positive rules. The colors aren't black and white, but grays of every degree.

Look at the following paragraphs of Narration from Bruce Catton. The excerpt is from *Glory Road,* the second book in his famous trilogy about the Civil War. The first was *Mr. Lincoln's Army,* and the last, *A Stillness at Appomattox,* won the Pulitzer Prize for history.

In historical writing, as in journalism which it resembles, there's more Description than is usual in the narrative form, which is only natural since the picture must be painted before the story can proceed. By Bruce Catton it is woven into the fabric of the narrative through beautiful language and unique style. The author has brought us to the climax of the Battle of Gettysburg, July 3, 1863—the dramatic event history calls Pickett's Charge. General Lee has thrown 15,000 men into the assault. At this point in the narrative they have crossed the deadly plain and are moving up against the high ridge held by Union troops:

Along the ridge and in the grove the Federals waited, and the foremost Federal brigade stood up to level its muskets, and the rebel line came very near. Then at last every musket and every cannon in this part of the Yankee line opened at once, and Pettigrew's whole Confederate division disappeared in an immense cloud of smoke and dust. Above this boiling cloud the Union men could see a ghastly debris of guns, knapsacks, blanket rolls, severed human heads, and arms and legs and parts of bodies, tossed into the air by the impact of the shot.

The mass rolled in closer, the Federals firing into the center of the storm cloud. The men with the improvised buckshot cartridges in smoothbore guns had a target they could not miss, and the XI Corps artillery on Cemetery Hill was sending shell in through the gaps in the Yankee line. Suddenly Pettigrew's men passed the limit of human endurance and the lines broke apart and the hillside was covered with men running for cover, and the Federal gunners burned the ground with shell and canister. On the littered field, amid all the dead and wounded, prostrate men could be seen holding up handkerchiefs in sign of surrender.

But if the right and left of the charging Confederate line had been smashed, the center was still coming on. Cushing fired his last remaining charge, and a bullet hit him in the mouth and killed him. Most of the Pennsylvanians behind the wall sprang up and ran back to the crest, and the few who remained were overwhelmed as the rebel line rolled in and beat the life out of them. Most of the rebels stayed behind the wall or crowded in amid the clump of trees and opened fire on the Yankees on the crest, their red battle flags

No wasted words, just plain, hard realistic reporting of chronological facts which drive the narrative into the reader's mind. Description and Narration are inextricably interwoven.

clustering thick, men in front lying prone or kneeling, men in the rear standing and firing over their heads.

A handful leaped over the wall, Armistead in the lead, and ran in among the wreckage of Cushing's battery. Armistead's horse had been killed and his hat was down on the hilt of his sword now, but the sword was still held high, and through the curling smoke the Union soldiers got a final glimpse of him, one triumphant hand resting on a silent cannon.

This was the climax and the bloody indisputable pay-off; the next few minutes would tell the story, and what that story would be would all depend on whether these blue-coated soldiers really meant it. There were more Federals than Confederates on the field, but right here where the fighting was going on there were more Confederates than Federals, and every man was firing in a wild, feverish haste, with the smoke settling down thicker and thicker. From the peach orchard Confederate guns were shooting straight into the Union line, disregarding the danger that some of their own men would be hit, and the winging missiles tore ugly lanes through the disorganized mass of Yankees.

A fresh Union regiment was moving up through Ziegler's Grove, and as the men came out into the open they heard the uproar of battle different from any they had ever heard before—"strange and terrible, a sound that came from thousands of human throats, yet was not a commingling of shouts and yells but rather like a vast mournful roar." There was no cheering, but thousands of men were growling and cursing without realizing it as they fought to the utmost limit of primal savagery . . .

Back on the crest, facing the clump of trees, the line swayed as men worked up their nerve. The mounted staff officer was shouting, men were yelling to each other, and a color-bearer jumped up and ran forward, waving his flag. The staff was broken by a shot, and he grabbed the stump and held the ragged colors above his head, and by ones and twos and then all along the crest men sprang to their feet and followed him, firing as they ran. Armistead was stretched out on the ground now with a bullet in him, and the other gray-coats who had got in among the guns were down too, and the Federals came in on the rebel mass among the little trees, and the smoke hid the hot afternoon sun.

Pickett's men were in a box now. On their left Pettigrew's division had evaporated, on the right they were dissolving under an unceasing flank fire, in front they were getting a head-on assault that was too heavy to take, and there was no support in sight. Longstreet had sent a brigade up to cover their right, but in the blinding fog the brigade had lost its direction and was heading straight for McGilvery's ranked cannon, which blasted it with deadly aim, and the Vermont regiments wheeled completely around and got the brigade

Narrative is movement. We have tremendous movement all through these passages.

in flank. It fell apart and its bits and pieces went tumbling back to Seminary Ridge.

And suddenly the tension was gone and the firing was dying down, and the Confederates by the clump of trees were going back to their own lines or dropping their muskets and raising their hands in surrender. Meade came riding up to the crest just now, and an officer met him and told him that Lee's charge had been crushed, and Meade raised his hand and cried "Thank God!" The last fugitives went back toward their starting point, Federal gunners following them with shell, and Gibbon's weary soldiers were sending a great mass of rebel prisoners back to the rear. The fighting was over.

The author uses almost every classic narrative device in these paragraphs of non-fiction. Conflict is, of course, supreme in the writing of history, particularly military history. This conflict is at several levels—national, geographical and personal—in the story of a battle like Gettysburg. Because battles involve human beings, particularly when these battles are fought hand-to-hand, conflict creates enormous personal suspense despite the fact that most readers know in advance how the story comes out.

By limiting the incidents to dramatized highlights, such as the desperate struggle for possession of the vital ridge, Catton creates emotional tension through suspenseful conflict. Yet in order to do this adequately, he has freely used Description interwoven into the Narration to give the reader a clear picture of the physical background of desperate fighting.

Catton's superiority as a writer owes much to his eye and ear for detail. He not only tells that such and such happened; he takes you there; you actually see every bloody, terrible minute of the climactic battle of the Civil War through telling, factual, realistic narrative.

The trained writer highlights incidents

Narration in advertising

Advertising copywriters use a combination of Narration-Description in almost every ad they write. Here's part of a *Reader's Digest* advertisement in *Time* magazine, telling readers why the *Digest* is a good magazine for a growing company to advertise in. The story concerns the Tappan Company, manufacturer of gas and electric ranges for the home. It's done in narrative style:

One basket of beans, six bushels of corn, three pounds of corn-meal . . .

Seventy-eight years ago the late W. J. Tappan sold his cast-iron cooking ranges the best way he could—often by barter. With his inventory packed into a wagon, he made the rounds of the Ohio River Valley swapping his stoves for fresh vegetables, plus whatever cash the thrifty farmers' wives would scrape together.

From this humble start, the Tappan Company has grown into the largest independent manufacturer of gas and electric ranges for the home.

Tappan has grown by inventing and marketing better products. It developed the more convenient, divided cooking top, the "see-through" oven door and the chrome-lined oven, which made cooking easier and got better results. More recently, Tappan brought out its "Fabulous 400" which it called "the first new step in range designing in 35 years." This space-saving range hangs from the wall or sits on a cabinet, the oven is at eye level and the burners recess like drawers.

Tappan's search for better methods extended to its advertising, too. As a result, it succeeded—in the middle of a prolonged recession for the rest of its industry—in setting new sales records.

Narration and Description are inextricably interwoven in the preceding quote, as in much modern advertising copy. Let's look at one of a series of ads written for the John Hancock Mutual Life Insurance Company in *The Saturday Evening Post*. The copy is the work of Louis Redmond and is written in narrative style but filled with descriptive phrases under the title: "He Sold Happiness for Nickels and Dimes." The following copy appeared with a painting in color showing the original Woolworth 5-and-10-cent store in upstate New York:

Suspense is part of good Narration

Frank Woolworth knew what was in the heart of a child when she stood with her nose pressed against the pane of a store window.

He, too, felt the weight of unsatisfied longing. He supported a family on the $10 a week he earned as a clerk in a small-town store He knew what aching hopes, what dreams of a better life, lay in the nickels and dimes that were left after the family bills were paid.

So in his mind there grew a picture of a new kind of store for America.

It was a make-a-wish store. It was filled with things that people wanted out of life. There were things to eat, to wear, to read, to build with. There were things to make children happy and to make women beautiful—things for health, for laughter, for work, for comfort.

And anybody in America could walk into that store with a dime *and buy anything he saw*. There, with life's bounty spread before you, was nothing you couldn't afford.

With a bucket of red paint for gaiety and $300 in cash, Frank Woolworth opened his store. At first there were only a few things on the counters. But each week there were more. For a wonderful thing began to happen. *The more people bought with their dimes, the more their dimes were able to buy.* Frank Woolworth's little red store had proved a great American truth—that the power of people's nickels and dimes, working together, can accomplish anything.

It made him rich. And it made us richer still. For he showed us, in a way we can never forget, that most of the good things in life are within the reach of everyone who works towards them in this land of opportunity.

Summing up

Narration is designed to represent a succession of happenings, to transform "stationary" facts and information into writing that has suspense, action and life. While Description concentrates on the representation of people and things through our senses, on the physical background and setting for a story or article, Narration goes the next logical step. It gives writing energy, pace and movement. Narration changes facts and people and backgrounds from a still photograph to a moving picture.

Don't begin with a dull point

There's a classical division to Narration which can be reduced to the words Beginning, Middle and Ending. These distinctly separate parts of any narrative story or article are implemented by narrative techniques which include the use of (1) flashbacks or antecedent action to bring the reader up to the point where the story begins; (2) Dialogue or verbatim quotation; (3) selection of incidents for dramatic peaks in the narrative; (4) conflict which leads to (5) suspense and emotional reaction in the reader.

Finally, as in all writing, there is no such thing as a story or article which is pure Narration. Frequently, Description and Narration overlap to a remarkable degree, especially in journalistic writing. Nevertheless, techniques of Narration which apply to fiction are fundamental in writing narrative non-fiction.

In order to understand more about the relationship of the first two forms to the third form, *Exposition,* we now examine the latter in detail. We shall see that the primary aim in *Exposition* is to *explain* things and ideas to the reader, rather than to describe characters or set a stage through the senses (*Description*), or tell a story which gives energy, pace and movement to these characters (*Narration*).

Lesson fifteen

Principles of good writing

Writing exposition

When you write *Exposition,* you're writing to inform the reader, to explain something to him, to give him directions. Since the field of Exposition is enormous—indeed, almost unlimited in subject matter—we should quickly settle upon a definition of the word. The simplest way to define it is to use the common synonym: *explanation.*

In short, we are not out to please the reader by stimulating his emotions or imagination; we are out to *instruct* him.

Writers usually think of Exposition in these broad areas:

1. Explanation of facts.
2. Explanation of events.
3. Explanation of ideas.

We shall take up these three categories one at a time. But first we must examine techniques common to *all* expository writing.

In basic Exposition, *clarity* is the primary goal. Without clarity, no satisfactory explanation is possible. Therefore, certain specific devices which promote clarity are helpful to all expository writing right from the start:

1. Logical organization of thought.

2. Use of specific detail.
3. Use of examples.
4. Contrast or antithesis.
5. Comparison or analogy.

These five clarifying devices apply to Exposition in all of its standard forms, whether explanation of facts, events or ideas. Explanatory writing is made understandable by logical organization, by use of specific details, by examples to illustrate your points, by the use of contrast (including antithesis), and by comparison or analogy.

These helpful devices are constantly used by professional writers to *fix the meaning*—to convince the reader of the truth or the logic of what the writer has put into words.

Your organization
must be logical

1. Logical organization of thought

In order to fix the meaning of your words in your reader's mind, it's wise to organize and develop your thought logically, from a beginning through a middle to an ending. You won't explain very much to a reader if your expository writing is all mixed up, with the conclusion in the middle, your ideas disorganized and your thoughts illogically formed.

If you start a mystery story by giving away the ending, you'll lose your reader right away. If you argue for or against something, you must logically organize and develop your points until, on the basis of what's been presented to the reader, you make a strong case in your summation.

Let's look at an example:

Paragraph One—A writer starts to explain how to put aluminum storm window-screen combinations on your house. He describes the combination in the first paragraph.

Paragraph Two—He jumps suddenly to the changing weather pattern in your state. It's getting warmer all the time, his facts indicate—the result of a receding Greenland icecap. One day, he states, palm trees will grow in Canada.

Paragraph Three—He leaps to another topic, this time the nuisance of mosquitoes and flies and other reasons why all houses should have screens. In this same paragraph he switches abruptly to a detailed explanation of why aluminum is better than wood for storm windows and screens.

Paragraph Four—All of a sudden the writer is talking about where aluminum comes from and how it's processed. He goes into detail about its discovery and modern uses.

Paragraph Five—Now he goes back to the physical act of fitting the combinations into a window frame, but uses a lot of technical terms for which there's no preparation or explanation. The last two sentences in the paragraph identify stores where aluminum combinations can be bought, except that the last sentence also returns to the reported changing weather pattern in your state, which never quite seems to make sense to the reader's mind.

This writer's copy lacks organization and logical development. It would have been better if he'd put his thoughts in this carefully prepared order:

Paragraph One—An explanation of what a combination storm window and screen looks like, what its functions are, and why it's better than separate storm windows and screens.

Paragraph Two—What aluminum is, what factors make it superior to other metals and woods for storm-screen use, its properties of lightness and durability, its stainless quality, etc.

Paragraph Three—Why aluminum is better than other types of frames, based on logical facts and sound references.

Paragraph Four—First steps in putting up the combination frames, with each step logically explained.

Examples should always be clear

Paragraph Five—Next step in securing the screens. Then an explanation of how to fit them properly and how to lock them in.

Paragraph Six—Final paragraph returning to the opening premise —why combination sash is superior to separate screens and storm windows, the ease of changing from one to the other, and perhaps a short dissertation on changing weather patterns pertinent to this problem.

In the second version, logical order has made things easier for the reader, developed the explanation from one premise to the next without digressions, and removed ambiguities arising from the first and less logical presentation.

2. Use of specific detail

You aren't going to convince your reader of your points by generalities and fuzzy statements. Facts are facts—and you transmit them to paper through details which evoke precise images in your reader. Non-fiction is essentially factual and of all forms of non-fiction writing, Exposition most needs *the fact*.

In Lesson Three we set forth one of the basic rules of writing: use enough specific details so the reader can picture what's in your mind.

We pointed out that it wasn't enough merely to write: "Mr. Willets was a lazy man" and let it go at that. We had to give sufficient details to make it clear to the reader that Mr. Willets *was* a lazy man.

In Exposition this principle is always true. Being factual writing, Exposition deals in one commodity only: the fact, whose strength is the detail. Facts without details fail to convince. Details fix the meaning in the reader's mind through his identification with places, events, sights, sounds, dimensions, feelings and ideas which first occurred to the writer and have now been transmitted to the other end of a telegraphic wire by an impulse we call the written word.

Don't give facts without details

3. Use of examples

One excellent way of assuring clarity is to *give an example,* since it is the best writing device to convert a fact or situation in the writer's mind into the image he wants the reader to get. Here's one from a handbook on public relations:

Suppose your company has a strike on its hands and the other side is bombarding your community with inflammatory handbills. It's up to your public relations department to answer these accusations in some way, and the carefully worded statement to the press is as good as any. Under no circumstances, however, let the other side go hog-wild without being answered. You're just asking for trouble.

By the example, which recalls other cases or makes one up to suit the occasion, you fix the meaning in the reader's mind. The example makes him think to himself: "Say, that's right. I must remember that. It's a good point!"

Law is frequently taught through examples. The "case system" of law requires the student lawyer to read one example after another of prior cases in which our legal precedents have been set. Exposure to examples is an extremely effective teaching technique. It's used in this Course when we give you quotations from authors. Each quotation is an example, setting the detail in the reader's mind as nothing else seems quite able to do.

4. Contrast or antithesis

Contrast is achieved by emphasizing significant differences when comparing facts, events, things or ideas side by side. When you contrast direct opposites, you call it *antithesis*. Of all the uses to which writers of Exposition can put contrast, the extreme form of antithesis is the most effective, because it's the most dramatic and telling in the reader's mind.

Contrast stresses
major differences

Here's an example of antithesis from classical writing. Alexander Pope, the great English poet-stylist, wrote:

Now trips a lady, and now struts a lord.

Pope was trying to explain to his reader the flagrant difference between a dainty, feminine lady-in-waiting and a loud, brusque, masculine peer. He did it by simply changing his verb from "trips" to "struts," an effective and economical writing technique. The contrast is so extreme it fulfills the definition of antithesis, or direct opposites.

You might be explaining on an editorial page the qualifications of one political candidate as contrasted with those of another. So you write the following:

Woodward has voted in favor of every progressive social advance offered in the Legislature in the last five sessions. Thompson has voted against them all, and boasted of it on the Assembly floor.

Woodward has never felt so much as the breath of scandal in a generation of public service. Thompson's record contains uncounted accusations involving fraud and graft.

Woodward served the Navy gallantly in the last war. Thompson used a dubious medical excuse to avoid military service.

Now trips a lady . . .
now struts a lord

The contrast is so great the reader cannot escape a conviction that candidate Woodward is far superior to candidate Thompson. This is expository writing with Argument its ultimate purpose, but the principle is clear. The contrast is extreme. One man seems to the reader to be the antithesis of the other.

Antithesis might be used in explaining why sportsmen and naturalists combined in support of a legislative measure setting up preserves for the protection of wild life:

Both sportsmen and naturalists—often at dagger's point over government policies toward wild life—have joined together to secure passage of the Marshall Bill setting up preserves for the protection of wild ducks. They differ widely, though, on the reasons for their support. The sportsmen see the measure providing them more wild fowl to shoot at. The naturalists know that such preserves will maintain areas in which not only ducks but a varied collection of birds will find protection.

The violent contrast between these opposite viewpoints, hunter on one side, conservationist on the other, is a sound example of antithesis. Particularly in Exposition and Argument a writer can score points with this sharp and useful weapon.

5. Comparison or analogy

Analogy, on the other hand, derives from similarity, not contrast. Where in contrast you fixed the meaning by opposites, you now reverse the method and use similarities to give your reader reference points from his own experience. You compare something in your writing to something he's familiar with, thereby clarifying your point.

For example, if you were trying to explain the game of cricket to an American audience, you'd probably use baseball as an analogy. The two games aren't exactly alike, but similar enough to supply understandable reference points. The same would apply if you were trying to teach the principles of rugby to an American audience. You'd probably write in football terms.

Let's take another analogy from sports:

Driving a racing car at 140 m.p.h. is like driving an ordinary automobile 70 m.p.h. on glare ice.

Or the traditional grade-school example of analogy:

The earth is round, like a ball or orange.

In each of these examples of analogy, the writer explained something in terms familiar to the reader.

Let's try an analogy involving household items:

This dishwashing machine works like an electric fan under water.

Most people have seen an electric fan, so by comparing something with which they may be unfamiliar with something they have seen, you've given them a reference—through analogy.

Another example:

The way an old-fashioned propeller plane works is similar to a propeller-driven ship. As the ship's propeller turns, it works like a brace-and-bit, twisting its way through water. The plane propeller operates similarly, but through the air instead. It pulls the plane ahead as it turns, the way the propeller moves the ship through the water.

The analogy here is clear. For generations, ships have used propellers. By comparing the new idea to the old, you transmit to your reader's mind the picture of a plane propeller.

Explanation of facts

On the first page of this Lesson we said that Exposition is divided into three general categories: explanation of facts, events and ideas. Let's first take up explanation of facts.

The purest factual Exposition, as in a cooking recipe, is something which gives bare instructions or tells clearly how something operates. It is often narrative in style—that is, it goes along a fairly straight path from a beginning to a conclusion, step by step. In this form, Exposition quite often suggests a title beginning with the word "How." "How to Drive a Car," "How to Mix Concrete," "How to Plant Golden Bantam Corn," "How to Compute Your Income Tax."

Below are two sets of tax instructions from the same source which illustrate the definition of factual Exposition. Yet one is clear and concise, the other confusing.

The confusing example is typical of "Federalese," a bureaucratic jargon also called "Officialese." It happens to come from a Federal income tax instruction sheet, and the item selected is all one sentence—212 words long. The sentence appears under the heading: "Additional Charge for Underpayment of Estimated Tax," and reads as follows:

"Federalese" stops the reader cold

The charge with respect to any underpayment of any installment is mandatory and will be made unless the total amount of all payments of estimated tax made on or before the last date prescribed for the payment of such installments equals or exceeds whichever of the following is the lesser—

(a) The amount which would have been required to be paid on or before such date if the estimated tax were whichever of the following is the least—

    (1) The tax shown on your return for the previous year (if your return for such year showed a liability for tax and covered a taxable year of twelve months) or,

    (2) A tax computed by using the previous year's income with the current year's rates and exemptions, or,

    (3) Seventy per cent (66⅔ per cent in the case of farmers) of a tax computed by projecting to the end of the year the income received from the beginning of the year up to the beginning of the month of the installment payment, or,

    (b) An amount equal to ninety per cent of the tax computed, at the rates applicable to the taxable year, on the basis of the actual taxable income for the months in the taxable year ending before the month in which the installment is required to be paid.

What the sentence deals with is this: for Americans who must file an estimate of the coming year's revenue and taxes, there are certain rules and penalties.

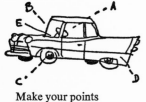

Make your points
clear and specific

Most taxpayers don't have to file an "estimated return" for the coming year—all they do is make out a return for the year just past, since most of their tax money has been withheld at the source. A minority of taxpayers, however, have to estimate ahead and send the government certain tax money in addition to what will be withheld in the coming year. The penalties mentioned in the 212-word sentence attempt to cover legally all possible situations—minimums, exceptions, tax computations of whatever nature.

Lawyers and lawmakers frequently write what is supposed to be English but actually it's a sort of gibberish the layman cannot comprehend. This is true here. Why is it true? Where has the writer missed the boat?

For one thing, he has violated the first rule of good expository writing. We said on the first page of this Lesson that in basic Exposition, "clarity is the primary goal." The income tax sentence isn't clear—to anyone, lawyer or layman. After the first clause it's very hard to see which idea refers to which antecedent, which subsequent clause modifies which prior thought.

The sentence has a certain organization of thought, but it's so obscure that the reader can't follow it. A thought is projected in the first clause, then subdivided in (a), then subdivided again in (1), (2) and (3). By the time you get to (3) you can't remember what alternative to the first rule you're now examining. The connection has been lost between this idea and the original idea to which it refers.

To compound the felony, it's all one sentence. If the thought were broken up into half a dozen sentences, the reader might have a chance. But he's hopelessly beaten at the end of the 212th word of a single sentence. Bergen Evans says of this one-sentence tax instruction: "The winner is really the Treasury Department."

Contrast the confusing, unclear 212-word sentence with the following paragraph from another part of the same tax sheet, under the subtitle "Changes in Marital Status." This proves that it's perfectly possible for tax writers to state something complex with clarity, precision and logical organization:

> If married at the close of your taxable year, you are considered married for the entire year. If divorced or legally separated on or before the close of your year, you are considered single for the entire year. If your husband or wife died during the year, you are considered married for the entire year, and may file a joint return. You may also be entitled to the benefits of a joint return for the two years following the death of your husband or wife.

Always show your reader the way

This understandable, straightforward explanation of a complicated tax problem is the result of (1) short sentences, (2) clear sentences, (3) well-constructed sentences and (4) logical organization of thought.

You start out with a simple statement of fact, that if the taxpayer is married at the close of the tax year he or she is considered married—for tax purposes—for the entire year. Nothing could be plainer. Then come the alternative situations: if the taxpayer was divorced or legally separated, or if his or her spouse died during the tax year. Every contingency is anticipated.

But it's taken care of one item at a time. These are short, declarative sentences, not a complex-compound sentence of 212 words.

At no time is there the slightest doubt in the reader's mind what a clause is modifying or to whom or what the pronouns refer.

Compare the two examples again—and remember they came from different pages of the same tax form. What the comparison illustrates is the fundamental rule of Exposition stated earlier in this Lesson: *clarity is the primary goal.*

Explanation of events

All news stories fall into this category. True-experience narratives also belong here since they are a natural extension of journalism. The difference is that the daily newspaper story is written with more immediacy and seeks quicker communication with the reader. True-experience narrative is usually in the first person. News seldom is.

News has to explain or instruct or it isn't Exposition. Here's an excellent example from a press service:

Explaining the essential problem of space travel.

> Fresh data from the satellite Adventurer gave further indication today that human space travel may first hinge on solving problems of intense radiation.

Logical organization of thought, starting with the basic statement in the first paragraph, then going back to the sources and bringing the parts together, step by step, with great clarity.

> Carl E. McIlwain, University of Iowa physicist, released preliminary findings after examining decoded space radiation information from about fifty of Adventurer's first 200 recorded passes.

Use of specific details fixes the facts in the reader's mind.

> He said that, starting 250 miles up, the intensity of space radiation appears to double with every sixty miles of altitude. Radiation intensities of 1,200 miles above South America, he said, represent an exposure level of about ten roentgens an hour. The average radiation you get in a whole lifetime from natural causes is about seven roentgens.

Another in the events category of Exposition is the diary or journal—although strictly speaking the diary is not for anyone else's eyes but the writer's. Keeping a diary at home is perhaps the easiest of all writing for the beginner—and one of the most satisfactory means of expression, requiring only a few minutes each day or week.

A famous Englishman used a diary as his way of reporting to the world one of the most dramatic of all events. He was Captain Robert Falcon Scott of the Royal Navy. In January, 1912, he led an expedition to the South Pole, only to discover that Roald Amundsen, the great Norwegian explorer, had a month earlier become the first human being to reach that goal.

Throughout his amazing adventure, Captain Scott kept a diary of events, which was found later where the expedition broke down on the cruel return trip from the South Pole. With death only hours away, Scott concluded what is probably the most poignant of all diaries:

I can only write at lunch and then only occasionally. The cold is intense, minus forty degrees at midday. My companions are unendingly cheerful, but we are all on the verge of serious frost-bites, and though we constantly talk of fetching through I don't think any one of us believes it in his heart.

We are cold on the march now, and at all times except meals. Yesterday we had to lay up for a blizzard and today we move dreadfully slowly . . . My right foot has gone, nearly all the toes—two days ago I was the proud possessor of best feet. These are the steps of my downfall. Like an ass I mixed a spoonful of curry powder with my melted pemican—it gave me violent indigestion. I lay awake and in pain all night; woke and felt done on the march; foot went and I didn't know it. A very small measure of neglect and have a foot which is not pleasant to contemplate.

Bowers takes first place in condition, but there is not much to choose after all. The others are still confident of getting through—or pretend to be—I don't know! We have the last half-fill of oil in our primus and a very small quantity of spirit—this alone between us and thirst . . .

Sledge dreadfully heavy. We are 15½ miles from the depot and ought to get there in three days. What progress! We have two days' food but barely a day's fuel. All our feet are getting bad—Wilson's best, my right foot worst, my left all right. There is no chance to nurse one's feet till we can get hot food into us. Amputation is the least I can hope for now, but will the trouble spread? That is the serious question. The weather doesn't give us a chance. . . . Blizzard as bad as ever.

Since March 21st (eight days ago) we have had a continuous gale from WSW and SW. We had fuel to make two cups of tea apiece, and bare food for two days on the 20th. Every day we have been ready to start for our depot only 11 miles away, but outside the door of the tent it remains a scene of whirling drift. I do not think we can hope for any better things now. We shall stick it out to the end, and the end cannot be far.

It seems a pity, but I do not think I can write more.

R. Scott

Last entry
For God's sake look after our people.[1]

---

[1] Captain Scott is referring to his party's families left at home. It is the only time he becomes anything but factual or calm in all the long and painful writing of his last journey. Here and here alone he leaves Description, Narration and Exposition for Argument.

Captain Scott reproduces the dreadful setting in which he and his men will freeze to death. Specific details—the subzero cold, the frost-bite, the dread of death.

Pure Exposition. Examples and factual details "fix the meaning," increase clarity and conviction.

In subzero weather, this fact is highly important. By the use of antithesis (extreme contrast) Scott has made his point securely. Contrast and comparison are powerful aids to expository writing.

You suddenly realize that it's been more than a week since they've had anything but blizzard.

Perhaps the most courageous lines written by a courageous man close the diary.

Ultimately, Exposition of events must, of course, be history in some form. History is narrative Exposition, with its chief purpose being to teach or inform the reader about the past. There are many avenues of history—folk tales, wars, subject history (as a history of the American labor movement or a family tree), and the longer streams of history where the chief requirements are also clarity, accuracy, thoroughness and honesty.

Few writers have combined the sense of news with the sense of history better than Winston Churchill, who once told a friend that he was essentially a writing man who had had to take time off from his profession to steer the British ship of state around some dangerous rocks.

On June 4, 1940, Churchill delivered an historic speech in the House of Commons after the British Expeditionary Force had been successfully evacuated from Flanders. This was Dunkirk, a miracle of World War II, and Churchill, the historical writer, was not unaware of the drama of the occasion. His speech follows in part. It is explanation in the ultimate degree, and the famous ending moves into the fourth and final writing form, Argument. Churchill put this speech in writing before delivering it, as do most public figures and great statesmen.

Churchill uses all of the five devices by which writers promote clarity.
1. Logical organization of thought.
2. Use of specific detail.
3. Use of examples.
4. Contrast or antithesis.
5. Comparison or analogy.

Pure expository writing. Here he is tracing the events leading up to Dunkirk. This logic helps "fix the meaning" in the mind of the reader, through clarity of explanation. He is using dozens of facts reinforced by specific details.

The surrender of the Belgian Army compelled the British at the shortest notice to cover a flank of more than 30 miles in length. Otherwise all would have been cut off and all would have shared the fate to which King Leopold had condemned the finest army his country had ever formed.

In closing this flank, contact was lost inevitably between the British and two of the three corps forming the First French Army who were still farther from the coast than we, and it seemed impossible that a large number of the Allied troops could reach the coast. The enemy attacked on all sides in great strength and fury and their main power—the power of their far more numerous air force—was thrown into the battle or was concentrated upon Dunkirk and the beaches . . .

For four or five days an intense struggle raged. All armoured divisions or what was left of them, together with great masses of German infantry and artillery, hurled themselves in vain upon the ever narrowing and contracting appendix within which the British and French armies fought. Meanwhile, the Royal Navy, with the willing help of countless merchant seamen and a host of volunteers, strained every nerve to embark British and Allied troops. Over 220 light warships and more than 650 other vessels were engaged. They had to operate upon a difficult coast, often in adverse weather, under an almost ceaseless hell of bombs and an increasing concentration of artillery fire.

Nor were the seas themselves free from mines and torpedoes. It was in conditions such as these that our men carried on with little or no rest for days and nights on end, making trip after trip across the dangerous waters, bringing with them always men whom they had ·escued. The numbers brought back are a measure of their devotion and their courage.

Now, suddenly, the scene has cleared. The crack of thunder has for the moment, but only for the moment, died away. The miracle of deliverance achieved by valour, by perseverance, by perfect discipline, by dauntless service, by resource, by skill, by unconquerable fidelity, is manifest to us all.

Narration and Exposition are closely interwoven throughout Churchill's essay. To explain, he must often tell the story. His contrast between land fighting and the escape by sea follows the classic technique of "contrast and analogy."

The enemy was hurled back by the retreating French and British troops. He was so roughly handled that he did not dare molest their departure seriously. The Air Force decisively defeated the main strength of the German air force and inflicted upon them losses of at least four to one. And the Navy, using nearly 1,000 ships of all kinds, carried over 335,000 men—French and British—out of the jaws of death and brought them back to their native land and to the tasks which lie immediately ahead . . .

Nevertheless, our thankfulness at the escape of our Army and so many men whose loved ones have passed through an agonizing time must not blind us to the fact that what has happened in France and Belgium is a colossal military disaster. The French Army has been weakened, the Belgian Army lost. A large part of those fortified lines whereupon so much faith had been reposed is gone. Many valuable mining districts and factories have passed into the enemy's possession.

Explanation of the statistical miracle and the incredible heroism of the Navy and the amateur sailors who did a fantastic job. Specific details follow our rules for basic clarity. Comparison and contrast between Nazi and Allied forces helps fix the point the author is trying to make.

The whole of the Channel Ports are in his hands with all the strategic consequences that follow from that, and we must expect another blow to be struck almost immediately at us or at France. We are told that Hitler has a plan for invading the British Isles. This has often been thought of before. The whole question of home defence against invasion is, of course, powerfully affected by the fact that we have for the time being in this island incomparably more powerful military forces than we have had at any moment of this war or the last.

This will not continue. We shall not be content with a defensive war. We have our duty to our Allies. We have to reconstitute and build up the B.E.F. once again . . .

Explanation of why the war cannot be won with defensive miracles. Perfectly logical on the basis of the organization of his thought.

Even though large tracts of Europe and many old famous States have fallen or may fall into the grip of the Gestapo and all the odious apparatus of Nazi rule, we shall not flag or fail. We shall go on to the end.

The famous declaration of faith by one of the greatest masters of the English language and of the expository form. Now, on the premise of his clear explanation, he is arguing a cause (the fourth form) based on facts whose meaning is fixed in his countrymen's minds.

We shall fight in France; we shall fight on the seas and oceans; we shall fight with growing confidence and strength in the air; we shall defend our island whatever the cost may be; we shall fight on the beaches; we shall fight on landing grounds; we shall fight in fields, in streets and in hills. We shall never surrender and even if—which I do not for a moment believe—this island or a large part of it was subjected and starving, then our Empire beyond the seas, armed and guarded by the British Fleet, will carry on the struggle until, in God's good time, a new world with all its power and might steps forth to the liberation and rescue of the old.

In this and other examples of writing so far in this Lesson, you've been aware of the devices each writer used to explain his facts clearly.

1. Logical organization of thought.
2. Use of specific detail.
3. Use of examples.
4. Contrast or antithesis.
5. Comparison or analogy.

When you write *Exposition,* constantly keep these five devices in mind. You may have other names for them, you may split them into definitions which suit your own writing better. But, by whatever names, these devices are vitally important, since by no other fundamental techniques can you prove to your reader that your facts are believable.

Explanation of ideas

When a writer wishes to explain ideas, he moves into a less concrete field, since ideas aren't as easy to put clearly on paper as facts or events. Here, writers often employ a form that is called the *essay*.

The essay is classified as one of two kinds—informal and formal. The first leans back in the direction of Exposition through Narration and Description, while the latter is nearer Argument, our fourth and final form.

The formal essay aims to instruct, and the informal to give pleasure. The difference between them is suggested by their names. Formal essays are serious in tone, weighty in matter and written with obvious care. The informal essayist, when he presents ideas, doesn't expect them to be taken too seriously.

Almost all columnists write informal or familiar essays. Christopher Morley, E. B. White, James Thurber, Stephen Leacock, Bernard de Voto, Heywood Broun and many other famous writers have been masters of the familiar essay. How is it different from the other forms of expository writing?

The informal essay presents ideas which the writer tries to explain, defend, condemn or promote, but the ideas frequently are trivial and the writing is almost always personal. The author takes a point of view and plays with it, sometimes with humor, sometimes with satire, sometimes with pathos or melancholy, always with an intensely personal interest in his subject.

The familiar essayist frequently laughs at himself and the world, his own shortcomings and doubts—which, he makes clear, are everyone's. This mock-serious style is ingrained in such popular newspaper columnists as Robert Ruark and Art Buchwald. They, like all familiar essayists, are chatty, gossipy, often urbane, and usually intensely interested in the subject. What they are doing is writing a sort of personal letter to all their readers at once. But all the basic techniques of Exposition still apply to their material.

Let's look at a typical syndicated columnist in the daily news field, Inez Robb, whose subject is not usually profound but whose lighthearted, familiar style is capable of carrying the reader right to the end. Besides lightness of touch, another rule is almost sure to apply to the familiar or informal essay—it will be written in the first person.

If I were President, (1) every girl would have a husband and (2) school curriculums would be sharply upgraded and intellectually stiffened. In re No. 2, there would be no more snap courses and no more sandbox activities, especially in high school.

The phrase "sandbox activities" explains immediately how she feels about current school curriculums. To explain her idea she will lightheartedly "fix the meaning" of her facts and points—through contrast and comparison—for her readers by Exposition.

However, I would try to get the girl and the curriculum better integrated for the long haul which, in this context, is the management of a home. I am a dandy housekeeper and homemaker, if I do say so myself, in all respects save one: I am completely baffled by machinery.

Machinery baffles her— the basis of the article.

This is the age of the mechanized household in which every woman should know what to do with a screw driver, a monkey wrench and a fan belt. But I still belong to that old-fashioned school that believes a good, swift kick is the proper treatment for recalcitrant household equipment.

Logical organization of thought, supported by specific details and examples, fixes her idea.

Often a good kick will do the trick. But there are times when the dishwasher, the air conditioner, the radio, television, record player, floor waxer, vacuum, the mixer and the attic fan refuse to respond and continue to play dead.

Exaggeration for effect clarifies her point. She pretends to have a phone conversation which so dramatizes the absurdities of the situation that the reader gets the idea, through contrast with what you'd expect in such a call. This call is the antithesis of the way such a call should be.

I am forced then to call in the repair specialist or service-maintenance man—a misnomer if ever I hear one—to cope with the situation. The telephone dialogue with this misanthrope, whose minimum charge for a house visit is $12, goes like this:

"Okay, lady, what's the matter with the air conditioner?"

"It won't work," I say.

"Yes, but why won't it work?"

"Because it quit."

"Yeh, lady, but why did it quit?"

"Because there wasn't any electricity."

"Why wasn't there no electricity?"

"Because it blew the master fuse."

"Why did it blow the master fuse?"

"That's what I want you to tell me!" I scream, and like a Comanche. "For $12 minimum per house visit, I should also make the diagnosis?"

Informal essay writing always has a point of view, and this is now made clear. Details of her dilemma help fix the meaning of her idea in your mind.

This recurrent dialogue has convinced me not that a housewife really needs a degree from M.I.T., but rather a basic course in household mechanics. It is obvious that the bored maintenance or quote service unquote expert expects the housewife to act as an internist who diagnoses the patient before handing it on to the specialist.

As a specialist, he wants a good prognosis and fever chart of the invalid, with blood count and metabolism already on paper. He arrives in the operating theater with his tools, and hopes not to be bothered with details. I'm probably just in luck that these surgeons deign to come to my house at all when I am unable to take so much as the patient's temperature.

Exposition turning into Argument. The essayist almost always ends by arguing for or against something.

By overstating her case, by overemphasis and exaggerated contrast, she makes her idea stick. Columnists love antithesis, or violent contrast.

Perhaps school curriculums should include—not for credit but for future sanity—a diagnostic course in the diseases, care and treatment of household gadgets. I foresee a day when the housewife who is unable to case an ailing hi-fi will have the invalid on her hands for the rest of her life. If she can't describe the symptoms, she won't get service.

The informality of this piece shows in subject matter and writing style, both considerably lighter than the subject matter and style of the formal essay.

The formal essay

The formal essayist almost always explains and expresses his ideas in serious writing—his meditative, reflective, often profoundly abstract thoughts about the general laws of life or nature or art. Criticism, for example, is usually formal. It seldom follows the "familiar essay" form.

Take a symphony concert. The music critic is rarely informal in what he has to say about the way the music was played. His subject, moreover, is far from the trivia which form the bulk of informal essay subjects, and only on very infrequent occasions is his writing at all narrative.

Just before he died, Dr. Albert Einstein wrote some essays in which he tried to explain to the new generation how the world had changed as a result of Hitler and the subsequent rise of Soviet Communism in an atomic world. His writing is truly in the classic form of the formal essay, an "explanation of ideas." Dr. Einstein is conveying information and explaining something difficult for a new generation to understand:

Conscious man, to be sure, has at all times been keenly aware that life is an adventure, that life must be wrested from death. In part the dangers were external: one might fall downstairs and break one's neck, lose one's livelihood without fault, be condemned though innocent, or ruined by calumny. Life in human society meant dangers of all sorts; but these dangers were chaotic in nature, subject to chance. Human society, as a whole, seemed stable. Measured by ideals of taste and morals it was decidedly imperfect.

Explanation of the hazards of normal life, prior to the atomic explosion. This logical start indicates good organization. By building up what life was like before the atomic bomb, Einstein will create antithesis or great contrast to what life is like now. This is an effective way of pinning home an elementary point.

But, all in all, one felt at home with it and, apart from the many kinds of accidents, comparatively safe in it. One accepted its intrinsic qualities as a matter of course, as the air one breathed. Even standards of virtue, aspiration and practical truth were taken for granted as an inviolable heritage, common to all civilized humanity.

To be sure, the World War had already shaken this feeling of security. The sanctity of life was vanished and the individual was no longer able to do as he pleased and to go where he liked. The lie was raised to the dignity of a political instrument. The War was, however, widely regarded as an external event, hardly or not at all as the result of man's conscious planful action. It was thought of as an interruption of man's normal life from the outside, universally considered unfortunate and evil. The feeling of security in regard to human aims and values remained for the main part unshaken.

Even before the atom bomb, world war had violated the sanctity of individual life. Einstein is explaining this to prepare for explanation of the remarkable change the bomb has made. Contrast and comparison again.

The subsequent development is sharply marked by political events that are not as far-reaching as the less easily grasped socio-psychological background. First a brief, promising step forward characterized by the creation of the League of Nations through the grandiose initiative of Wilson, and the establishment of a system of collective security among the nations. Then the formation of Fascist

Logical organization and development. In Exposition, this factor is at a premium. It is one of the fundamental explanatory techniques.

states, attended by a series of broken pacts and undisguised acts of violence against humanity and against weaker nations.

The system of collective security collapsed like a house of cards—a collapse the consequences of which cannot be measured even today. It was a manifestation of weakness of character and lack of responsibility on the part of the leaders in the affected countries, and of shortsighted selfishness in the democracies—those that still remain outwardly intact—which prevented any counterattack.

There is simply no substitute for the fact—unadorned fact—in Exposition. Facts drive home to the reader the point Einstein is making.

Things grew even worse than a pessimist of the deepest dye would have dared prophesy. In Europe to the East of the Rhine, free exercise of the intellect exists no longer, the population is terrorized by gangsters who have seized power, and youth is poisoned by systematic lies. The pseudo-success of political adventurers has dazzled the rest of the world; it becomes apparent everywhere that this generation lacks the strength and force which enabled previous generations to win, in painful struggle and at great sacrifice, the political and individual freedom of man.

Awareness of this state of affairs overshadows every hour of my present existence, while ten years ago it did not yet occupy my thoughts. It is this that I feel so strongly in rereading the words written in the past.

And man does not change very much over the pages of world history. This is comparison, highly effective in fixing an idea in a reader's mind by relating it to something he knows.

And yet I know that, all in all, man changes but little, even though prevailing notions make him appear in a very different light at different times, and even though current trends like the present bring him unimaginable sorrow. Nothing of all that will remain but a few pitiful pages in the history books, briefly picturing to the youth of future generations the follies of its ancestors.

This is true expository "idea" writing, though differing greatly from the informal essay, the news story, history, diary or instruction sheet. Exposition is, as we have said, essentially explanation, although it may be expressed in a great variety of ways and involve infinite subjects.

Summing up

Whether you write an informal or formal essay, a news story, sermon, business report or explain your ideas to a reader in some other form of writing, the principles of good Exposition are applicable.

All writing needs logical organization so it will flow in ordered sequence and you won't lose your reader by bumps and digressions. Through logical organization you tend to prove to your reader the explanation you're making.

Two devices help fix the meaning of the facts in your reader's mind: use of details and examples. Details communicate the reality of facts. Examples increase reader interest, as well as help communicate. Between them, these devices help to support the statements you're making because they evoke reader identification. Therefore they explain better what you have in mind.

Contrast is a useful device because it establishes in the reader's mind noticeable differences in facts, events and ideas placed side by side. When contrast is extreme—a direct opposite, for effect—the device is known as antithesis. Of all the uses to which contrast is put by writers, antithesis is the most productive because it's the most dramatic.

Comparison is another useful device. You line up events, facts or ideas side by side, but this time you show your reader the similarities. You explain something to the reader in terms already familiar to him.

Fix facts through details and examples

Exposition essentially means explanation, and writers usually think of Exposition as falling into three broad areas—the explanation of facts, events and ideas. But techniques for writing all three types have common ground. Underlying these techniques is the fundamental premise that Exposition deals with facts, for which there is simply no substitute.

One further step is explanation solely for the sake of Argument, and it is this fourth basic form that we shall take up next—the art of persuasive writing.

Clear thinking comes first

The essence of satisfactory writing comes down to a matter of saying what you have to say in the clearest possible manner, so that the person who reads will understand precisely what you are trying to convey. It goes without saying, therefore, that you have to have something to convey in the first place. If your thoughts are hazy to begin with, what you write will also be hazy.—Bruce Catton

Lesson sixteen

Principles of good writing

Writing argument

Argumentative writing seeks to convince readers of the rightness of certain ideas and of the wrongness of others. Although the indirect purpose of all writing is to persuade the reader of something, however small, it is the sole purpose of *Argument,* the fourth and last of the general writing forms.

Argument is a close relative of Exposition. As we have pointed out, Argument first explains certain facts, instructs the reader, then goes one step further. It tries to convince the reader of a specific point, to make him think or act as the arguer desires.

Argument is not so clearly defined a form of writing as Description, Narration and Exposition because some kind of Argument is present in virtually all types of fiction and non-fiction. The mere act of writing is an act of persuasion on the writer's part. The purest form of Argument is found in political tracts, editorials, essays, legal opinions and similar kinds of writing in which the author seeks only to get his own views across. Then, too, in the field of public speaking, Argument plays a predominant role, since most speakers are trying to sway their audiences to one or another point of view.

Consider the relationship of Exposition and Argument. The

following example presents views for and against two travel routes between Grand Rapids, Michigan, and Milwaukee, Wisconsin. First the routes are explained in expository form—factually. Then we're going to pretend that two different people are writing a mutual friend who is coming to visit Milwaukee from Grand Rapids. Each writer will, by letter, try to argue the friend into going the way he suggests.

First let's assume these expository details:

(A) Route A is entirely by road, running south from Grand Rapids through Holland, South Haven, Benton Harbor, Bridgman and New Buffalo, Michigan; west through Michigan City, Gary, Indiana Harbor and Whiting, Indiana; and north through Chicago and Evanston, Illinois, to Milwaukee. This route covers 250 miles and should take seven hours of driving or less.

(B) Route B is to drive from Grand Rapids to Ludington, Michigan, where there is an auto ferry to Milwaukee. It takes about an hour to drive to Ludington and to load on the ferryboat, and the 60-mile trip directly across Lake Michigan consumes about six hours. So the total time is about the same as the all-land trip—seven hours.

Not everyone agrees on travel routes

Now for the letter containing Argument A:

There's no use thinking about the expensive Ludington-Milwaukee ferry if you haven't made a reservation way ahead. Some days as many as 400 motorists are stranded in Ludington, unaware that they should have reserved space on the limited-capacity steamer. And if you've never been caught in one of those sudden Lake Michigan storms, you don't know what it is to be seasick. Unless you're a good sailor—and have made reservations well in advance—*drive*. Then you'll be motoring through some of the most beautiful fruit country in the world as you skirt the bottom of Lake Michigan. Pick up a winter's supply of home-made grape and peach jam at farm discounts. Eat a wonderful supper at a country inn overlooking the big, blue lake below. No more lovely drive in spring, summer or fall than around the curve of Lake Michigan!

And now for the letter containing Argument B:

If you like bumper-to-bumper traffic, exhaust fumes, and seven hours (if you're lucky) of the worst driving in the Midwest, go by road. But if you want to limit your frustration and fumes, go to Ludington and relax on the deck of one of the world's best ferryboats. While your opposite number is cursing in the heat of an endless highway, you'll be eating a fine sea-voyage dinner or taking a snooze on deck while someone else worries about the miles. The trip actually costs less than driving—and it's a third the distance. If you take the Ludington-Milwaukee ferry, you'll arrive in Wisconsin refreshed and relaxed.

Argument A ignores the traffic jams and hazards of the all-land route. Argument B ignores the fact that the ferry is apt to be crowded beyond capacity. Argument A cites the advantages of driving through fruit orchards and avoiding seasickness. Argument B sidesteps sudden lake storms but plays up the refreshing voyage.

Each writer emphasizes exactly what he wants to emphasize, and no more.

Rules for writing argument

This brings us, then, to fundamental rules for writing Argument. Since Argument is essentially persuasion, it might be well to begin with two specific techniques of developing persuasion in writing: *personalized persuasion* and *narrative persuasion*.

Some Argument
is personalized

1. Personalized persuasion

In this form of persuasion the writer uses *you* and *your* and addresses the reader directly. A modified variation of this form is personalized argument in which the writer uses mainly *I* and *my*.

But the difference can readily be imagined: in the *you* and *your* technique of persuasion, the writer addresses the reader directly; in the *I, me* and *my* technique, there is little or no direct address to the reader.

Here's an example of *you* and *your* personalized persuasion:

This is your school district and the building proposed will be attended by your children. Do you want to pay out good money for a firetrap? Do you want your children to be caught one day in a building that doesn't have elementary fire precautions which would cost only pennies more? It doesn't make sense if you'll think it through. You and you alone can force the Board to adopt fundamental fire precautions in the new building plan. But you have very little time. Your present school blueprint has none of these precautions. It's up to you and your neighbors to make changes before ground is broken. Remember, it's your school and these are your children you'll be sending into a firetrap.

An example of the modified, *I*, *me* and *my* technique might read this way:

I have studied the Board's blueprint for the new school and my own architect has gone over it with me. He tells me that the plans lack fundamental fire precautions which would cost only a few pennies more. It seems ridiculous to me that I should send my children to a brand new school less safe than the one condemned by this same Board. I would hesitate to send my children to a new school built to the present blueprints. It does seem absurd that I should pay heavy taxes for years to come for an expensive new school more dangerous than the one being demolished.

Let your instinct
govern your choice

Which personalized persuasion should you use on which occasion? Your own instinct has to govern your choice. You'll know your reader and tailor your technique to suit the audience. It is true, however, that the *you* and *your* approach, addressing the reader directly, probably contains more persuasive pull in the average situation than the *I*, *me* and *my* indirect approach. This follows a basic truth in the craft of writing: that if you can get the reader to identify himself with what you've put into words, you've undoubtedly established communication.

2. Narrative persuasion

Narration is effective in Argument. The writer creates typical narrative characters who, through talk and action, expound the Argument the writer seeks to make. For example, two parents are discussing this same school situation and here is the way a writer might use narrative persuasion to put his point over:

I overheard two mothers of children in this school talking it over last week in a supermarket. One mother said:

"It doesn't make any sense to condemn the old school building as a firetrap, then build a big, new expensive one that's just as dangerous."

The other woman replied: "What makes me mad is that our taxes will go up 20 per cent when the new school is started. And what'll we have? Something worse than what we have now."

"Isn't there something we can do about it?" said the first mother.

"There certainly is," I said, breaking in. Then I told them what my architect had said and explained the purposes of our new committee to force the Board to adopt fire-prevention measures in the new building blueprint. Both women agreed to join the committee and said they'd bring their husbands along to the next hearing.

You can also handle narrative persuasion through a monologue in which a make-believe character relates his or her story to argue a point of view. This is effective if you know your audience will accept occasional satire (making fun of the Board, for instance) and if you use a style slightly off the beaten path. Here's one way a satirical monologue might be handled, with the writer pretending to be the Board chairman for purposes of catching interest through satire:

I'm Board chairman of the new school committee and I'm here to tell you we've got just about the perfect plan and we don't want anyone interfering with it. I'll admit the new blueprint doesn't call for fire doors, but who needs 'em? We'll probably never have a fire anyway, so why not save the money? Then, there's the matter of the fire escapes. We don't have any in the blueprint, because they cost $500 apiece and we'd need ten of them. Why, that's $5,000! We'd have to cut out the oak-paneled Board room and the hi-fi system in the junior girls' recreation room. Why was the old building condemned, you say? It *was* a fire hazard . . . that is, well, we needed a new school building anyway and don't you try to interfere with your Board.

Persuasive writing calls for examples

Narrative persuasion is used in practically all Argument and is particularly effective when you're certain the average reader will quickly see your point. Reader identification with your narrative characters is easily established through Dialogue, action, and standard narrative procedures. By telling a story the reader can understand, you'll persuade him faster and more surely than by preaching to him.

The two fundamental methods of Argument—personalized persuasion and narrative persuasion—have common techniques to make them effective. Some of these techniques are:

1. You have to have something *specific* to argue about, for Argument over a vague generality won't interest or convince many readers. Therefore, all written Argument must be about a *proposition*. This can be a statement which is believed, doubted or denied. But whichever side of the discourse you take, a proposition represents a judgment. In general, there are two kinds of propositions: *policy* and *fact*. A proposition of policy asserts that a certain action or line of action is desirable. A proposition of fact asserts that something is true.

2. Your proposition should not express more than *one basic idea for Argument*. You may be expressing several propositions in the course of a single document, but take them one at a time. They must

be argued individually or they won't be persuasive.

3. A proposition is stronger if it appears to be *unprejudiced*. Nothing in your proposition should imply a foregone conclusion to the Argument.

4. Your proposition should be *clear*. It shouldn't contain fuzzy terms your readers won't understand. No Argument can proceed until all concerned, writer and readers, have accepted the definition of what's being argued and the organization of your thought.

5. Your persuasive writing should contain many *factual details*. Nothing in Argument is as telling as a *fact*, particularly a fact spotlighted by an *example* so familiar to the reader it really strikes home.

6. In Argument, as in Exposition, *contrast* and *comparison* are extremely useful writing techniques.

We would like to reiterate the close relationship between Exposition and Argument:

Argument first explains, then goes one step further. It also tries to convince the reader of a specific point and make him think as the arguer desires.

Exposition is factual and fair. Expository facts should not be slanted: they are like the news columns of a paper. Argument, on the other hand, is like the editorial page: it is only partly factual; it is essentially and intensely partisan. Nevertheless, Argument must be based on facts. If it isn't, it won't be very persuasive.

Examples of argument

Most letters employ persuasion as well as factual reporting. The letter writer rarely wishes merely to state facts, but almost always feels a compulsion to explain them and persuade the recipient of something. Because letters are personal things, Argument in letter form is normally personalized persuasion.

A classic example is Abraham Lincoln's letter to his stepbrother, John D. Johnston, written on January 2, 1851. The stepbrother had borrowed money from many people, including his own family. He seemed incapable of doing a day's work, yet would make rash and elaborate promises to all concerned if only one more loan were granted.

Lincoln's reply is not harsh but firm; nowhere in all the writing of one of America's truly great writers is his power of Argument more persuasive:

Don't make use
of fuzzy terms

Dear Johnston: Your request for eighty dollars I do not think it best to comply with now. At the various times when I have helped you a little you have said to me, "We can get along very well now" but in a very short time I find you in the same difficulty again. Now this can only happen by some defect in your conduct. What that defect is, I think I know.

You are not lazy, and still you are an idler. I doubt whether, since I saw you, you have done a good whole day's work in any one day. You do not very much dislike to work, and still you do not work much, merely because it does not seem to you that you could get much for it. This habit of uselessly wasting time is the whole difficulty; it is vastly important to you, and still more to your children, that you should break the habit. It is more important to them, because they have longer to live, and can keep out of an idle habit before they are in it, easier than they get out after they are in.

You are now in need of some money; and what I propose is, that you shall go to work, "tooth and nail," for somebody who will give you money for it. Let father and your boys take charge of your things at home, prepare for a crop, and make the crop, and you go to work for the best money wages, or in discharge of any debt you owe, that you can get; and to secure you a fair reward for your labor, I now promise you, that for every dollar that you will, between this and the first of May, get for your own labor, either in money or as your own indebtedness, I will then give you one other dollar. By this, if you hire yourself at ten dollars a month, from me you will get ten more, making twenty dollars a month for your work. In this I do not mean you shall go off to St. Louis, or the lead mines, or the gold mines in California, but I mean for you to go at it for the best wages you can get close to home in Coles County.

Now, if you will do this, you will be soon out of debt, and, what is better, you will have a habit that will keep you from getting in debt again. But if I should now clear you out of debt, next year you would be just as deep in as ever. You say you would almost give your place in heaven for seventy or eighty dollars. Then you value your place in heaven very cheap, for I am sure you can, with the offer I make, get the seventy or eighty dollars for four or five months' work.

You say if I will furnish you the money you will deed me the land, and, if you don't pay the money back, you will deliver possession. Nonsense! If you can't now live with the land, how will you then live without it?

You have always been kind to me, and I do not mean to be unkind to you. On the contrary, if you will but follow my advice, you will find it worth more than eighty dollars to you.

Affectionately your brother,

A. Lincoln.

Lincoln, called by literary critic Jacques Barzun "the maker of a style that is unique in English prose" and "a literary genius," had a knack for clear, forcible English. The last two sentences are miracles of succinct structure.

Lincoln's kindness and patience show here in a clear exposition of his stepbrother's habitual difficulties; sparse, bare, right on target, the basis of his personalized persuasion.

The kind offer of one dollar for every dollar earned. His logic helped Lincoln's writing style, as well as his powers of persuasion.

This is a classic illustration of personalized persuasion. The words "you" and "your" appear 21 times in this one paragraph!

These last two paragraphs are masterpieces of Argument. The final paragraph brims with love of all mankind. It's definitely marked by the human touch, and powerful personalized persuasion.

People use the argumentative form every day in speech and writing. It is part of a human being's make-up to wish to persuade someone else to his or her viewpoint. This may be simply a struggle between a mother and child over wearing rubbers on a rainy day, yet what they say to each other involves the rudiments of Argument. When it is reduced to paper, this kind of expressed thought is the essence of Argument.

Rudolf Flesch argues in his book, *The Art of Readable Writing,* that almost all writers start their letters the wrong way. He makes a flat statement at the beginning of his Argument, then proceeds to prove it effectively. This is how he does it:

The proposition.

Almost all reading matter in this country gets off to a false start. This is not an exaggeration; it is a statement of fact which I am going to prove.

Quickly Dr. Flesch uses personalized persuasion, first "me" and "us," then "you" and "your."

Let me first define my terms. What is a false start? It's a beginning that doesn't do what a beginning *ought to do.* Psychologists tell us that an effective piece of writing should start with something that points to its main theme. In other words, you must put your reader in the right frame of mind; you must start by getting him interested in what's going to come.

Dr. Flesch always uses factual examples.

Look around you and you'll find that most reading matter doesn't start that way. It usually starts in routine fashion—with a stale, humdrum opening that does *anything but* whet your appetite for the main dish. Take one of the most common pieces of writing in American life: the business letter.

Ninety-nine out of a hundred business letters start with an acknowledgment of the addressee's last letter. Have you ever asked yourself why? The only plausible answer I found is that it's always been done that way. It's an old, old custom. There's a quaint, old-fashioned composition textbook on my shelves that contains the following model business letter:

4 Park St., Boston, Mass.
May 26, 1882

Factual examples (one of the basic techniques of Argument) help make his point about the writing of business letters. Dr. Flesch likes contrast and comparison as techniques of Argument.

Mrs. M. E. Dawson
Jacksonville, Ill.

Dear Madam, — Your letter of the 23d inst is at hand. We do not sell single poems from the Leaflets in quantity, but we have published "The Building of the Ship" in a pamphlet with "Evangeline," and supply teachers with the same at the rate of fifteen cents per copy. There are notes to the poems, but no illustrations.

Yours truly,

Houghton, Mifflin & Co.

I have purposely copied the letter here in the original form; I hope this will remind you of the fact that "Your letter of the 23d inst. is at hand" is something that goes back to pre-typewriter days. It's time to stop furnishing your letters with this shabby antique.

Of course, people who have the souls of file clerks always say this stock opening is needed for filing purposes. But that's no argument: there's always room for a reference somewhere in a corner of the letter; and quite often it doesn't make a bit of difference to anybody who wrote what on what date. Mrs. Dawson didn't need to be told that Houghton, Mifflin & Co. had "her letter of the 23d inst. at hand"; she knew that before she opened the envelope.

There's been some progress since 1882, but not much. Not long ago I conducted a little survey: I went through my files and assembled all the answers I got when I asked for permissions to quote in my book *The Art of Plain Talk*. (I had written the same letter to about two dozen writers and publishers.) Result: Two-thirds of the replies began by acknowledging my letter, one-third began by saying yes or no.

At one end of the scale was a letter from a textbook company that began like this:

Dear Mr. Flesch:

We have your letter of July 21 and note that it is your intention to include—in your book on modern English prose style, to be published by Harper & Brothers under the title *The Art of Plain Talk*—a few brief passages from our Wirth's *The Development of America*.

After reading these fifty words, I knew exactly as much as before.

At the other end of the scale was the reply from the well-known writer on popular science, J. D. Ratcliff, who returned my letter with the following note on it:

By all means—J. D. Ratcliff

Naturally, you can't always follow Mr. Ratcliff's method in your correspondence, but the basic principle is sound: Say what you have to say, and then stop. Watch your letters perk up once you've thrown the acknowledgment phrase out the window.

Another example of argumentation

Bennett Cerf argues in the paragraphs below that reading is here to stay, therefore writers are here to stay, and that there will never be a substitute for a really good book. This excerpt is from

Though not unprejudiced, this Argument is effective through contrast with new, modern writing styles in business correspondence.

Factual information tends to hit the target of the reader's inner understanding.

Contrast—far better to give the example than merely talk about it.

Publishers argue about books

the introduction to Cerf's best-selling anthology, *Reading For Pleasure*.

Cerf's proposition is clearly set forth here.

Statistics reveal that a million or so more Americans are "reading for pleasure" every year, although you never would believe this by listening to the moans of the publishing fraternity. Publishers cry more easily than anybody else on earth. A simple, routine inquiry like "How's business?" is enough to make their tears flow like water, diluting their vintage wines and drenching the decks of their private yachts.

Here is that something specific the arguer needs. He makes a point by recalling publishers' cries of doom several generations ago.

To hear them tell it, there's always something threatening to bankrupt half the publishers in America. Seventy years ago, believe it or not, a spokesman for the industry predicted that interurban trolley cars would be the doom of the reading habit! So many people were swinging and swaying aboard these dangerous contraptions that there soon would be nobody left to appreciate Shakespeare and Aristotle!

Factual Argument. Hard examples, not generalities.

Then came the menace of the bicycle, followed closely by cheap automobiles, magazines, giant economy-size Sunday newspapers, motion pictures, radio, and now, of course, television.

This clearly defined proposition precludes prejudice in the writer, so it's more potent. Also, there's but one basic Argument.

Anybody fortunate enough, however, to have learned the joys of reading in his formative years—usually through the inspired guidance of one wise, gratefully remembered, and disgracefully underpaid schoolteacher—knows that there never has been, and never will be a substitute for a really good book. All the wisdom of the ages, all the tales that have delighted mankind for generations, are there at your fingertips, at negligible cost, to be picked up, savored, digested, and laid down exactly as your fancy dictates. That's why more good books are sold in America every season, despite all other gimmicks and distractions.

Bennett Cerf has first set up his premise—that the publishers of America continually talk poor, yet nothing on earth can doom the reading habit in America. He lists the menaces to reading over the years. He again makes his statement or proposition (sometimes called a "peroration" at the end of a formal speech) which sums up what he thinks of reading as a pleasure and why it will never be replaced.

Oliver Wendell Holmes, Jr., one of the nation's famous Supreme Court Justices, defined in these words the end purpose of Argument: "Every idea is an incitement." Hence, there is justification for the view that the true purpose of Argument isn't to make the reader think *or* act, but only to act.

Take Patrick Henry's legendary speech to the Virginia Convention in 1775:

Is life so dear, or peace so sweet, as to be purchased at the price of chains and slavery? Forbid it, Almighty God! I know not what course others may take, but as for me, give me liberty, or give me death.

The famous patriot wasn't pleading for men to agree with him —and do nothing about it. He was asking them to lay down their lives if need be in defense of liberty. This was the only purpose of his Argument.

Another American patriot, Daniel Webster, believed that the Union must be preserved or the American dream would vanish. In 1830 he made perhaps his most famous speech in the Senate, ending with a plea not for agreement in thought but for action:

When my eyes shall be turned to behold for the last time the sun in heaven, may I not see him shining on the broken and dishonored fragments of a once glorious Union; on States dissevered, discordant, belligerent; on a land rent with civil feuds, or drenched, it may be, in fraternal blood . . . Liberty and Union, now and forever, one and inseparable!

Webster's famous lines probably saved the Union for the time being, although the Civil War did come thirty-one years later and fraternal blood did drench American soil. What Webster, Henry and all other patriotic orators have tried to do with words matches precisely the dictionary's definition of Argument: "The act of forming reasons, making inductions, drawing conclusions and applying them to the case in discussion."

Argument in the business world

Of all the fields in which Argument is used by writers, advertising is the most common. Advertising, says Mark Wiseman, "is the most prolific form of writing which seeks to convince readers of the rightness of certain ideas."

Our daily newspaper ads are full of Argument. We see Argument on the billboards and in buses, subways and trains. It's on the jackets of the books we read, in the mail we receive daily. It's in the pages of our magazines. We hear it on radio and see it on television. Advertising indeed contains many fine examples of the fourth form of writing. For instance:

Facts are vital
to good Argument

Wherever children gather these days
You're Sure to Find Germs!

The Saturday afternoon double feature is a good old American institution. But with colds and resultant sore throats going the rounds, every mother ought to protect her youngsters against *germs*.

Before they go and after they return, have your children gargle Listerine Antiseptic full-strength. Listerine kills germs on mouth and throat surfaces on contact, by millions—germs that cause much of the misery of a cold.

Tests over 12 years proved that those who gargled Listerine twice daily had fewer, shorter and milder colds than those who did not.

Reach for Listerine—your No. 1 protection against infection.

In every legitimate ad you ever saw or heard, the copywriter was obeying the basic principle of Argument: *explanation, then persuasion to action!*

Business uses Argument every hour of every working day. Let's take an example from the company which issued the following public relations statement of its financial condition:

Businessmen use
Argument every day

James Felton & Sons declared the usual 50 cents dividend at its quarterly meeting October 5. Mr. Felton, Chairman of the Board, told stockholders that while gross business was slightly below a year ago, net income increased from $1,650,000 to $1,890,000.

This situation was made possible, said Mr. Felton, by elimination of several unprofitable items on the company's old production list, which reduced over-all income but enabled Felton's to increase its net. Mr. Felton scoffed at rumors that the company was for sale, pointing to the net income rise and to new lines which will result from absorption last month of Steele & Company, makers of roller-bearings used in Felton products.

Mr. Felton also stated that he expects the net income to rise in the coming year to a figure in excess of $2,000,000, which suggests the possibility of a slight increase in dividend.

What is James Felton really doing? He's trying to persuade the stockholders, the financial editors and the public at large that, despite rumors, his firm is not only perfectly sound but on the upgrade. He is factual in his explanation, knowing that in business nothing substitutes for facts and logic. Having explained, he tries to persuade the public (and the editors) not to sell his company short and to put an end to the rumors.

Summing up

Argument seeks to convince readers of the rightness of certain ideas and the wrongness of others. All writing, in fact, tries indirectly to convince the reader of something. But in Argument there is no other goal.

Since Argument is a close relative of Exposition, facts are vital. But where Exposition merely explains facts to a reader, Argument goes the next logical step and tries to persuade the reader to a specific point of view and to take action along the argued lines.

There are two basic ways to persuade through the written word. Writers call them personalized persuasion and narrative persuasion. Most argumentative writing falls into one of these categories, frequently both.

In personalized persuasion you address the reader directly, frequently using *you* and *your*. In another form, personalized persuasion uses *I, me* and *my* to win the reader's assent.

In narrative persuasion the writer creates typical narrative characters who, through action and talk, give the writer's Argument in story form. Sometimes narrative persuasion takes the form of a monologue which can be satirical or ironic in tone.

Characters give
form to Argument

Common techniques to advance these methods of persuasion include (1) having something specific to argue about, called a proposition, which the writer immediately sets out to prove to his reader (2) by limiting himself to one basic idea at a time, (3) by appearing to be unprejudiced and avoiding foregone conclusions, (4) by being clear and factual, by dodging fuzzy terms, (5) by the use of hard, realistic examples, and (6) by employing contrast and comparison.

Never forget the notebook

I am never without a notebook in my pocket—nor should you be. You never know when a bright notion for a story will strike you. The mind, being a capricious organ, often lets you forget some truly valuable ideas. If you have a notebook and make your notes instantly, you don't have to rely on your memory.—Max Shulman

Lesson seventeen

Principles of good writing

Writing dialogue

Besides the basic forms of Narration, Description, Exposition and Argument there is one special form writers call *Dialogue*. It doesn't fall precisely into any main category but it overlaps them all with problems and purposes of its own.

Whenever you wish to quote exactly what someone has said, whether the someone is a character in a fiction story or a person you've interviewed for a non-fiction article, you use quotation marks so there can be no question which are his words and which are yours. This is the standard practice in Dialogue.

Plays for stage, screen, television or radio are written entirely in Dialogue, except for occasional stage directions the audience doesn't hear, or offstage narration which can also be Dialogue in itself. In novels and short stories, particularly modern ones, whole pages will be devoted to theaterlike conversation in which the writer seldom uses the phrases "he said," "she replied." The reader knows who is talking by the simple fact that the characters speak alternately.

John O'Hara and Ernest Hemingway, among the first to do this well, set a style which often reads like this excerpt from O'Hara's short story, "No Mistakes":

"Mac! You old rat. How are you? Were you at the Mass?"

"I sure was. Okie, I want you to meet my wife. Jean, this is Father O'Connor."

"How are you, Jean?"

"How do you do, Father?"

"When did all this happen, Mac? And why didn't I get an invitation?"

"Well," said McDonald, "There weren't any. We, uh—"

"Waterbury girl?" said Okie.

"No. New York."

"You should have waited—when'd you say you were married?"

"About six months ago."

As it happens, all four basic forms overlap in the above Dialogue. We have a bit of Description. We know that McDonald's wife is named Jean and she's probably not a Roman Catholic, while McDonald, having been at Mass, is one. We know that Father O'Connor is a priest and that Jean isn't a Waterbury girl but comes from New York.

You must know
your characters

There is also a good deal of Narration in this passage of Dialogue. We learn that Mac and Okie (Father O'Connor's apparent nickname) haven't seen each other in quite a while and that Mac and Jean have been married for six months—but probably not in the Catholic Church and definitely not by Father O'Connor. We know it was a comparatively secret affair: there weren't any invitations. We have Jean meeting Father O'Connor and we suspect they don't approve of each other. The phrase "Mac! You old rat" tells us that McDonald and Father O'Connor are familiar friends.

Exposition and Argument also are involved, though to lesser degrees. Author O'Hara has explained briefly to the reader that McDonald and Father O'Connor are old friends and that the McDonalds probably were married outside Father O'Connor's (and McDonald's) church.

In fiction, Exposition is used to explain antecedent action, or what has happened up to the time the story opens. This is frequently done by Dialogue in a short story or novel, and practically always by Dialogue in plays, movies, television and radio fiction.

O'Hara argues implicitly in these sparse lines that McDonald shouldn't have married outside the Catholic Church and should have had his old friend Father O'Connor at the ceremony.

Dialogue violates rules of grammar because people usually violate these rules when they talk. Dialogue seldom is made up of complete sentences and a great deal is implied. For instance:

> "Gone yet?"
> "Not yet. Soon I hope."
> "What a night!"
> "Whose idea was this, anyway?"
> "Mine. I'm sorry."
> "You ought to be. Three o'clock in the morning!"
> "Well, they're only young once."
> "But they can sleep tomorrow. We can't."
> "Not tomorrow. Today."

Dialogue violates
rules of grammar

Little detailed description has been given the reader about the people involved here, yet we know a great deal about them through a handful of incomplete sentences. This is the essence of Dialogue—an emotionally concentrated version of the English language in which much is *implied* or *indicated,* rather than spelled out.

We assume the people in this Dialogue are parents and that one of them has given permission for a party. The party is most likely going on downstairs, which prevents the parents from sleeping at 3 A.M. We also know the older people have a regular daily routine to face all too soon.

We know whoever is downstairs is young ("Well, they're only young once"). We suspect that the parents have consciously refrained from breaking up the party, and we surmise from "Whose idea was this, anyway?" that it's the first time they've let the youngsters have a late party. Indeed, we know something about several human beings through nine slight lines of Dialogue, in which no name has been mentioned and which can be read in a matter of seconds.

Dialogue is true to life

Dialogue must
be true to life

Only in Dialogue can a writer legitimately write as people really talk. Before Twain, Lardner, Hemingway, O'Hara and other American writers displayed an ear for accurate speech, certain kinds of Americans were supposed to talk certain ways. Seldom if ever was their Dialogue true to life.

An Irishman always said "Begorra" in written Dialogue, even

if he'd never said it in his life. A Negro talked like Br'er Poss'm whether he had a college degree or had never gone to school at all. An Italian traditionally ended all words with vowels, usually -a or -o, though he might be a Ph.D. Certain women talked baby talk and nothing else. Cowboys used only such words as "reckon" and "chuck wagon" and "dogie," regardless of context or background.

Then Twain and Lardner opened the gates of American literary realism, as many a French writer had done before them, and soon it was possible for all writers to write Dialogue as it was actually spoken in life.

An illiterate ball player could say in print, "I should *of*" instead of "I should *have*," "like *I*" instead of "like *me*," or "*ain't*" when the story called for it. Lovers now said things to each other in print that lovers really said, not glossed-over generalities and type-cast clichés. Words which had long been taboo were soon common in rough Dialogue, because rough characters would talk that way in real life. Newspapermen were now able, for the first time, to quote an interviewee precisely, with resultant realism for the reader. Dialogue had come of age.

The chief thing, then, to remember in writing Dialogue is that the characters in your story must sound natural, must talk the talk of real life. If you're at a press interview, try to get down the words the way they actually come from the interview subject. Eavesdrop on spoken talk. Listen to the sound and swing of words, to the way language is misused in real-life Dialogue. Write down bits of speech when you hear them. That's what your notebook is for.

With Dialogue, a good writer can put across the personalities of his characters or make his reporting real to the reader. Dialogue is important in re-creating emotional scenes, in sketching local color, in developing lines of Argument. An accurate ear for human speech is a gift, it's true, but practice—notebook in hand—will help anyone write natural Dialogue.

One thing Dialogue writers should avoid is the adverb. Adverbs tend to tell a story twice, once in the Dialogue, once in the unquoted material between speeches. For instance:

"What train goes to Pensacola?" Art demanded in a querulous tone, his eyes glinting *brightly*.

"The 2:45 train," *firmly* replied Bob.

"How about Tallahassee?" asked Art *wonderingly*.

"The same train," Bob answered *irritably*.

"How will I find Georgia Street in Pensacola?" demanded Art *insistently*.

"I'd ask when I got there," *gloomily* asserted Bob.

This is nonsensical Dialogue, as you can see, but the example is a useful one. The adverbs—*brightly, firmly, wonderingly, irritably, insistently* and *gloomily*—ruin the Dialogue. Take them out, then reread the passage. You've lost nothing by dropping the adverbs.

The purposes of dialogue

Why do writers use Dialogue? What are its specific purposes?

Well, most important of all purposes is to aid in characterization. In real life you rarely know much about someone until you hear him talk. The way he says things, the words he uses, the emphasis, the dialect, the subject define his real personality.

So, in writing a story, an author has his characters talk in certain ways, using certain language and speaking about certain topics to indicate the characters' personalities to the reader. Let's suppose you want to tell your reader that one of your characters is an Englishman. You might do it very quickly this way—via Dialogue:

Dialogue reveals the real person

"Where do I find the Home Secretary?"

"Beg pawdon?"

"The Home Secretary or his clerk."

"Home Secr't'ry? Oh, his *clark*. One moment and I shall ring up."

"I already have an appointment."

"Oh, raw-thair."

This is obviously overdone, but it makes the point. Through Dialogue, the average reader soon grasps what you're driving at: one of the two people in this Dialogue is undeniably English. The way he has said things has characterized him at once and given him at least the beginnings of a personality.

Let's try another. You're writing a short story and you want to make it clear that a young college student has just fallen in love. He has come home late and his roommate wakes up:

"Hi, Roger."

"Sorry I woke you, Red."

"That's all right. How is she?"

"She who?"

"Don't kid me. Your date. I can tell by the way you're acting that you like her."

"Fine. She's fine."

"Does she like you?"

"I guess so."

"Now I know you're in love."

"Don't be silly."

"So she's really that good?"

"Yes. No. I don't know what you're talking about."

The embarrassment of a young man freshly in love, his roommate's candor and perception give the reader quick insight into the character of both boys. No other form of writing could do it more quickly and accurately than Dialogue.

Good dialogue techniques

Here are some good techniques for writing Dialogue:

I

Pretend you're actually talking, then write what you and the others are "saying." Some writers have found they must "talk" their Dialogue, listen to it, before it begins to sound real. Then they put it on paper.

II

Pretend that you're actually talking

To write good Dialogue you must know your characters inside out, how they're apt to feel and react in various situations and with various people. If you don't know your characters well, they won't seem real to your reader. They'll be one person one page and quite another the next. It isn't too much to say that if, after beginning to write a story, you have to imagine what your characters will say, they are shadows, not real people. Galsworthy, Conrad and Hemingway have testified that they have gone to great lengths to "learn" their story people and that when they have come to know them completely, the writing of their Dialogue came as naturally as breathing.

III

You don't need such old-fashioned crutches as "he said" and "she replied" on every line of Dialogue. Much modern Dialogue is written without any conversational tags. The fact that the characters speak alternately makes clear who's talking, quickens the pace and heightens reality.

IV

Natural Dialogue is the most effective. Try making your characters sound as though they were flesh-and-blood humans expressing flesh-and-blood thoughts, not ponderous essays. If you're characterizing a slangy teen-ager, don't have her suddenly use oratorical, philosophical phrases. Use slang—*her* kind of slang. Above all be conversational in writing Dialogue.

Flesh-and-blood
words are needed

V

Since Dialogue can advance the action of a story very swiftly, use Dialogue instead of straight Narration from time to time. In other words, let the characters instead of you tell your story. For example, two of your characters may reveal in a brief Dialogue what would require pages of development if you used Narration and chronological action.

VI

When you've written page after page of unbroken Description or Narration and need some "air" in your pages, use Dialogue. Long paragraphs and heavy blocks of type are sure to kill your reader's interest—so break them up with indented Dialogue. Change of pace is good in all writing, and Dialogue will give you this change of pace very neatly.

VII

In Dialogue you must "stage-manage" your characters wherever possible. Don't let them talk to each other too long without moving them about or giving the reader a quick description of their facial expressions and gestures. Toss in an occasional comment as to how your character is reacting physically, how and where he or she is moving, what changes may be occurring in the background, what terminates one piece of Dialogue and initiates another.

VIII

In their haste to avoid using "he said" and "she replied" over and over again, writers in the past have substituted such words as "he *hissed*," "she *breathed*," "*grunted*," "*smiled*," "*ejaculated*," "*supposed*," "*asserted*," "*declaimed*," "*soliloquized*," "*voiced*," "*divulged*," "*giggled*" etc. Now, while it's possible to *assert* or *voice* something, people in real life rarely *declaim* or *hiss* a sentence. They *say* it. So, *said, said, said* is better than a lot of fancy synonyms.

But you don't even have to use *said* most of the time. Modern technique permits you to write Dialogue without conversational tags or adverbs, the bare fact of alternate speaking being enough to identify each speaker.

Dialogue in television

The play *Patterns* made history on television. Written by Rod Serling, it was repeated many times through popular demand and eventually became a first-rate movie. It concerns the struggle for power in a corporation office and the way some big companies go about making their none-too-human decisions.

In the following excerpt from the script of the TV play, Serling has Ramsey, a tough, icy, predatory but honest corporation head, presiding at a meeting at which Fred Staples, a young and sensitive new executive, is introduced to the Ramsey methods. We also meet Andy Sloane, an older and not unfeeling executive who has been with the company too long and is on the way out.

Know your characters
inside and out

The scene is Ramsey's conference room and, as the Dialogue suggests, all the department heads are present. They are discussing the purchase of a plant which will have to be closed, throwing 200 men out of work.

Ramsey: Before we go any further, gentlemen, I'd like you all to meet our newest member of the firm—Fred Staples. He's from Cincinnati. He's a production engineer by training, an industrial relations man by instinct. I expect good things from him. Reading from left to right, Mr. Staples—Mr. Smith, comptroller; Mr. Jameson, head of purchasing; Mr. Vandeventer, chief engineer; Mr. Gordon, head of sales; Mr. Latham, head of service; Mr. Granningan, record control; and Mr. Portier, head of operations. (*Each in turn nods and Fred murmurs how-do-you-do's.*) You've met Mr. Sloane—he's our assistant general manager in charge of everything everybody else forgets to be in charge of.

There's laughter, but it's pleasant laughter. Andy laughs with them, and then Fred chuckles along.

Ramsey: Now back to this Anderson thing. Look feasible to you? Look practical?

There's general agreement, rather dutiful enthusiasm.

Ramsey (*Looking at Andy*): How about you, Sloane? You look injured by it all. (*He says this absolutely pleasantly, and smiling.*)

Andy (*Wetting his lips*): You mention here probable time of purchase as sometime next spring. The plant'll be in receivership until then?

Ramsey: That's what it says. Bother you?

Andy: That means six months with improper maintenance of equipment. Loss of good will. Deterioration of—

Ramsey: If you'll forgive me for interrupting, it also means a savings of a quarter of a million dollars in the purchase price.

Andy: The plant employs two hundred men. That's half the working force of the village.

Ramsey: So?

Andy (*Sorry he's gone so far, but unable to turn back*): So it means the disrupting of an entire village's economy!

Ramsey: That is very true. Anything else?

Andy (*Flushing*): Aside from the . . . the consideration I mentioned, I think the purchase plans are adequate.

Ramsey: Adequate? (*To the others, and amused*) Mr. Sloane thinks it's adequate. Well, Mr. Sloane, if I can't induce any more enthusiasm than that from you, I'll be satisfied with what little crumb of agreement you may toss at me.

Jot down Dialogue in your notebook

Andy: I . . . I didn't mean to imply just . . . just adequacy, though I must admit to feeling a concern for two hundred wage earners suddenly deprived of a livelihood.

Ramsey (*This time nothing humorous*): Mr. Sloane, if you'd do me the goodness to listen closely to what I think is a fairly elementary thing. By putting two hundred men out of work, we ultimately may employ twice that number—by paying less for the plant, by being able to cut production costs as a result, by then competing more favorably in the market, we'll be able to sell more goods. We're not going to ruin that town; we're going to make it. I should think, Mr. Sloane, after twenty-odd years you'd be able to think beyond the tongue-clucking stage and come up with an analytical point of view!

Andy: I was under the impression I'd given you a point of view.

Ramsey: I saw none. I perceived what amounts to a little emotional tidbit that is decidedly more charitable than it is corporative, and by no means thought through. I asked, I believe, for an objective view of a business venture. From you I got—and I seem to be constantly getting a very negative response if any at all. Adequate, I think you said. Well, Mr. Sloane, this little move will save us two hundred and fifty thousand dollars, which we'll be able to put back in the business. Sloane, you take a liberal view of adequacy!

Andy: I didn't . . . didn't mean just . . . just adequacy. I meant—by and large—it sounded very good. Very good indeed.

Ramsey: Thank you, and bless you, Mr. Sloane. (*To the others, grinning again*) Mr. Sloane approves.

There's laughter now, but a little forced, because the kidding has become something infinitely deeper, more cutting. Andy tries a grin, but it's sickly and fades fast.

Ramsey: Now, Mr. Staples. You have an opinion?

Fred: I'm . . . frankly . . . because I've looked at this for just five minutes. I know nothing about the plant—its corporative set-up, causes of bankruptcy, *or* its product, for that matter. I'm afraid I'd have to pass on this one at the moment.

Ramsey: I would call that a solid, intelligent and conservative answer. Had you come up with an intensive program of your own after five minutes I'd have wondered about your sanity. There are times, gentlemen, when dynamics are plain idiocy. I respect thoughtful judgment. Congratulations, Staples. That's it for now. I want each of you to try to pick this analysis to pieces—we'll discuss it further. If there are any flaws in it, I want to find them now.

He rises, and this is the signal for general exodus.

Rod Serling wrote this scene by imagining himself present at it. He "heard" Ramsey and Andy talking to each other, and he told his TV audience that Ramsey was a tough, icy, predatory corporation chief by the way Ramsey talked, especially by the way he talked to the softer-hearted Andy. Ramsey would put Andy on a spot by making fun of his sentimentality over workmen losing their jobs—in front of everyone at the conference. And, in doing so, tough Ramsey would take on one personality and Andy another.

The author knew his characters inside out: they spoke as they would speak in real life. Ramsey would call everyone present by his last name, not his first, and so he does in the Dialogue. Andy would think of the human factors in closing a village's only plant, and he says so in the Dialogue. Even the words Ramsey uses are clipped and hard, while Andy's tend to be more gentle and, occasionally, timorous. In the end, Ramsey has bullied Andy into reversing his position and done it cruelly, which characterizes Ramsey for the viewer-listener, characterizes him through Dialogue alone.

Serling's characters are stage-managed to give the audience further insight into the characters of his play. After Ramsey has cut Andy to ribbons, the stage directions say:

There's laughter now, but a little forced, because the kidding has become something infinitely deeper, more cutting. Andy tries a grin, but it's sickly and fades fast.

The sickly grin, the hollow laughter, the nervous movement of other persons at the conference table will create for the audience still deeper insights into the human (and inhuman) traits of Serling's puppets, who have become living people.

Dialogue, as we can see from this script, can be a very powerful writing weapon. We know a great deal about Ramsey's character and methods by the end of the scene (of which this is only the last few minutes). We also know something about Staples and Sloane. In fact, we have fair descriptions of all three leading male characters in a few short lines of Dialogue.

We are also aware of at least a section of narrative—whether the company will buy the Anderson plant and throw 200 people out of work, but save the company a quarter of a million by doing it. We are equally aware of Ramsey's cruel practicality and Sloane's sentimental business approach, the basis of the conflict on which the TV play moves to its tremendous climax.

Be an eavesdropper
when people talk

Methods used by some big businesses are explained rather abruptly but pointedly in the brief Dialogue above, and the author is obviously presenting these facts because he disapproves of the Ramseys of the business world, while understanding their function. In short, all four basic forms come into play through the Dialogue alone. Yet the author of a play has only Dialogue and stage directions with which to express the gamut of Description, Narration, Exposition and Argument.

Dialogue in non-fiction

A writer of biography is likely to use Dialogue from time to time, yet what he writes isn't fiction but non-fiction. He's trying to re-create scenes, it's true, but theoretically the Dialogue he uses was actually said by someone involved with the biographee. It is, therefore, non-fiction.

The following non-fiction excerpt is from *McCall's* magazine. In order to make the article more realistic for her reader, Sabra Holbrook used Dialogue at several points in "I Was a Thief at Fourteen." This is a sample involving an older boy who is trying to help rehabilitate other children through planned recreation:

As "President" of Children's Village and football star I felt pretty big—*too* big in fact. One night after a football game, when a group of girls was brought in for a dance, I waited until I spotted the prettiest, then walked up to her and said:

"What do you say, kid, do you want to shake your dogs?"

She replied: "Sorry, but my dogs are barking now."

I would have retired from the scene, but the recreation director took me aside and told me not to be afraid of using manners if I wanted to get results.

"Try plain American language," he said, "like *please, may I?* and *thank you.*"

I spoke respectfully to the next girl.

Characterization of two people in two lines of Dialogue.

Journalism constantly uses Dialogue through quotation from real life. Something in the nature of Dialogue lends reality to any news story in which a man or woman is quoted directly. Red Smith, writing a pre-season baseball story from Miami, does it in the following humorous squib about a teen-age baseball rookie who can hit but can't field:

That juicy bonus ($115,000) got attention from the papers when the Orioles signed him out of Southwest High in St. Louis, and when he went to camp with the Orioles in Scottsdale, Ariz., a year ago he was eyed with what must have been pretty agonizing appraisal for an 18-year-old. Gordon Cobbledick, sports editor of the Cleveland *Plain Dealer,* dropped over several times.

"To be sure," he wrote, "he hasn't caught any fly balls yet, but he's getting closer to them."

An exaggerated quotation gives us perfect characterization.

The quote tells more about a teenage rookie with a big price tag on him than columns of Description about his inability to catch a fly ball.

One more example of non-fiction Dialogue comes from the memoirs of Queen Wilhelmina of the Netherlands, as briefly reviewed in *Newsweek* magazine:

After years of stern palace regimen, the rigors of two world wars and the decline of a once-sprawling empire, retired, 78-year-old former Queen Wilhelmina of the Netherlands found release from her bitterness and frustration by publishing her memoirs, *Lonely But Not Alone.*

"Because of immovable conventions, I had to grow up in a cage," wrote Wilhelmina, who became Queen at the age of 10. "I never had the opportunity to come into touch with common life . . . Ordinary conversation with other children was unthinkable in the cage atmosphere . . ."

Even in non-fiction, the character of the people you write about is etched more sharply by their own words than in any other way.

After abdicating to her only child, Juliana, in 1948, Wilhelmina recalled: "I needed a long time to find peace . . ."

Whether Dialogue is used for fiction or non-fiction, its hazards and uses are about the same. The Dialogue must be realistic or it won't come off. The fascinating realism of question-and-answer reporting of any famous courtroom trial justifies the many columns newspapers devote to it. Genuine Dialogue is the most readable writing there is; everybody knows that. And while Dialogue is the fiction writer's stock in trade, well-handled Dialogue, as we have seen, can be amazingly useful in non-fiction, too.

Whatever you write, there's no excuse for using the indirect approach instead of the direct quotation. In modern times, when authors of fiction or non-fiction may quote human beings exactly as they speak and not paraphrase them in mid-Victorian niceties, you simply must use Dialogue, the special form which invokes Description, Narration, Exposition and Argument simultaneously, yet moves the reader under its own power and through its own techniques.

Dialogue puts
air in writing

Summing up

Dialogue is a special form which doesn't fall into any of the four main categories yet overlaps them all. Modern writing, fiction and non-fiction alike, uses Dialogue to a greater degree than ever.

The purpose of Dialogue is essentially to aid in characterization. In real life you don't know much about someone until you hear him talk. The way he says things, his words, emphasis, dialect, subject matter define his real personality. So it is in writing. There's no quicker way to indicate a character's personality to a reader than through competent Dialogue.

The basis of all good Dialogue is conversational style. You must *hear* what your characters are saying to each other. They have to *talk* naturally or they won't become real to your reader. You must know your own characters inside out and when you do, they'll speak for themselves, characterize themselves without help from adverbs, even tell your story for you—through Dialogue alone.

It isn't necessary any longer to put in such old-fashioned crutches as "he said" and "she replied" at every line. Alternate speaking logically takes care of that. Avoid conversation-tag verbs like "hissed," "breathed," "ejaculated," "divulged" and "declaimed" when "said" will do as well.

Be careful when using adverbs, for they can weaken your Dialogue. In this Lesson, you noticed how the adverbs *brightly, firmly, wonderingly, irritably, insistently* and *gloomily* ruined a short passage of Dialogue. Let the things your people say in the Dialogue itself tell the reader how they're reacting.

Natural Dialogue holds your readers. Try making your characters or the people you're quoting in non-fiction sound as they would in real life—flesh-and-blood human beings expressing flesh-and-blood thoughts in real language, not ponderous essays.

You can use Dialogue instead of straight Narration from time to time. In other words, you may sometimes let your characters tell the story instead of you.

**Listen to yourself
as you write dialogue**

Dialogue even helps hold readers because it gives a printed page "air" by changing the pace and physical appearance from solid blocks of type to a page with more white space.

Writers must remember to stage-manage their characters wherever possible, not letting them talk to each other too long without moving them about or describing some new environment.

Dialogue is useful in non-fiction, though normally closer in technique to fiction. This is true because Dialogue is the most readable of all writing forms, accurately reproducing the essence of human character through what people actually say to each other.

Where style must come from

People constantly ask me whether the student of writing should confine himself to the style of any given period or branch out on his own and experiment as freely as he wants. If he wants to experiment with the style of any period, it would just be an exercise. It might help him to try to write one story in the Victorian style of George Meredith and try to write another in the Faulknerian style. Or he might try the style of Scott Fitzgerald or the people who came after him—

people like Thomas Wolfe or even J. D. Salinger. But this would only be exercise.

Young writers should never model themselves faithfully and slavishly after another writer. They should be themselves. When you sit down to write, express yourself the way that comes easiest and most naturally, without deliberately aping somebody else's style.—Bennett Cerf

Giving pleasure to others

Do you realize what a writer can contribute to the world in which he lives? He can contribute a thousand things: amusement, relaxation, escape; he can contribute the springboard for serious thought, ideals and standards; he can contribute pleasure and pondering; he can evoke happiness or pain, both of which every reader has experienced. And more than that, he can give of himself. For all writing in fiction and non-fiction must, to be valid, contain something of the writer—experience, principles, desires and belief.

Writing does much for the writer in an inward, even a spiritual sense. As you write of people, as you share their misery or joy, their insecurities and fortitude, their hesitancies (for you must share in order to communicate to the reader), you are learning more and more about people; the good, the evil, the in-between (which most of us are) and what's more, you are giving to others an immeasurable gift of entertainment and pleasure.—Faith Baldwin

Advice from Sinclair Lewis

You learn to write by *writing*. Sinclair Lewis once said to a Columbia University writers' club: "What are you people doing here? Why don't you go home and write instead of coming to look at me?"

Section V

Lesson eighteen

Principles of good writing

Writing for your reader

If there were no need for writing beyond the persistent urge of the writer to put words on paper, the craft would have died long ago. But since writing is not only a means of self-expression but also the basis of communication, its value is twofold. It satisfies the writer's compulsion to express himself *and* it satisfies the reader by entertaining, stimulating and informing him.

In the profession of writing you have to have readers. A book, an article, a short story or a business report is only half done until it finds an audience. Or to put it another way, a piece of writing doesn't really exist until someone reads it. For example, a letter lost in the mails never serves as a communication between the sender and the addressee. It needs the reader to make it come alive, just as a seed needs soil, sun and rain to germinate and grow.

One thing, then, is elemental to writing: most of the millions of words written every day are designed to tell something. Just the same, all of these words are of no value whatever until they begin growing in the minds of their readers. Writing is communication only when there's a receiver at the other end.

Is this true of fiction and non-fiction? It is.

Consider businessmen, lawyers, engineers, doctors, teachers, students, scientists, newsmen, civic workers, clubwomen—all of these people write letters, reports, briefs, minutes, memorandums, articles, speeches and papers. The purpose of their non-fiction writing is to educate, to influence, to inform, to argue or to fulfill some specific requirement.

When it comes to fiction, the authors of short stories, novelettes, novels and serials also have a purpose. They seek to entertain, to amuse, to thrill, to sadden, to stir the reader. Fiction is, then, also designed to tell somebody something—to communicate. Thus we can say that in *all* writing, the writer and the reader are an inseparable team.

As Max Shulman puts it:

There is always an unseen attendant looking over my shoulder when I am at the typewriter. He represents the reader I am trying to reach. When I have to make a decision between my taste and his, I always yield to his. I avoid the esoteric, the private joke and the personal idiosyncrasy. I do not underrate my reader but neither do I regard him as a reflection of myself.

Writer and reader
are a team

You as a beginning writer should bear this in mind. If you have noticed that certain things make only you laugh out of the whole crowd, or that only you are moved and affected, do not therefore assume that the rest of the crowd are a bunch of Philistines and you are the sole possessor of wisdom. Remember that a writer without an audience is a writer only in his own eyes.

No reader can benefit from your story, article or letter until you, the writer, tell him why you are writing. Before he starts reading, he cannot possibly know what you have to say about the subject because you, the writer, are his sole informant and guide. If he fails to become informed, the fault is yours, not his. Your aim is to capture his curiosity and interest, and through them arouse the feelings you intend to arouse.

Sometimes the reader eagerly awaits what you've written—a letter to Mother, a confirming sales order, a press release of the President's Inaugural Address. At other times, the reader hasn't asked you to write anything: he already has plenty of reading material. In such instances, what you've written must compete for his curiosity and attention with other words created by other writers on the same subject.

In our era of high-speed presses, television, radio, movies and other instruments of communication, the competition for the reader's time is severe. This fact sharpens the need for knowing your particular reader before writing something aimed in his direction.

Knowing your reader is somewhat like gardening—you must understand the nature of your soil to ensure a good crop. The gardener knows that celery grows best in rich black loam, blueberries do well in acid soil, earth for some vegetables needs lime each spring. So it is with the writer. He must understand his reader or he will find his words falling on barren ground.

Such being the case, how do you go about discovering your reader's interests and desires? Let's look at six general areas of writing where knowing your reader is vitally important:

1. Personal notes and letters.
2. Diaries, journals and minutes of a meeting.
3. Magazines and books.
4. Journalism for the printed page.
5. Radio and television.
6. Advertising and business.

Always keep your reader in mind

1. Personal notes and letters

Writing a winning, warm and informative personal letter or note isn't as easy as it seems. Too many letters, personal *and* business, leave the reader puzzled, bored, patronized, misinformed, irritated or keenly aware of the indifference of the writer to his problems or existence.

In any form of communication, it's not only *what* you write; it's the *way* you write it. A letter may contain all the facts you wish to communicate to your reader, yet be cold in tone and fail in its purpose.

The Veterans Administration in Washington publishes a useful pamphlet called *The Winning Letter* in which the following questions apply just as well to personal as to business communications:

It all depends on what kind of hand we write. Is your hand—
a. like a fist with brass knuckles, unfriendly and threatening . . .
b. like the smooth gestures of a sleight-of-hand artist with a now-you-see-it and now-you-don't motion . . .
c. or is it like a sincere, friendly handclasp?

This last kind of hand might be called "the human touch," but it doesn't mean being overly sentimental, falsely sympathetic or apologetic. It's essentially a matter of applying the Golden Rule to this field of elementary writing:

Write to others as you would have them write to you.

Read this letter written by a teen-ager to her brother in the Army and see if you don't feel a certain lack of warmth and understanding, despite the love and friendship which undoubtedly exist between them:

Dear Bernard:

I've been very busy reviewing my lessons for the mid-term exams and have not written. My history exam comes tomorrow afternoon and my civics exam on Thursday morning. I think I passed English lit' but I'm not as sure with geometry or French. That Miss Giddings in French has got it in for me as I told you before. I'll let you know of my progress after my marks come in . . . , etc., etc.

There's nothing in this letter so far which shows the girl's concern for the safety, well-being, hopes, fears or plans of her uniformed brother. To the contrary, she seems to think only of herself.

In fact, there is little in this letter about anyone except the writer, a great mistake in personal communication. The letter brims with *I, my,* and *me,* but seldom gives *you* much attention, though *you* are the reader and interested in your sister's awareness of *your* existence, problems, plans, small disasters and triumphs. Bernard, lonely in some distant military post, would enjoy reading a letter starting like this:

The reader's age
is important

Dear Bernard:

The whole family is excited over your promotion from Private First Class to Corporal. Though you say it doesn't amount to much, we think *Corporal Foley* is much more impressive than Private First Class Foley, and we drank your health last night, in grape juice of course. You know Mother and teen-age drinking! And how cold it must be up in Labrador—just wait until you get home. We'll have a roaring fire and you can stick your feet up and we'll wait on the Corporal hand and foot. It won't be long now, either, because do you realize you have only six months . . . etc., etc.

This letter makes Bernard feel warm and comforted, certain that his young sister cares about *his* life and problems, not wholly about herself. After she has talked of Bernard's promotion, the warming fires of home, and the fact that he's happily nearing the end of his tour of duty, Bernard will gladly listen to girlish talk about her own school, friends, problems and progress. In fact he'll *want* to hear about it from anyone as thoughtful as the writer of this kind of letter.

How do *your* personal letters sound? Do they have too much of yourself in them and too little concern for the reader? Do they offend the reader?

Phrases and expressions common to your own way of life or surroundings may jar your reader or conjure up pictures in his or her mind quite different from those you want to portray. For instance, local slang doesn't always translate accurately a thousand miles from the sender.

You have to keep your letter-reader in mind at all times, just as you keep your readers in mind when you write a short story or magazine article. Some close friends you can joke with or gently ridicule and they'll understand, taking it for what you meant it to be . . . friendly joshing. With others you may never dare to joke by letter because you know in advance they won't understand and may even take offense.

Some friends can take a joke

Six basic points in letter writing

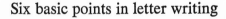

Here are good basic points to remember about any personal communication:

I

Never reply to an unreasonable or offensive letter by adopting the same tone. This hurts your own case and simply invites more invective. Perhaps the letter you received is so offensive you can't think of a fair, decent way to reply to it. In that case, don't do anything.

Many a businessman has saved himself money and mental grief by writing a vitriolic reply to an offensive letter, then tossing it in the wastebasket. Personal letter writers might follow his example with profit.

You have received a highly personal letter which reads this way:

I warn you that if your child ever comes to play with my child again, I shall have to take the matter up with the authorities.

Obviously, this isn't a matter for letter writing, but for a family council, neighborhood inquiry, perhaps a personal call on the writer. Undoubtedly things aren't as bad as they sound in the letter, but this is no time to put your own mixed, highly-charged emotional reactions into black and white.

II

Don't "exceedingly regret" anything trivial. Few things are more irritating to a letter-reader than overstated personal feelings. There may be infrequent times when you actually do "exceedingly regret" an act or word, but don't use the phrase or others like it when you're simply calling attention to an overdue bill or writing someone you don't know about the death of a person you never met.

For example, don't write this kind of letter to someone you scarcely know:

In your inconsolable bereavement thank God for your precious memories of her whom you adored and for the multitude of gifts which must have been given you by your beloved one during her marvelous lifetime. I am exceedingly distraught at the news of her demise and deeply regret not having known her during her blessed time on this earth. In humility before the ever-increasing picture of your present grief, and with assurances of my personal wretchedness over your heartbreaking sorrow, I remain . . .

Indeed, don't write this sort of letter to anyone. The flowery language, the overstated personal feelings, don't ring true. Far better to write a letter like this:

Your sister Katherine, who works next to me, tells me the sad news about your husband. While I didn't know him, Katherine has said many times what a fine person he was and I have heard from many others how much he will be missed. There is very little a stranger can do at times like these, but I do have a car which might be of use to you or someone in your household during the coming week. If you can use it, you need only tell Katherine, who sees me here. Sincerely . . .

This is a courteous, truthful letter and a sympathetic one. It doesn't gush; the reader won't be embarrassed. It offers a specific service which may well be useful at such a time.

III

The third point is never "write down" to your audience. Say what you have to say simply, plainly and quickly. If your audience is young or someone you consider to be your inferior, the way you write can be a giveaway of your own lack of tact and understanding.

Don't, for instance, write like this to a less fortunate stay-at-home neighbor:

> Our non-stop jet plane made the trip in less than three hours. You have probably never been in a jet plane so I won't go into detail about our flight because you wouldn't understand it. But take it from a seasoned traveler, this was a rich experience, though I would suggest that you start with the old-fashioned propeller plane as the jet would be too frightening for you. Then when you've become used to flying, as I have, you can venture something like this. Anyway, we arrived in Florida at lunch time and had tree-ripened orange juice at the airport. I won't even attempt to describe the difference from the canned orange juice. You wouldn't understand because you've never been to Florida . . .

Don't "write down" to your audience

If you got a letter like this, you'd feel like throwing it in the wastebasket. Who does the writer think she is, Mrs. Marco Polo? Others have taken plane rides to sunny Florida. There's nothing so superspecial about it all. Far better to write a letter starting:

> Our jet trip was exciting, under three hours, and far less noisy than planes we've been used to. When you come this way be sure to try the jet, if you haven't already. For one thing it's so steady they don't even give you a removable tray—you just pull down your tray from the back of the seat ahead of you! At 22,000 feet we seemed to be standing still, but of course we weren't. We were going almost as fast as the speed of sound! In any case, Florida is as nice as ever, warm and relaxing, the sort of vacation you people had a couple of years ago when you drove to Arizona. I've never seen the desert but I imagine sun country is equally wonderful anywhere and in wintertime, Western tree-ripened orange juice must be the same delight it is down here . . .

IV

Never be afraid to put factual truth in a letter. If this seems strange advice, think back over letters you've received—personal and business—which evaded questions and issues raised by you in prior correspondence. Some people are apparently incapable of "putting things in writing," preferring to leave this to person-to-person communication. While it's not a good idea to gossip or to disclose secrets you will one day regret having revealed, there are ways of modifying almost anything you write.

You're trying to tell your mother and father of a personal crisis and you must communicate in writing because they live halfway around the world from you. Perhaps you put the news in your letter like this, which is far better than withholding it:

So many things can happen to marriages, particularly overseas marriages, as you two dear people must know, it's a wonder there aren't more disasters than there are. In our case, Jerry has simply fallen in love with another woman, one I don't even know. On an Oriental assignment like ours there's little for him to do on his trips to Japan, Hong Kong and Singapore except go to parties with company friends. And I think that's where the trouble started, though one never really knows.

Perhaps I am more at fault than I believe, which wouldn't be surprising. In any case, Jerry wrote me day before yesterday from Tokyo that he isn't coming back because he has found someone he "really loves." I thought at first I should try to spare you, but we have to face facts and you'd know eventually, so in all candor I must tell you now, however unpleasant it is for all of us. I do love you both. You know that.

V

If your letter is especially important, don't hesitate to use notes and outlines. This isn't often true of personal letters, but in modern business the best writer is the one who marshals the facts, knows what to say and what must be said—in the right order.

Just the same, writing a letter of any sort requires forethought. For example, a college boy keeps notes during the week of things he wants to write home about each Sunday. He keeps his jottings on a small pad near his bed and by the end of a week the notes might read like this:

1. Send for white evening jacket.
2. Need cash for Denver trip. Explain.
3. A— mark in history survey paper.
4. Ran into Mrs. McClellan at the Student Union.
5. Tom's new car.
6. Wyoming, Utah games.
7. Honor society chances.
8. Spring vacation dates.
9. Laundry mailing carton broken.
10. Chemistry test poor.

This isn't an outline in the strict sense, but it's good journalistic practice. Note-taking is admirable at any time. Letters are no exception.

VI

Letters should be lively. Robert Moses, the letter-writing Park Commissioner who laid out the parkway system around New York City, discusses in the *New York Times Magazine* the perils and fascinations that lie between "Dear Sir" and "Yours truly":

Letter writing became an art long before the telegraph made communications shorter and the telephone made them interminable; before the daily press, radio and television spread the news much faster than the mail or even gossip and rumor; and before stenography, stenotyping, disk and tape recording spared the busy executive the ignominy of doing his own work . . .

In looking through various collections of letters, some conclusions seem inescapable. Most of these effusions, whatever the claims of experts, were palpably open letters written and rewritten for posterity. Few were intimate in the sense that they were intended to be seen only by the addressee. I doubt whether there was anything impulsive in the various Epistles of Saint Paul . . .

Keep your letters lively and "adult"

Good talkers, like Dr. Johnson, are usually good writers, especially if they have friends like Boswell to memorize, keep notes and insure enduring fame.

On the other hand, some who are dull in conversation write astonishingly good letters, maybe because they pause to think.

Most people become paralyzed when they grasp the pen. They affect elegant periods, become stilted and self-conscious and never slip into the vernacular. Some of them act as if they were matadors in a bull ring, acting under the compulsions of an elaborate, traditional code.

Robert Moses is talking about the dull, trite letters so many people send to family and friends—letters written in a childish style that the writers would be ashamed to use in personal conversation.

Here's a paragraph from a letter written by a fairly interesting young person, though you'd never know it from the way she writes:

We went to the zoo where we saw many wonderful sights. Then we went and had expensive chocolate sodas, but they weren't as good as the ones at home. After that we took a sightseeing bus up Fifth Avenue and Riverside Drive and returned by subway to our hotel, more dead than alive!

What zoo? *What* animals did they see? Were there any *unusual* ones? If so, *what* colors and shapes and noises made impressions? *Where* did the party have sodas? If they had them outdoors under an umbrella, was it *gay*? If they had them in a famous Fifth Avenue hotel, *which* hotel? *How much* were the sodas—three times what sodas are at home? Was it a glass-roofed bus? What sights and smells and sounds made the trip memorable? Same for the subway ride—surely they don't have subways like this back home.

You see, most of the things this young woman will breathlessly describe to her family and friends when she returns aren't in her letter at all. Perhaps her letter would have been more interesting if written this way:

Play on your reader
like an instrument

> We went to the new Central Park Zoo on Fifth Avenue just below the Metropolitan Museum of Art. It isn't as large as the Bronx Zoo, I understand, but it does have just about every animal you could name: tigers, leopards, elephants, lions, polar bears, all our native American animals such as skunks, badgers, possums, foxes and raccoons, plus a water buffalo, a bison (I always call them buffaloes) and a giraffe. They even have a tiglon, which is half tiger and half lion. The cages were spotlessly clean, but still I don't care for the smells of a zoo. The cockatoos were lovely, every color in the rainbow. Yet I still can't get over feeling sorry for caged birds and animals, silly as it seems . . . etc. . . .

Now compare the paragraph originally written by the zoo visitor with a descriptive letter written many years ago by the young English poet Robert Browning to Elizabeth Barrett, prior to their marriage. Elizabeth, a chronic invalid, took to her London bed in wintertime and stayed there until warm weather. Her father encouraged it, possibly because he wished thereby to keep her to himself. In February, 1846, the young poet-suitor writes to the girl he loves and wants to marry:

> Then see the bright weather while I write—lilacs, hawthorn, plumtrees all in bud; elders in leaf, rosebushes with great red shoots; thrushes, whitethroats, hedge sparrows in full song—there can, let us hope, be nothing worse in store than a sharp wind, a week of it perhaps—and then comes what shall come—

You can feel hope in the lover's heart as he sees movement, sound, color and life beginning to burgeon all about him. Although naturally reserved, Browning as a writer is probably capable of putting on paper perhaps more, not less, than he's able to say in person. What he describes has specific appeal to the senses of his reader.

Letters should indeed be lively but they shouldn't offend the reader or seem smart aleck. When writing to verify arrangements for an interview, for instance, you should always make your request succinct and specific. You should ask for a short quick favor—then name the specific area of questioning you have in mind. For example:

Dear Dr. Tennyson:
This is to confirm in writing our telephone conversation of yesterday regarding an interview you have been kind enough to grant me.
Green Book magazine has assigned me a short article on the hibernation of animals. As Curator of Mammals at the Zoological Park, you are one of three prominent zoologists I plan to interview before writing the piece from notes I have already carefully researched. The other two to be interviewed are your colleagues, Dr. Fuller and Dr. Meade, of the University staff.
I can match my plans to suit your schedule, but some day early next month would be best for me. I don't plan to bring a photographer as this piece is to be illustrated by rather amazing pictures I already have of hibernating animals.
A self-addressed, stamped envelope is enclosed and I would appreciate a reply as soon as you can arrange a convenient time.
Sincerely yours,

This letter has two merits. It will not irritate a busy and important man, but rather verifies facts he will want to be certain about. Secondly, it saves you time because you've answered pertinent questions in advance—where the article will appear, who else will be interviewed, what the general area of information will be, the important fact that no photographer will accompany you. This is common courtesy. It's also sound letter-writing technique.

2. Diaries, journals and minutes of a meeting

In basic writing, a natural step beyond notes and letters is the keeping of personal diaries, and the minutes of a meeting that keep your members informed. Many people are familiar with these writing forms: others find them helpful in learning how to write simply, clearly and factually. The diary or journal is especially useful to the student because it does three things:

1. Satisfies the longing for self-expression.
2. Perpetuates the habit of daily writing.
3. Gives him material on which to base his future writing.

Thousands of articles and books have been based on day-to-day entries kept by people in all walks of life. Many professional writers would have been helpless without the chronological, fact-filled pages which gave them marvelously accurate reminders of times and details long past.

Many great books
stem from diaries

Thoreau's amazing life and philosophy as an individualist at Walden Pond and Brook Farm might never have been fully known had it not been for his journals, posthumously collected and published two generations after his death in 1862. We might never have known the true story of Florence Nightingale had she not kept a Crimean War diary in the 1850's, from which *Notes of Nursing* became a best-seller and revolutionized the nursing profession.

Winston Churchill readily admitted writing his magnificent six-volume history of World War II, *The Gathering Storm, Their Finest Hour, The Grand Alliance, The Hinge of Fate, Closing the Ring* and *Triumph or Tragedy,* from wartime diaries and journals. Without day-to-day entries, Anne Lindbergh could never have written *North to the Orient,* her book about pioneering air travel with her famous husband. Eleanor Roosevelt's autobiographical books were founded on her syndicated public journal, "My Day," and diaries going back to her childhood. William L. Shirer's famous best-seller, *Berlin Diary,* was one of dozens of World War II journals which became books with little change from the day-to-day entries.

From king to commoner, men have been keeping diaries or journals since man first wrote down his thoughts. How many of these private diaries and journals supplied their authors with material for important books no sensible man would guess. We know far more, for instance, about life in the Confederacy from 1861 to 1865 because a society leader named Mary Boykin Chesnut kept *A Diary from Dixie.* Literally hundreds of Civil War authors have used this diary to give them authentic material for their stories.

Daniel Defoe, author of *Robinson Crusoe* and *Moll Flanders,* once wrote a best-seller called *Journal of the Plague Year* which could well serve the student as a model of diary or journal writing—except that Defoe's *Journal* wasn't real. He made it up.

Defoe wrote his celebrated journal in 1722; the Great Plague had struck London in 1665, when Defoe was only five years old. Hence, the remarkably acute statements of "eye-witnesses," which make some of the most fascinating reading in English literature, weren't fact at all but pure fiction.

Daniel Defoe was merely using the diary *form* to intrigue and then hold his readers.

The point is that intense personal involvement does something for writing. It gives it certain authenticity. The reader feels he or she is being let into the very core of human emotions, reactions and opinions. Reading a diary or journal is like eavesdropping or listening to family gossip. In short, what's been written in a private diary is usually nearer candid truth than something written with public readership in mind.

Nothing is more satisfactory to the beginning writer than keeping a diary, nor more useful later on. We recommend it to you if you don't already keep one. Most writers have done so at one time or another, and professional writers often keep a journal going all their lives. Arnold Bennett kept one: few books of the past century give a clearer picture of the life of a professional writer than Bennett's *Journal*, from which the following excerpts, written in France, are taken:

Keeping a diary
is soul-satisfying

Wednesday, October 9th—Yesterday I began *The Old Wives' Tale.* I wrote 350 words yesterday afternoon and 900 this morning. I felt less self-conscious than I usually do in beginning a novel. In order to find a clear three hours for it every morning, I have had to make a timetable, getting out of bed earlier and lunching later. This morning I calculated that I could just walk to the Croix de Montmorin and back in an hour. I nearly did it this morning without trying, in heavy rain. A landscape of soaked leaves and thick clouds and rain—nothing else. But I like it.

Thursday, October 10th—A magnificent October day. I walked four miles between 8.30 and 9.30 and then wrote 1,000 words of the novel. This afternoon we penetrated into the forest with our bicycles and without a map! Had to walk miles, got lost gloriously, and at last reached home after two hours 40 minutes of labour. Far off, in an unfrequented path, we came across three old women sitting in the hedge and discussing mushrooms.

Wednesday, October 16th—I have now written 7,000 words of the first chapter of the novel, and am still far from the end of it. Regarding it objectively, I do not see that it is very good, but from the pleasure I take in doing it, it must be.

Nothing but rain. I walked four miles in 59 minutes this morning in the rain. And this afternoon I went with Marguerite to Moret in pouring rain. A promenade on a thoroughly bad day in autumn is the next best thing to a promenade on a fine spring morning. Now it is dark, and I write this by my desk lamp (after only one and one-half pages my eyes feel fatigue) and it is still raining on the window.

Monday, October 21st—Today I finished the second chapter. I seem to be rather uneasy as to its excellence. The date of the first part worries me, as my own recollections don't begin till 10 years later than 1862. However, the effect of the novel will be a cumulative one.

Lately I have been overworking, in spite of all resolutions to the contrary. I rise at 6.30 or so, and after reading Italian, one hour's walking, etc., I begin on the novel at 9.30 and work till 12.30. Then my afternoons are often taken up with articles. I had meant to keep my afternoon quite free of composition. Nevertheless, my health, thanks to walking four miles in an hour each morning, is simply admirable, and I sleep well. But my eyesight is weakening.

Wednesday, October 23rd—Still much rain. The forest all yellow and brown. Leaves falling continuously. Horse-chestnuts quite yellow.

I have written over 2,000 words of third chapter yesterday and today. I planned the chapter perfectly yesterday in the forest.

Saturday, October 26th—The forest is now, for me, at nearly its most beautiful. Another fortnight and the spectacle will be complete. But it is really too close to our doors for us to appreciate it properly. If we had to walk five miles instead of 500 yards in order to get into one of these marvellously picturesque glades, we should think we were exceedingly lucky in being only five miles off and not 50 . . . The sound of voices is very clear in the forest in this mushroom weather. I have learnt a little about mushrooms. I have tremendously enjoyed my morning exercise in the mist or rain.

In general, slightly too much work. 18,000 words of *Old Wives' Tale* in two weeks, four days. Much tempted to throw up my Italian and my piano, on account of stress of work, but I still stick to both of them.

Monday, October 28th—I began work on the scenario of an operatic libretto from *Antony and Cleopatra* yesterday afternoon, and I finished the whole thing this morning before lunch—complete in all details. I ripped to pieces two copies of Hunter's student's edition of the play in order to save myself the trouble of copying. I have never done as much work before in the time.

Autumn in the forest. The colours get richer and richer; and one's fingers colder. Many parts are now quite covered with new red leaves. Fogs every morning. In my morning exercise I have timed myself and find I can walk uphill at the rate of seven kilometres an hour for at least a quarter of a mile. I could no doubt do several miles at this speed.

*Thursday, October 31st—*First day of St. Martin's summer today apparently. As soft and treacherous as a day of spring. In four days I have written probably about 10,000 words.

*Monday, November 4th—*I finished first half of first part of *Old Wives' Tale*. 8.30 to 11, walk by Seine and in forest. Thinking about next chapter of *Old Wives' Tale*.

*Wednesday, November 20th—*Regularly I have been doing 2,000 words a day at least. 1,200 to 1,500 words of my novel in the morning, and pieces of articles in the afternoon. I am now almost sure to do 365,000 words in the year.

When you walked briskly with Bennett, you felt the rain and the rapid pace, you were keenly aware of his accumulative creative writing, you triumphed with him when he got past the first half of *Old Wives' Tale*.

Compare his accurate, honest and compelling sequence with the following paragraph from the alleged diary of a movie star, printed in a Hollywood fan magazine:

*October 10—*If only Ron and I could work together with faith, I know we'd find happiness. And maybe we'd even find love again. I can remember the first time our eyes met and his lips were soon on mine, a flame, searing my very soul. It seems so remote, foreign now. If only Ron had my faith this would never have happened to us, this awful divorce, this final parting.

The reader knows, after several pages of this, that not a trace of sincerity or honest observation went into the writing of the entries. If diaries and journals aren't honest, they are worthless.

Here are two basic statements to keep in mind about diary and journal writing:

1. Since intense personal involvement does something for writing, makes it more interesting, intimate and real, the diary or journal can be a delight for any man or woman learning to write. Here all the inhibitions of publication may be avoided and the very heart of human workings exposed, but only to private eyes. This is very good psychologically, since it frees your desires to express inner feelings in material that will not be published.

2. Since a diary or journal is personal, the *whole truth* is of prime importance. Anything less than candidly honest entries—accurate, factual and real—discredits this most private of communications. Indeed, some colleges have courses in the diary and journal which are almost always called in the catalogue, "*Intimate* Types of Writing." And so they are. Take advantage of this fact.

Writing the public journal

**Records are needed
of public gatherings**

Differing from the personal diary is the public journal, which includes records kept by an organizational secretary, minutes of professional societies, medical, engineering and law review notations, such publications as the *Congressional Record* (verbatim record of Congressional sessions), public listings of real estate transactions, etc.

Here's a simple example of minutes, taken from the records of a high school art club:

The regular meeting of the Art Club was held in the high school auditorium on March 29, 19— at 3 o'clock, with Grace Curry presiding and Louise Horvath acting as secretary. The minutes of the previous meeting were read and approved. The treasurer, Harlan McGee, reported a deficit of $4 in the treasury. A motion made by Edwin Knight that the Art Club sponsor a party to raise funds was carried. Chairman of the various committees for the event were appointed as follows: Betty Phelps, decoration; Mary Hall, orchestra; Walter Franklin, publicity; Mary Jane Kennedy, refreshment; Charles Gordon, cleanup; Pauline Lengel, entertainment; Ann Peterson, invitation; Josephine Timberlake, tickets; Nancy Eberman, hostess. Lee Manning was appointed to ascertain a suitable date for the event. On a motion made by Margaret Smith, the meeting adjourned at 4 o'clock.

Respectfully submitted,
Louise Horvath, Secretary

Relatively simple, this art club's report nevertheless records for all its members a clear recapitulation, essentially journalistic. To someone who hadn't been present, the idea of sponsoring a party to raise club funds (and the mechanics of same) would have been communicated successfully—who was to do what, where, when and why.

Let's take another simple set of minutes, this from a social club of university women graduates who want to raise money for charities. It requires legal motions to start the ball rolling. These particular minutes were printed in the local newspaper just as written by the club secretary:

The midwinter meeting of the Exeter County Alumnae Club of New Hampshire University was held at the home of Miss Eloise Dupree in Fall River on Tuesday, January 23. Plans for the coming year were discussed.

Mrs. William Howard of Topping Lane, Jackson, new President, announced that the second annual benefit dance will be held May 2 at the Shore and Country Club, Jackson, from 9 to 1. Proceeds from the dance will go to the Exeter County Rehabilitation Center. As a result of last year's dance, $300 was donated to the center for the care of children suffering from cerebral palsy.

The theme of this year's dance will be "Silhouettes in Rhythm." Mrs. James Rhodes of Fall River will be in charge of decorations. Chairman for the dance is Mrs. Knight McCready of New Bedford; she is to be assisted by Mrs. William Wordsley of Noroton. Reservations are being handled by Mrs. Allen Kelley of New Bedford (TE 8-4573) and Mrs. Richard Forrest of Fall River (LO 2-5592).

The Community Swing Six, popular Exeter County dance band, will provide the music again this year for the dance.

There being no other old or new business, the meeting was adjourned after the treasurer's report, which showed a balance of $82.55 as of January 1.

Organizations like the Board of Education, the vestry of a local church, the Rotary Club or the Volunteer Fireman's Association are quasi-public and require detailed recordings similar to those of assemblies of a legislature or court. Fixed policy requirements place great responsibility on the recording secretary or stenographer at such meetings or assemblies. Robert's Rules of Order prevail, motions are entertained and procedural maneuvers are quite common.

Following is an exact reproduction of the minutes of a monthly vestry meeting called to discuss a new rectory. Only the names, dates and places have been changed:

Community Church Parish
Minutes of Vestry meeting at Parish House, June 16, 19—

Present: Messrs. Cunningham, Larned, Leary, Manuelli, Munger, Noonan, Smith and Younger; Mesdames Albertson, Shaw and Williams.

First order of business was the report on the new house for the second minister by Mr. David Cunningham, reporting to the Vestry for the Building Committee composed of Mr. Thomas Smith, Chairman, Mr. Cunningham and Mr. John Larned. It was reported that the Assembly approved the building plans and clearance was received from the Chairman and the standing committee. The house plans and specifications are in the hands of George Manuelli and it is hoped that all details and signing of the contract will be completed within the next week or ten days. However, Mr. Cunningham reported that the Building Committee questions whether we can have the house completed and ready for occupancy on September 15. It was estimated that November 15 might be a more realistic date. Mr. Cunningham added that they hoped to start the road and house excavation in approximately ten days. Ledge conditions have been noted and may cause change of plans for house site.

Mr. Manuelli reported that the County Trust Company today had granted a $30,000 20-year mortgage and approved the plans for the house. Mr. Manuelli also advised that it would be necessary to have firm specifications at time of signing the contract.

Mr. Larned suggested we look ahead to the problem of housing the Thompsons during the interim period. Mr. Leary agreed and said we ought to fix responsibility and plan for this contingency. Later in the meeting Mrs. Williams and Mr. Larned accepted the responsibility for working on this and will report to the Vestry at the next meeting.

Minutes refresh members' memories

Mr. Younger reported that a gift of 10% of the house cost ($3,000) had been offered by an anonymous donor, contingent upon the Vestry's making a serious and honest effort to raise additional funds for this purpose. Mr. Younger noted that the giver did not restrict his offer to the success in raising additional funds, but merely stated that an honest effort should be made. This matter was the subject of long discussion by the Vestry as to ways and means of complying with the anonymous giver's wishes.

Some debate centered upon the question of what would or would not constitute an "honest effort." Mr. Noonan suggested that a letter be sent to the Parish stating the terms of the gift. Mr. Munger expressed some concern (shared by several other members of the Vestry) that such a campaign could hurt the Every Member Canvass. Mr. Younger mentioned that the giver had remarked that it might be possible to contact a selected list of parishioners who would consider following the giver's example.

Following this discussion Mr. Noonan moved that (1) a letter be sent to the Parish outlining the terms and intent of the anonymous offer; (2) prior to the sending of this letter Mr. Younger consult with the prospective donor to determine if he or she would be satisfied with this effort and to acquaint that individual with the Vestry's thinking regarding the Every Member Canvass; (3) the Vestry may take further action to pursue this effort, based on its success and the feeling of the prospective donor. This motion was seconded by Mr. Manuelli and unanimously carried.

Mr. Cunningham requested Mr. Younger to write the letter for the Vestry.

Mr. Leary then reported for the Education Committee and presented an extensive typewritten resumé consisting of reports from members of the various educational groups. Mrs. Barbara Shaw participated in this presentation and was also helpful in clarifying and explaining the work and aims of the Education Committee. The Vestry indicated strong interest and considerable time was devoted to discussion.

Mr. Cunningham asked if the Seabury Teaching Method had any effect on Sunday School attendance. Mrs. Shaw replied that this was a difficult correlation to make. Mr. Cunningham asked if we should do more to publicize the Seabury Series to the Parish. Mrs. Shaw answered that we are always trying to do this in every way and this meeting is a good instance. One of the large problems faced by the Education Committee is the irregular attendance at Sunday School. After discussion the Vestry recommended that the report be summarized and published in a Parish News Letter—and further, that such reports from the Education Committee to the Vestry should be continued each year.

A motion was passed unanimously approving the Stewardship Committee's statement on giving.

Mr. George Noonan reported for the Finance Committee. Due to the lateness of the hour it was decided to have him report more fully at the next Vestry meeting. However, Mr. Noonan called attention to the fact that it was now time to consider the purchase of a new car for the Rector. The present car has over 40,000 miles and is becoming increasingly costly to maintain. The matter was discussed and Mr. Larned moved that Mr. Noonan be authorized to negotiate the purchase of a new car at a price not to exceed $1,850, and to close the deal if Mr. Noonan considered it favorable. Motion was seconded and unanimously passed.

Mr. Smith reported that he has ordered envelopes and plans to send them to all parishioners next year. He also made the following treasurer's report, covering the first four months of the year, comparing last year's income with this year:

19— Pledges: $ 8,237   Plate Collections: $1,860
19— Pledges: 10,482   Plate Collections: 2,279

Meeting adjourned at 11:00 P.M.

Respectfully submitted,
Andrew B. Younger
Clerk Pro Tem

Agenda for July Vestry Meeting—8:15 P.M.
1. Treasurer's report—Mr. Noonan
2. Education Committee—Mr. Leary
   Adult Program for Fall
3. Thompson home—Mr. Larned
   Temporary housing—Mr. Larned, Mrs. Williams
4. Social Responsibility Committee—Mr. Noonan
5. Leadership Conference in September—Mr. Manuelli
6. Other matters?

How do you write minutes of a meeting so they will be clear to any future reader, whether he was present at the meeting or not? There are rather definite rules, based on some principles of journalism. For example, minutes of a meeting require that the following questions be answered:

1. *Who?*
2. *What?*
3. *When?*
4. *Where?*
5. *Why?*

Let's start with *who:*

1. Which organization is it?
2. Which members are present? Is there a quorum?
3. Who are acting in what official capacities?
4. Who propose, second and vote on what issues?
5. Who is writing and signing these minutes?

All right, now go to *what:*

1. What's this meeting about?
2. What topics were debated? What were the arguments?
3. What resolutions passed or were defeated?
4. What other business was transacted?
5. What is the organization's financial status?

A great many questions arise under *what,* but you also need to say *when:*

1. Specific date, by name and number.
2. Specific time of day or night. Regular meeting or extraordinary?
3. Specific season or occasion.

Where is next:

1. Is the meeting being held in regular quarters?
2. What town, county, state, etc.?

Erect your structure
with the five W's

Why is much the same as *what* or *how,* but explanation is also essential:

1. Why is the meeting being held?
2. Why did these questions arise?
3. Why does the organization need money?
4. Why (or how) were these decisions arrived at?
5. Why did the meeting adjourn?

Keep in mind that you must record what is done and what is decided rather than what is said. When a count is called for and when the voting is done by ballot, you should record the number of votes on each side. In the case of a committee report in which resolutions are included, you must enter the resolutions as finally adopted.

It's a good plan to make your notes during the meeting on sheets of scratch paper—and guard them carefully till you can make a copy. After the meeting, while the events are still fresh in your mind, use the first available moments to write the minutes in orderly fashion, so that everyone understands when you read them at the next meeting (as most organizations require) for any additions or corrections the members may want to make before giving approval. Once they are approved, you can then type them cleanly for the permanent records.

But *be accurate* when you make the final copy. Looseleaf notebooks are quite suitable for secretarial records. However, it's always wise to strengthen the sheets by using gummed reinforcements around the ring holes. Because these minutes are the most important documents of your club, you must be careful not to mislay or lose them.

Inaccurate records aren't worth keeping

Before you read the minutes at a meeting, be sure you read them over once or twice yourself so that you can present them attractively to your group. When you read them, speak in a loud, clear voice and hold your head up. Secretaries who mumble and swallow the ends of their sentences are always ignored at meetings—and usually at the next election, too.

3. Magazines and books

Having covered two fields of elementary writing, we now move on into other areas where knowing your reader is also vitally important. However, these areas involve far more than elementary writing: they are the province of the professional writer and hence require detailed examination. In this Lesson we will merely define the areas and give you some guideposts to follow. Then, in the special sections devoted to these topics, we will return to these areas, analyze them thoroughly and, by the use of examples, show you various ways of improving your writing.

In the magazine field, successful writers learn everything they can about their readers—*before* they begin writing. No sensible author would write an article for the *Ladies' Home Journal* the same way he would write it for *Field & Stream*. He might write on the same topic, perhaps, but even this would be unusual. It's certain, however, that the article would be written differently for the two readerships. For *Field & Stream* you might write a hunting story and become quite technical about firearms and the reader would understand every word. But the women readers of the *Journal* wouldn't get beyond the first few paragraphs that talked about rifles and shotguns. On the other hand, *Field & Stream*'s male readership would be bored with a psychological *Journal* romance about a marriage that was saved on a camping trip.

To know magazines, you must read them

Magazine articles and short stories are written to be read. The professional writer doesn't exist who puts words on paper with no thought of writing for print. Usually he has some publication in mind before the article or story is begun, and he follows the specifications for the reader at whom this magazine is aimed.

An extension of this logic applies to writers of novels and non-fiction of book length. The contemplated result is firmly fixed in the author's mind long before he sends his manuscript to a publisher.

4. Journalism for the printed page

Keeping your reader in mind, you'll write differently for the sports pages of a newspaper than for the editorial page. In an editorial, sentences and paragraphs are apt to be longer, more complex. The thought content will be for a higher level of intelligence. In a sports story you'll use sports slang, a good deal of humor and lightness, and you'll discuss ideas and events of far less moment to the world at large.

Technical words aside, the fashion writer also has to think of her audience or she won't hold her readership. Sentences about pleats and darts and sheaths, velvet and dacron and faille, won't win her readership on the sports page but will ensure it in the women's section. Like the sports writer and all other specialists in journalism, the fashion writer must constantly keep her reader in mind.

5. Radio and television

Radio news writing differs from news written for the printed page in at least three techniques involving the listener: (1) radio news has to be capsuled rather than thorough; (2) it has to be repeated because the listener (the "reader" in radio) can't go back with his eyes to make sure who's talking or what's happened; and (3) the composition of the audience varies by time of day.

In midafternoon, your audience will be predominately feminine and you'll lose it if you broadcast a half-hour about bullfighting. At 11 P.M., when radio stations traditionally report the news, you'd be foolish to substitute a soap opera. Your audience would tune you out and go elsewhere for the news. As in the other categories listed in this Lesson, radio writing is written to attract and hold an audience, not discourage it. You have to have a reader (or listener) in every field of the written word.

Television programs vary with the hour

In television, you aren't going to write a script the same way for a 3:30 P.M. audience as for a 9:30 P.M. audience. The former will be composed largely of women and your writing will require considerable emotional flavor. The subject matter will differ—perhaps you'll need fewer facts than in a script for a mixed audience later in the evening. If your audience is for a weekend sporting event, you will use more "male" words and facts than for a soap opera on a weekday afternoon or a children's suppertime show.

6. Advertising and business

In the world of advertising, the copywriter faces the same problem of knowing his audience before he begins to write. You won't get very far with male readership by using such words as *darling, sweetest, cute* or *fashionable*. On the other hand, *pal, sportsman, rugged* or *feel like a king* are masculine. Such words as *free, extra, new, how to, pleasure* and *enjoyment* are words an advertising writer can use almost anywhere for almost any audience.

Business reports written for one kind of client or associate won't do for another. The same goes for letters and memos. You'll become sharply aware of this if you imagine writing a business letter to the president of your company and the same letter to an old friend in the company's sales department.

Be sure to follow this important rule for all writers: always know your audience and tell them things that interest them in a way they understand. Try to match your audience and your writing by subject matter, style, pace and length. This common-sense principle applies whether you're writing notes or letters, journals or minutes of a meeting, magazine articles, stories or books, news or features, radio or television scripts, advertising copy or business communications.

Whatever your target as a writer, you'll attract more readers, listeners or viewers if you consistently keep in mind this simple slogan: *Know your audience!*

Summing up

Since writing is not only a means of self-expression but also the basis of communication, its value is twofold, for it satisfies the writer's compulsion to express himself and it satisfies the reader by entertaining, stimulating and informing him.

In the profession of writing, therefore, you have to have readers, so every writer must keep his reader constantly in mind. Six general areas where knowing your reader is vitally important are the following:

1. Personal notes and letters.
2. Diaries, journals and minutes of a meeting.
3. Magazines and books.
4. Journalism for the printed page.
5. Radio and television.
6. Advertising and business.

In personal notes and letters you keep your reader in mind by remembering to be sincere, friendly and informative, not too belligerent or too smooth. What it boils down to is "the human touch," to applying the Golden Rule to the field of elementary writing: "Write to others as you would have them write to you."

Diaries, journals and minutes put down on paper, in chronological order, precious facts of great interest and usefulness to you and others. The diary or journal is especially useful to the student writer because it satisfies his longing for self-expression, perpetuates his habit of daily writing and gives him material on which to base future writing. Truth and honesty are of prime importance in this intensely personal yet factual type of writing for the record. In writing minutes of a meeting, the five W's of journalism must be met and satisfied: Who, What, When, Where and Why. You have to keep your reader's needs in mind.

Knowing your reader is absolutely essential to writing for magazines and books, provinces of the professional. In the magazine field, successful writers learn everything they can about their readers before they begin writing. No sensible author, for example, would do an article for the *Ladies' Home Journal* the same way he'd write it for *Field & Stream,* and not very often on the same topic, either. Magazine articles and short stories are written to be read, and no professional writer puts thought on paper without readership in mind. An extension of this logic applies to all writers of book-length fiction and non-fiction.

Book readership
varies widely

Keeping your reader in mind, you'll write differently for the sports pages of a newspaper than for the editorial page. Even the vocabulary will differ. So will length of sentence, let alone topic.

In writing for radio and television, you write most carefully for specific audiences. You aren't going to do a script the same way for a 3:30 P.M. audience as for one at 9:30 P.M. The emotional flavor, factual content and subject matter will differ between a sporting event and a soap opera—because the audiences are different.

Advertising and business are no exceptions to the rule for writers that they must constantly keep their readers in mind. Advertising copywriters won't get far with a male audience using such words as *darling, sweetest, cute* or *fashionable.* On the other hand, if their ad is directed at women they'll avoid words like *rugged, sportsman, pal* or similar man-words. Business writing (including business letters) varies widely, depending on the reader. You aren't going to write the same business letter to an old friend as to the president of your company.

In summary, let's repeat a good rule for all writers: always know your readers and tell them interesting things in a way they'll understand, using their kind of language and writing about what interests them. In short: *Know your audience!*

A lesson from rejection slips

The first rule for the beginning writer is constant practice. One lesson to be learned from early rejection slips is that the tyro-writer has not practiced long enough at his craft. In fact, the production of a good deal of unsalable writing is a necessary prelude to successful writing for publication.—Gorham Munson in *The Writer's Workshop Companion*.

Getting the right attitude

Don't be careless when using words

When you are writing you are a writer, no matter how fumbling or poor your work may be. If you assume an attitude seriously enough and often enough and intelligently enough, it is likely that the attitude will become a part of you.—Roger H. Garrison in *A Guide to Creative Writing*.

Your words must be precise

One of the primary needs of the good writer is to be precise in word meaning. Mathematics is an exact science, and answers to mathematical problems can be proved. This isn't true of writing. Hence, the need for precision in words. The writer must pay just as great attention to word meaning as is required by the theorems of the mathematician. Samuel Butler said that definitions are the cross each writer must bear. "A definition," he wrote, "is a wall of words surrounding a chaos of ideas."

Should you talk about your work?

Without question there is value in discussing your work with your friends, your family and other writers. But there is also a great danger—especially for a beginning writer. Writing is a private affair—it is not done in committee. Gathering a large number of uninformed opinions can only compound your confusion. The blind cannot lead the blind. Find one or two people whose taste you trust. They do not necessarily have to be professional writers or editors—just people with sound judgment. Show your manuscripts only to them and nobody else.

A word of warning: don't show your manuscript to anyone at frequent intervals during its composition. You cannot expect a baby to be born if you pull it out every few hours and pass it around. There may come a point in the composition of a story when you are stuck and need help—but try your best to lick your problems by yourself. As a general rule it's wise not to show a story until it is completed.— Max Shulman

Let your feeling guide you

The new writer can probably write best about that which he knows from personal experience. He's still functioning on a new level. He's unsure of his tools and will be unsure for a few years to come. Under those circumstances, it's best that he doesn't take on the added pressure of research into alien fields.

But this rule can never be hard and fast. If in the beginning you have something to say about a subject which is not a part of your own experience and yet you have a strong feeling about it and interest in it, you should write about it. There is nothing that begets better writing than the process of writing. It's as simple as that.—Rod Serling

Lesson nineteen

Principles of good writing

Developing
your style

If Charles Dickens were alive today and writing as he did at the height of his fame, few American editors would publish his novels, splendid as they were, without making style changes. Just as the clothes of the overdressed woman of the Victorian era have been replaced by feminine styles far freer and less cumbersome, so has Dickens' Victorian prose given way to today's simple, conversational, modern writing style.

Rudolf Flesch puts it this way:

The writer today writes for a vastly larger audience. On both sides of the Atlantic, many millions more have acquired the habit of reading. These added millions are a different kind of people. They don't have the literary background of Victorian ladies and gentlemen; they don't have their leisure and patience; they are unwilling to put more effort into reading than they would do in watching a movie or listening to the radio. A reader of today, reading Dickens with his customary newspaper-reading speed, would stop, turn back and have to reread.

Style, then, is a distinctive way of expressing something, whether in women's clothes, automobile design, architecture or writing. Dickens isn't modern enough for current readers although, as we shall point out later, many superb passages from

Dickens and other classical writers stand up very well today.

Since style is a distinctive way of expressing something, writers' styles, like styles in other areas, vary from generation to generation. As Bergen Evans says, the writer must listen to the actual speech of his time, must know every shade and nuance, so that without his readers in the least perceiving *how* he does it, he can speak to them in words and phrases that move them. Dr. Evans continues:

> The writer must reach their hearts, draw strength from their experiences, catch the quality of their laughter, hold pathos on its narrow line between sadness and sentimentality. He must be simple, direct, clear. And that means he must know the speech of the millions, because his style must be utterly transparent.
>
> They must not for a moment know there *is* a style. The ideas must *seem* to them to just come out of his writing. And that requires complete immersion in their speech.
>
> I'm afraid that in my student days, I thought there were fixed rules—and I felt guilty because I didn't know them. I didn't then have the courage to notice that the few rules I did know didn't always conform to the practice of contemporary writers. Indeed, like most students, I didn't know much about contemporary writers. We were reading writers of at least two generations ago.
>
> People have forgotten that when Sinclair Lewis, say, received the Nobel Prize, this was *not* hailed as a triumph for American letters— as it was—but as a disgrace. Two of America's leading professors of literature, Henry Van Dyke at Princeton and Stuart Sherman at Illinois, shrieked against the award. Now that Lewis is safely dead and a generation out of date, he is being taught in the schools.
>
> Maybe it has to be that way. Maybe you have to read the classical stuff first and then find out for yourself how the good men are actually writing now.

Writing styles
constantly change

Let's look at the specific styles of two different generations— one Victorian, one modern. The first example is from *Rose in Bloom* by Louisa May Alcott, whose prose, filled with old-fashioned moralizing, was lush and flowery. This passage is the beginning of love's dream for Charlie and Phebe:

The italicized words and phrases would seldom see the light of print nowadays. They have gone out of style— writing style.

> So Charlie *attitudinized unnoticed,* and was getting *rather out of temper* when Phebe began to sing; and he forgot all about himself *in admiration of her.* It took everyone by surprise; for two years of foreign training added to several at home *had worked wonders;* and the beautiful voice that *used to warble cheerily over pots and kettles,* now *sang out melodiously* or *melted to a mellow music* that woke a

sympathetic thrill in those who listened. Rose *glowed with pride* as she accompanied her friend; for Phebe was in her own world now, a lovely world where no depressing memory of poorhouse or kitchen, ignorance or loneliness, *came to trouble her;* a happy world where she could be herself, and *rule others by the magic of her sweet gift.*

Contrast these long, flowery sentences with the more modern style of Irwin Shaw from whose novel, *The Young Lions,* come the following paragraphs about young love in Brooklyn:

Roger had had a good time all one evening casting about among his old address books for likely candidates for Noah. And now, to-night, they were coming, six of them, besides the girl that Roger was bringing himself. There were going to be some other men, of course, but Roger had slyly selected funny-looking ones or slow-witted ones among his friends, so that the competition would not be too severe. As Noah looked around the warm, lamp-lit room, with cut flowers in vases and a print by Braque on the wall, and the bottles and the glasses shining like a vision from a better world on the desk, he knew, with delicious, fearful certainty, that tonight he would finally find himself a girl.

Noah smiled as he heard the key in the door because now he would not have to face the ordeal of greeting the first guests by himself. The door opened and Roger came in. Roger had his girl with him, and Noah took her coat and hung it up without accident, not tripping over anything or wrenching the girl's arm. He smiled to himself inside the closet as he heard the girl saying to Roger, "What a nice room. It looks as though there hasn't been a woman in here since 1750."

How much simpler or more direct is this prose than Louisa May Alcott's. Our world is less polite than the Victorian world, and Shaw's writing style matches the content.

The conversational style

Generally speaking, the best writing styles are the most natural styles. Few writers achieve fame or success if they think and talk one way and write another.

In the beginning, then, it's best to write pretty much as you speak—if you wish to achieve a characteristic style. The American trend toward simple, conversational, informal writing grows each year. It's easier to understand, it communicates faster and more accurately than the formal language of the classics. Bergen Evans says:

A natural style is the best style

Today, most good writing approaches the conversational, perhaps as a reaction against the more elaborate literary style of the nineteenth century. It may be a response to the enormous extension of education within the past fifty-odd years. In 1900, only the exceptional child went to high school and millions were totally illiterate. Today few people have ever encountered a genuine illiterate—that is, a basically intelligent person who never had the opportunity to learn to read or write.

A student should adapt himself to the conversational style by seeking models who have mastered that style—writers like Twain, Hemingway, Lardner—and by checking the conversational quality of his work by reading it aloud to himself.

How can you make your writing sound like conversation? The most important thing is to use the types of sentences used in conversation.

When we talk, we don't put all our thoughts into subject-predicate sentences—one following the other in much the same pattern. We vary our sentences. We start one sentence with the subject, the next with a prepositional phrase, the next with a conjunction; then we ask a question or answer with a word or two; then we interrupt ourselves with a casual side remark; and so on. So, to make our writing more conversational and more fun to read, we need *sentence variety*.

Strive for variety
in sentence openings

Sentence variety means mainly three things:

1. Questions and answers;
2. Short sentences sandwiched between longer ones; and
3. No sentence built exactly like the one before.

Suppose, for instance, you have written:

There was a lively debate among the students. There was great enthusiasm for the idea. There was hardly a dissenting voice. There was full agreement on the project in the end.

Now this doesn't sound like conversation at all. There are no questions and answers; all sentences are about the same length (between six and ten words); and all of them start *There was*. Let's try something different:

The debate was lively. Were the students enthusiastic? They certainly were. Hardly a dissenting voice was heard, and in the end, everybody agreed on the project—yes, every one of them.

Or let's take these sentences:

I am sorry for this long delay. I have not written for four weeks. But I have some excuse for my behavior. I have been working at the store weekends and evenings.

Again, all these sentences start with *I am* or *I have*. (The one *but* doesn't really make much difference.) And they are all built on the same simple subject-predicate pattern. Let's see how much sentence variety we can get into this paragraph:

What a long delay! Is it really four weeks since I wrote? I'm sorry —but there is *some* excuse for my behavior. All these weekends and evenings I've been working at the store.

How about using some participles, infinitives or prepositional phrases to add variety? Let's look at this passage in which the sentences start the same way:

I went to the library in the afternoon. I took out a book that was on the reading list. Then I went home to eat supper. I did not open the book until after supper. Then I discovered that it was the wrong volume. I was greatly annoyed. I should have looked at the book when I took it. I had nobody to blame but myself.

Now let's rewrite the paragraph, beginning each sentence differently:

In the afternoon I went to the library to take out a book on the reading list. *Then, armed with my book,* I went home for supper. *Opening* the book after supper, I was greatly annoyed; it was the wrong volume. *To take* out a book without looking at it was just like me. *I had nobody* to blame but myself.

No two sentences start the same way. In the previous paragraph every sentence began with "I" or "Then I."

It's not hard to follow simple rules and put variety into your sentences. The main thing is to pay attention to the pattern of your writing. Two or three similar sentences in a row have a way of cropping up by themselves. The trick is to foresee these boring repetitions and weed them out.

Awareness of such a simple thing as variety of sentence openings indicates an awareness in a writer of what professionals call *style*. In contrast to grammar (the structure of a language), style refers to the words and expressions the writer chooses to clothe his thoughts. It's the writer himself who makes the choice and the choice dictates his style.

The personality and characteristics of a writer also strongly influence his style. For example, certain men and women are apt to be formal in their talk, ultra-conservative in their clothes, extremely careful in their mannerisms and stodgy in their writing styles. Their letters are seldom fun to read. They almost never use contractions, colloquialisms or slang. They seem to regard conversational style as beneath their dignity and shun it.

On the other hand, some sports writers and columnists have overly developed a slangy, conversational style and abhor the normal English sentence. They tend to go too far in the direction of informality. Sometimes their lingo is all but unintelligible.

Somewhere between these extremes lies the best style technique for the modern writer. The important thing is to use the types of sentences, the kinds of words you use in conversation. Vary your sentence length and structure. Use questions and answers. Use direct quotations whenever you can, being sure to make them sound natural. Add, when possible, a personal touch or a bit of humor to your style. Don't write everything as though it were a doctor's thesis or an 18th-Century essay.

The number of words in your sentences changes your style, too. Milton averaged 60 words to a sentence, Spenser 50. Today's successful writers average 15 to 20. There are simply too many events and distractions in modern life for the average reader to take enough time to untangle a sentence that is 50–100 words long.

Examples from professional writers

Let's look at John Steinbeck, a modern novelist whose conversational simplicity in fiction is extremely difficult to imitate. Here is a passage from *Of Mice and Men:*

Steinbeck is master of the simple word in the right place. There isn't a descriptive word here that a child would stumble over, yet the writing comes off with great style.

It was Sunday afternoon. The resting horses nibbled the remaining wisps of hay, and they stamped their feet and they bit the wood of the mangers and rattled the halter chains. The afternoon sun sliced through the cracks of the barn walls and lay in bright lines on the hay. There was the buzz of flies in the air, the lazy afternoon humming. From outside came the clang of horseshoes on the playing peg and the shouts of men, playing, encouraging, jeering. But in the barn it was quiet and humming and lazy and warm.

Ernie Pyle, the great correspondent of World War II, was another master of natural, informal style. He had an ear for spoken language, like Steinbeck. Here's a sample of Pyle's easy, simple non-fiction on a tragic subject—American soldiers face to face with death for the first time on Anzio beachhead. It's from *Brave Men:*

The worst of all was when men had to join an outfit while it was right in the line. That happened there on the Fifth Army beachhead. There were even times when a company had to have replacements instantly; that was in cases where no front-line movement whatever in the daytime was possible. Hence the new men would have to be guided up at night, establish themselves in their foxholes in darkness, and inhabit those foxholes until it was all over.

I felt sorry for men who had to do that. All of us who have had any association at all with the imminence of death know that the main thing a man wants is not to be alone. He wants company, and preferably somebody he knows. To go up to the brink of possible death in the nighttime in a faraway land, puzzled and afraid, knowing no one, and facing the worst moment of your life totally alone—that takes strength.

Simplicity of style again. The words are short, clear, easy. The sentences are the same. The power of this style is deceptively facile and very hard to duplicate.

Ernie Pyle wrote as though he were talking to you. His conversational touch gave his writing readability. Even the last sentence, longer than the rest, is made of simple words.

Conversational style is now common even in newspaper editorials, foreign correspondence, intellectual essays and literary criticisms. For example, consider the use of the now commonly used contracted phrase.

Contractions weren't often used in the oldtime formal essay, and it's surprising how many people fail to use contractions in writing even now. This is particularly true of business writing, where sensible contractions would save business millions of dollars a year in paper and working time.

The most frequently used contractions in our everyday conversation and informal writing are:

it's	he'll	aren't
I'll	he's	wasn't
we're	she's	they're
can't	hasn't	we've
that's	couldn't	I've
don't	you'll	I'd
there's	doesn't	let's
isn't	you're	they'll
won't	they've	didn't

The contraction is definitely a factor in style. It's informal, talky and natural. Let's say there are ten words to a line, on the average, in a business letter. The contracted style of writing may save one line in twenty. If a firm writes a million letters a year (and some do), a saving of five per cent will add thousands of dollars in income—and also make the writer's meaning much easier to grasp.

The best business reports now written for company stock-

holders have a breezy, informal way of telling what has traditionally been a stuffy story. The story itself hasn't been stuffy;
far from it. American business has been and can be as exciting
as any subject on earth. But the approach in most annual reports
creates formidable barriers between company and public, rather
than offering a line of easy communication and relationship.

Here's a good example of informality from an annual stockholders' report of the Worthington Corporation, makers of
pumps and other machinery. This is scarcely the most romantic
company in the United States, yet here is the opening paragraph
of the report, far different from the dull wording so often found
in business:

Company reports are
often too formal

> You may think that a machine . . . is just a machine . . . But to us
> at Worthington, machines are the strong arms with which industry
> does its work. They give you
>   Food
>   Shelter
>   Comfort
> and all the necessities and luxuries of modern life.

Style, informal or formal, conversational or essay, is something that will probably come to you of its own accord. Your
writing style is like your body—it's shaped by your ancestry and
the normal course of your everyday living. Heredity enters into
style, childhood reading enters into it, as well as modes of speech
of those around you, teachers you have had in the past, adult
reading habits or lack of them. All these factors are part of the
characteristic way you express yourself in words, the characteristic writers call style. Here is what Dr. Evans adds about developing style:

> A man's style of expression is latent in the first word he ever
> writes—or speaks. I don't believe a writer develops a style. I think he
> stops imitating other people and writes his own way; and that's his
> style.
> The beginning writer should not imitate—except as a deliberate
> exercise. Rather, find something that you want to say, something
> that you feel strongly about, and "think it over," that is, hold it in
> your mind and turn it over in your thoughts—perhaps for weeks—
> until you begin to know how you feel about it. Then some day, when
> the tide of feeling about the matter rises to excitement, wade into it
> and you will probably hammer out not only the form but also your
> final judgments on the matter.

One word of caution, however. Not every writer needs a distinct style of his own. Businessmen often do better when they stick to the principles of clarity and brevity, forgetting individual style in their prose. In fact, any writer is much better off not trying too hard to develop his or her very own style. It will come by itself with practice based on the principles of clarity and brevity. Don't try to force it or to copy someone else consciously.

Vocabulary and variety

Every writer needs
a large vocabulary

No writer ever lived who didn't need to increase his vocabulary. A writer must have a working acquaintance with words, just as an artist has with colors. This doesn't mean that you're going to improve your style by using a lot of fancy, ten-dollar words when a fifty-cent word does a better job, but a good vocabulary vastly improves your chances of reaching the reader.

The most obvious mechanical aids to vocabulary building are a dictionary and a thesaurus or word book. As a simple example, let's say you're writing that someone's action has been "quick" or "rapid," but these words don't seem exactly right. So you consult your word book and come up with "rash" or "overhasty," which may be much better. Possibly "precipitate" is better still in this particular place, or "slapdash" or "rapid-fire."

The thesaurus is an excellent aid to vocabulary building, especially when you learn new words, alternate words, while going through its pages. This kind of learning is the secret to increasing your word power. But don't use your word book as a crutch for writing. Once you have looked up a word, add it to your mental store and it will always be there, ready to work for you at a moment's notice.

The good writer also picks up new and useful words as he reads, either for information or pleasure. In the works of professional authors, he also finds old and familiar words used in fresh ways. Variety of usage appeals to him.

All in all, reading is the best aid to vocabulary building. The more you read—with an eye to words and their usage—the more you will enhance your style and add to your mastery of the English language.

As we said earlier in this Lesson, one of the surest signs of a writer's style is the way he varies his sentence openings. There is a parallel to this in music. No two pianists play the same piece the same way; they vary their phrasing so you scarcely realize they are moving from one part to another.

Watch how Paul Gallico, the veteran craftsman, varies his sentence openings in a piece about skiing in *Farewell to Sport:*

By some miracle I got to the bottom of the run uninjured, having made most of the trip down the icy, perpendicular slopes on the flat of my back. *It was the thrill* and scare of a lifetime, and to date no one has been able to persuade me to try a jump. *I know when* to stop. *After all,* I am entitled to rely upon my imagination for something. *But when* it was all over and I found myself still whole, it was also distinctly worth-while to have learned what is required of a ski runner in the breakneck downhill race, or the difficult slalom.

No two of his sentences begin the same way. There is a constant change of pace. Even the next sentence beyond what is quoted here starts a new way: *"Five days later,* when I climbed laboriously . . ."

In Samuel Eliot Morison's *History of United States Naval Operations in World War II,* an entire section in Vol. IV is devoted to submarine patrols in the Pacific from May to August, 1942. He takes a dozen submarines on their courageous missions and for 35 closely written pages must find *new* ways to write about each *new* venture. Yet no two consecutive sentences begin the same way. Let's look at a few openings, noting the constant change of pace:

Keep your style
relaxed and easy

The most successful American patrol in the late spring of 1942 was made deep into enemy waters by *Trout. This was her third patrol under* Lieutenant Commander Frank W. ("Mike") Fenno. *Trout departed Pearl Harbor* 24 March and, a fortnight out, arrived off the south coast of Honshu after fueling at Midway. *On 9 April, two days after* arriving on station, two small freighters were sighted, chugging along toward Kobe. *Fenno could not get within* a mile of them but neither could he resist having a try at them because, as he later remarked, "We didn't yet know that the woods were full of ships."

Next day Trout followed the trail of a long smoke plume to a slow steamer. *Two single-torpedo attacks failed* to connect, and the freighter with an escort chased the submarine so persistently that her sailors believed they had tangled with a Q-ship. *But Trout was as hard to catch* as her finny namesake, and evaded her enemies. *Next, a fat 15,000-tonner* was sighted sneaking along the Honshu coast, her camouflage blending with the cliffs. *Fenno got in two shots* from a little more than a mile away. *One of them hit,* the ship's engines stopped abruptly and she fell off course with whistle shrieking, but she was not fatally stung and escaped to seaward. *Fenno could not surface* and give chase because he was only 3000 yards from an enemy shore battery, so he fired one more torpedo on an overtaking run, and it missed.

Admiral Morison hasn't begun any two consecutive sentences precisely the same. There's been a constant change of pace, an awareness of different approaches to narrative passages to keep them from becoming monotonous.

First he has used a sentence beginning with "The . . ." in the classic manner. Then one beginning with a pronoun. Then one beginning with the name of the submarine. Then a prepositional phrase involving time. Next the submarine commander's name. Different openings every time.

In the second paragraph he opens with a time connective, "Next day . . ." Then follow adjectives and their noun. Then a conjunction leading into the submarine's name once again. Then the connective "Next . . ."—a time-setting word. The commander's name comes back, for effect. Then a pronoun phrase referring to the two shots. Finally, the commander's name again, purposely repeated to give human drama to submarine action.

In some of his sentence openings the author has been direct, in others indirect. But all the time Morison consciously varies his beginnings and changes his pace, like the professional author he is.

The readers shouldn't be aware of style

Jack Denton Scott is another professional who knows the importance of sentence openings. Following is a descriptive excerpt from his book *Forests of the Night* in which he automatically begins almost every sentence a different way, yet occasionally starts consecutive sentences or clauses the same way —for effect. This supports the thesis that good writers deliberately use a change of pace, just as an expert pitcher seldom throws the same ball twice in succession.

The following passage describes a train trip into the interior of India:

The train made its way through the soft Indian night, sending its beam before us like a probing finger, reaching out and finding the dangerous spots that might lie ahead. *It was a large, rugged engine,* made by the Scotch, Rege said, and it tugged fifteen cars behind it. *It snorted like a living thing* and every now and then a burst of flame

Normal sentence opening with a noun preceded by "the" or "a."

Now a pronoun begins a sentence.

belched from its stack, coloring the dark sky like a Roman candle.

Something historic should be done about this shikar train, something to lift it into the fame of trains like the Orient Express. *It has a dogged determination* about it that deserves recognition. *Never—or seldom—*traveling over twenty miles an hour, it crept across the broad face of Madhya Pradesh, through orange groves and the rich agriculture section, stopping about every ten miles.

This Central Railroad can be compared with the heart in the human body, pumping life into the towns, the primitive villages and huts that are miles away. *Its narrow bed with* sun-silvered ribbons of track is responsible for the life of much of Central India, the link that makes it possible for the people of the back country to move. *They come from* the inland villages, walking many miles to get to the railroad and squat, waiting for this train that will carry them to Nagpur, Itarsi and Harda.

This railroad is the way to see the real India: *children sleeping on the* station platforms covered with flies and little else; men and women making their morning toilets on the edge of the platforms; *men in disheveled dhotis* and women and children in saris and other pieces of clothing that looked like long-tailed shirts or cast-off bed linen, sitting, sleeping, eating curds and a wheat mash that looked as if it had already been eaten and digested once; *the gray-headed Indian* house crows boldly swooping down among the outstretched people as they scratched themselves awake and began to stir. *And at every station* the loud cry of "Cha, cha ga run," sounding as if the turbaned food-butchers were bullfrogs talking to the moon, but really meaning, "Tea, hot tea!"

Here, then, is a good style rule for writers to remember: vary your sentence openings. Don't make them all the same, particularly in succession. If you start one sentence with a simple subject, back into the next one or use one of the connectives listed above—as Gallico and Morison and Scott have used them so well. As much as anything, this helps to give your writing a style of its own.

Even contemporary styles vary

Writers don't have to be of different generations to exhibit vastly different styles. Here are two passages from short stories in *The Saturday Evening Post*. At the left is the opening paragraph of "The Widow's Kid" by Arthur Mayse and at the right the opening paragraph of "Killers' Rendezvous" by Merle Constiner. Mr. Mayse likes the unusual, out-of-the-way style which purposely

---

Margin notes (left column):

"Something historic" is a complete change of pace and tone.

"Never—or seldom" does a nice job of pace change.

Now we refer directly to "This Central Railroad."

Now a possessive adjective.

Throughout this paragraph note how the separate clauses change pace in the descriptive opening:
a. "This railroad"
b. "children sleeping"
c. "men in disheveled"
d. "the gray-headed Indian"

Scott now shifts to "And at every station . . ," a good change.

slows a reader. Mr. Constiner uses a simple, flowing style which never gets in the reader's way:

I. *Unusual style*	II. *Simple style*
When word got round that the widow who'd gaffed Joe Beckett tended to look on any boy in thigh boots as a gypsy scamp, Joe's friends began to think twice before putting in at Protection Creek for a bite and a pow-wow. The boats would pass, fish-chasing their way along the British Columbia up-coast, and Joe Beckett would watch them, with sea gulls mocking him from the brown-earth furrows.	Night had fallen when Dayton Crandall rode into the little desert town. He was seventeen, small and wiry. Dog-tired, he stabled his sorrel and walked up the street, looking for a hotel. He had never bedded in a hotel and the idea embarrassed him, but he was too close to the end of his trip, to home, to take any risks. Blue Rock, said the post office. It wasn't much of a place—night sky, a railroad, a broken line of shabby buildings.

The point is basic: even contemporary styles vary widely, influenced by the way people live, by what they wear, read and eat, what television programs they like best. Style must fit the subject matter and the pressures of the time but it also matches a writer's background and habits.

No greater style contrast can be found than between the tough, lean American fiction of novelist James M. Cain and the flowery, often over-flowing style of Cain's contemporary, Thomas Wolfe. In the opening lines of *Galatea,* Cain's story-teller is a convict working out his parole by clearing stumps:

I chopped, grubbed, and shoveled, and the deeper I dug the keener I felt it: I was being watched. At first I tried not to mind, as a holdup case his first day out, on a cockeyed probation deal, could expect watching, especially if left alone on the farm he'd been put to work on. But it rattled me, and didn't help any that I was going about it all wrong, the job I'd been given to do. The order was to get out trees, and the right way was to hire a dozer.

But, maybe on account of the cost, maybe on account of me, to test the stuff I had in me, nothing had been said about that, and I was left with the tools that were there. With chain, rope, blocks, and stuff from the implement shed, and a ladder to help with the climbing, I thought I might get by shackling trees to each other and hauling them out by the roots. But it meant trenching around each one, and was slow, pesky and tough.

Notice how many sharp points are made by the verbs in Cain's writing. He does not waste a word, a phrase, but goes straight to the target in spare, lucid prose.

You'd have a hard time cutting one word from this bare, terse writing style.

Wolfe's writing style, on the other hand, is generous and flowing. Never by any stretch of the imagination could it be called terse or bare. The great Scribner editor, Max Perkins, slashed thousands of words from Wolfe's original novel manuscripts, yet what remains is still far from lean. Contrast the next paragraph, from *Of Time and the River,* with the Cain passage. Wolfe is seeing the great river as the link of human past and present, of one part of America with another:

And the slant light steepened in the skies, the old red light of waning day made magic fire upon the river, and the train made on forever its tremendous monotone that was like silence and forever— and now there was nothing but that tremendous monotone of time and silence and the river, the haunted river, the enchanted river that drank forever its great soundless tides from out the inland slowly and that moved through all man's lives the magic thread of its huge haunting spell, and that linked his life to magic kingdoms and to lotus-land and to all the vision of the magic earth that he had dreamed of as a child, and that bore him on forever out of magic to all the grime and sweat and violence of the city, the unceasing city, the million-footed city, and into America.

Always beware
of too-long sentences

Almost every phrase is childlike in its wonder and awe. The one sentence and every phrase begin breathlessly with ". . . and." Breathlessness is a Wolfe style pattern. Words are repeated— "haunted river . . . haunting spell," and other words are similar: "enchanted river," "magic kingdoms," "magic fire," "forever out of magic," "city . . . city . . . city." This is a giant-size word canvas filled with generalities, plurals, repetitions for effect—vague and unfactual.

Now contrast Robert Ruark's factual, journalistic style in the African novel, *Something of Value,* with Wolfe's breathless torrent. The Ruark setting is Kenya Colony, heart of the Mau Mau country. The boy, Peter McKenzie, is pretending to wage tribal war with a small native friend:

Peter McKenzie stripped off his faded shorts and his green drill shirt and reached for a bowl of ocher mud which had been softened to a pliant paste with water. He smeared the mud over his face, neck and shoulders, until his sunburned skin was dyed a deep coppery red. He picked up his trousers and took a small mirror out of his pocket.

Holding the mirror in one hand, he painted circles of white lines around his eyes and made traverse scar marks across his cheeks. He pushed his black forelock down over his eyes and gummed the hair

Details of costume and of boy are carefully woven into the description. The phrase: softened to a pliant paste" is telling, while the fact he frowns at himself fiercely in the mirror and seems satisfied gives the reader a revealing touch.

heavily with the ocher. He frowned fiercely at himself in the mirror and seemed satisfied. He tied iron rattles around his ankles and draped a goatskin from his shoulders like a toga. Then he put the mirror back in his pocket and hung the pants on a thornbush.

In contrast to Thomas Wolfe, Ruark is almost reporting, distinctly journalistic.

Contrast Wolfe's style with Willa Cather's sharply etched description of a train moving through the cornfields of the Middle West in the early 1900's. The passage is from her novel, *Song of the Lark*.

One warm damp June night the Denver Express was speeding westward across the earth-smelling plains of Iowa. The lights in the day-coach were turned low and the ventilators were open, admitting showers of soot and dust upon the occupants of the narrow green plush chairs which were tilted at various angles of discomfort. In each of these chairs some uncomfortable human being lay drawn up, or stretched out, or writhing from one position to another.

She tells you specific things. Her style uses the five senses but uses them with realistic factual word pictures, not generalities.

There were tired men in rumpled shirts, their necks bare and their suspenders down; old women with their heads tied up in black handkerchiefs; bedraggled young women who went to sleep while they were nursing their babies and forgot to button up their dresses; dirty boys who added to the general discomfort by taking off their boots.

These observations are earthy and real. No frantic beating of the air here, but a pragmatic, factual style.

Willa Cather's marvelously accurate picture of a train never generalizes when it can be specific, and Wolfe's powerful vision has been replaced by an eye for earthy detail and a pity for humanity. This is impressive when you look at the date of publication of the novel—1915.

Now compare Miss Cather with another realist, Thomas Hardy, whose prose style is about as complex as that of any writer of English. In *The Return of the Native*, he wrote:

A Saturday afternoon in November was approaching the time of twilight, and the vast tract of unenclosed wild known as Egdon Heath embrowned itself moment by moment. Overhead the hollow stretch of whitish cloud shutting out the sky was a tent which had the whole heath for its floor. The heaven being spread with this pallid screen and the earth with the darkest vegetation, their meeting-line at the horizon was clearly marked. In such contrast the heath wore the appearance of an installment of night which had taken up its place before its astronomical hour was come: while the day stood distinct in the sky.

"Embrowned" is typically Hardy.

The tent idea is remarkable.

Hardy's style is consciously obscure. He never writes a phrase as you'd expect it.

Looking upwards, a furze-cutter would have been inclined to continue work; looking down, he would have decided to finish his faggot and go home. The distant rims of the world and of the firmament seemed to be a division in time no less than a division in matter. The

The author is giving the heath human attributes— a valid personification which greatly helps his description.

face of the heath by its mere complexion added half an hour to evening: it could in like manner retard the dawn, sadden noon, anticipate the frowning of storms scarcely generated, and intensify the opacity of a moonless midnight to a cause of shaking and dread.

Nothing is plain or simple in the writing of this great English novelist. His people are simple people, his setting is rural, but his writing style is highly complicated. Like Dickens', Hardy's books make difficult reading for the average American today. Contrast Hardy's style with Dickens' *Hard Times,* which delineates the atmosphere of an English coal town.

The streets were hot and dusty on the summer day, and the sun was so bright that it even shone through the heavy vapor drooping over Coketown, and could not be looked at steadily. Stokers emerged from low, underground doorways into factory yards, and sat on steps and posts and palings, wiping their swarthy visages and contemplating coals.

Dickens' sense of realism is clearly demonstrated in these sensuous word images. The sense of smell is especially reflected in his words. Dickens was a master of sensuous style.

The whole town seemed to be frying in oil. There was a stifling smell of hot oil everywhere. The steam engines shone with it, the dresses of the hands were soiled with it, the mills throughout their many stories oozed and trickled it. The atmosphere of those fairy palaces was like the breath of the simoon; and their inhabitants, wasting with heat, toiled languidly in the desert.

Dickens exaggerates with tremendous effect. He also has a fantastic ear for sentence rhythm.

But no temperature made the melancholy mad elephants more mad or more sane. Their wearisome heads went up and down at the same rate, in hot weather and cold, wet weather and dry, fair weather and foul. The measured motion of their shadows on the walls was the substitute Coketown had to show for the shadows of rustling woods; while for the summer hum of insects, it could offer all the year round, from the dawn of Monday to the night of Saturday, the whir of shafts and wheels. Drowsily they whirred all through the summer day, making the passenger more sleepy and more hot as he passed the humming walls of the mills.

This comparison of coal cranes to bending, dipping elephants is a fine example of imagination. One of the characteristics of Dickens' style is using individual figures in his description.

The recognizable sounds of summer.

Sun-blinds and sprinklings of water a little cooled the main streets and the shop; but the mills and the courts and alleys baked at a fierce heat. Down upon the river that was black and thick with dye, some Coketown boys who were at large—a rare sight there—rowed a crazy boat which made a spumous track upon the water as it jogged along, while every dip of an oar stirred up vile smells.

The reader's senses are appealed to by the use of "thick with dye," "rowed a crazy boat," "spumous track," "stirred up vile smells." Realism was Dickens' basic style ingredient.

Varying styles in non-fiction

Style variation in writing is not confined to fiction. Styles differ in non-fiction, varying greatly even in contemporary magazines.

Here are contrasting examples from *Time* and *U.S. News & World Report,* newsmagazines covering the same field and with similar reading audiences:

Time	*U.S. News*
On swirl-dimpled, symbol-specked Weather Bureau maps, the storm gathered in classic pattern: polar air and Gulf of Mexico winds butted along a line that curled like an overturned roller coaster; winds overhead fluxed cold and warm. Translated into ground-level consequences last week, the winter's most severe storm heaved snow, sleet, gales, tornadoes and floods over most of the U.S. west to the Rockies, by week's end was responsible for more than 100 deaths.	Nearly two-thirds of all farm products still sell at less than the lowest ceiling prices allowed by law. These products could go up an average of almost 20 per cent before controls could be imposed. The ceiling prices, furthermore, do not stay put. Congress tied prices for what the farmer sells to prices he pays for what he buys. And prices for non-farm goods are sure to edge up gradually, experts believe.

Time style is quite evident in the above sentences, where a colon eliminates the need for several words, a comma is used in place of a conjunction. This terse, characteristic prose contrasts markedly with the more usual approach of *U.S. News,* which uses fairly standard writing style.

Styles also change in the business world, particularly in letters. Not so long ago, as we've said, many an executive was honor-bound to start his letters: "Yours of the 16th instant received and contents duly noted." A few still do, but not the progressive executives, who get down to brass tacks right away. Their style is less flowery, more direct.

Better to start a business letter like this: "Would you do me a favor, please? A Mr. George Larkin has applied for a job here as Assistant Accountant and he gives you as a reference . . . etc."

Advertising copywriters' styles likewise change. Here is copy for a Packard Motor advertisement of a generation ago:

Business letters are not flowery

Because it was a Packard, the soundness of Single-Six engineering was accepted from the first as a foregone conclusion. It can be judged now, however, both by time and by numbers—thousands of Single-Sixes having been in the hands of owners for more than two years. Its history may be summed up at this moment as one of individual instances of deep satisfaction, multiplied by thousands. Never in Packard history was the familar advice: Ask the Man Who Owns One, more pertinent—never was the answer surer than it is in the case of the Single-Six.

Compare this rather formal style with copy for a car of today:

Once there was a pitcher, believe it or not, who batted 1000. How? When he hit the majors, he wanted the finest car ever . . . so he bought the biggest one ever. But after his wife drove it, and watched it guzzle gas, she said: "Southpaw, on this one you struck out. Get me something we can afford!"

He got her a little European car. It just sipped gas, but wouldn't even hold four for bridge. Said his wife: "You're headed for the sand lots!" "Women!" he groaned, and sought a friendly haven.

But on the way he saw a Rambler showroom. "Wow!" said he, "big car room, European car economy!" He saw all-new Rambler jet stream styling, pushbutton driving . . . heard of Rambler's record economy. "Give me *two*," he said.

This time, the Little Woman gave him a big kiss and said: "Southpaw, with Rambler you've batted a thousand!" So will you, neighbor.

Whether it's a short story, an article, a business letter or copy for an ad, writing styles vary. It's somewhat like playing the piano. Every standard piano has the same 88 keys, yet no two of the millions of piano players in the United States play exactly alike, even from the same sheet of music. They phrase differently, they play faster or slower in certain passages, they make mistakes, they improvise. Each has a style of his or her own.

Here's a typical example of non-fiction style from the *Reader's Digest,* a magazine that is noted for its clarity and ease of understanding.

Notice how no two sentences begin the same way and how short and lean they are.

Of all the creatures with whom we share the globe, none is more senselessly slaughtered than the hawk. There are 32 species of American hawks, but most people simply classify all of them as "big" chicken hawks and "little" chicken hawks, and are quite willing to believe that they are bloodthirsty creatures that kill for sport.

The truth is that hawks kill only when hungry, never for sport. They can be trained to the affectionate obedience of a dog, and are as mischievous in the air as otters are around a pond.

The simplicity of *Reader's Digest* style is deceptive, as many a professional writer has found. The simple sentence style and artless wording are far from Alcott, Dickens or Wolfe.

Equally far from the complicated style of some professional

novelists is the following passage from Charles A. Lindbergh's amateur prose—his story of the most dramatic flight in history, the first transatlantic hop from New York to Paris.

I saw a fleet of fishing boats. I flew down almost touching one of the craft and yelled at them, asking if I was on the right road to Ireland. They just stared. Maybe they didn't hear me. Or maybe they thought I was just a crazy fool. An hour later I saw land.

There is not one difficult or remote word in either the excerpt from the *Digest* or the passage from Lindbergh's story. No attempt is made by either writer to say what he wants in any but simple style. Neither writer fights for the unusual phrase. The idea is simply to communicate quickly and clearly, in short sentences and plain words.

Even in political writing, trite as most of it is, a Woodrow Wilson, with a style all his own, can say in an address to Congress: "The world must be made safe for democracy," and in eight simple words arouse a nation to take up arms. Wilson's style is deceptively unsophisticated and plain.

Style has made
memorable speeches

In the same vein, consider Franklin D. Roosevelt's famous phrase of 1933: "The only thing we have to fear is fear itself." He might have said: "Most of our banks are closed because the people are afraid of the future." He might have said: "We have gone through panics before; we'll get through this one." But he said it in his own style, using the same word—*fear*—as a verb and a noun. Repetition of the word fixed the phrase in the minds of his countrymen and helped them to overcome hard times. His writing style made the people remember what he had written.

Summing up

Many factors shape a writer's style: his family background, education, reading habits, physical and mental interests, the time in which he lives, the audience he's writing for, his purpose in writing. Style is his own special, distinctive way of expressing himself in words.

Generally speaking, the best writing styles are the most natural. Few writers achieve success if they think and talk one way and write another. Conversational, informal style communicates faster and more accurately than the formal language of the classical essay. Indeed, the American trend in both fiction and non-fiction is toward simple, conversational writing style, sometimes called "spoken prose."

How can you make your writing sound like conversation?

Sentence variety is one way. Use of contractions also gives your writing a breezy informality. Using colloquial words and phrases instead of a formal vocabulary is another technique. Direct quotations help, even in non-fiction, if you make them sound natural.

A personal, homey touch or a bit of humor will sometimes transform stiff writing style to spoken prose, most readable of all writing styles. Cutting down the number of words in your sentences is vital to conversational prose.

No writer ever lived who didn't need to increase his vocabulary, for a good writer must have an acquaintance with words paralleling an artist's familiarity with shades, tones, textures and the limitless variety of color combinations.

The "classic" style
has faded away

Comparison of writing techniques in classical literature proves how individual a thing style is, and how each writer's personality, background and environment help mold his style. Here's how Faith Baldwin sees the problem from the viewpoint of the professional novelist:

Every writer worth his salt develops, after a time, his own style. A child learns to spell his name by printing it; afterwards he learns to write it and eventually develops a distinctive personal signature. Style is like that—a signature. If you give six writers the same plot and ask each of them to write a story around it, the bones of the story—the framework—will be the same in each case although the six stories they produce will be vastly different.

I haven't the least idea when I developed a style. I suspect it began to emerge in the early Thirties when I started to write serials. Yet looking back at the first books, which were not written under editorial advice or criticism, I can see a turn of phrase, an attitude of mind which was, perhaps, the foreshadowing of a style. That is probably the way it will be in your case. Your style will grow, just as will your other aptitudes.

Style variation isn't confined to fiction. In general, simple sentences, plain conversational words and spoken prose are an admirable trend in modern America, both in works of imagination and in practical writing.

However, not every writer has the same need for developing a style of his own. The businessman, for instance, may be better off sticking to clarity and brevity. In any case, style always comes with practice and no writer should consciously adopt someone else's style or force one of his own.

The tennis angle on writing

Every year, I join the thousands at Forest Hills watching the tennis champions. Somehow, by watching a flawless backhand again and again, I get more fluency into my own hambone stroking than I can find in many hours on the court.

And it is even more true in writing than tennis. If you live only with the best, some of it may rub off on you. Do you remember the neat story about the famous international banker, Baron Rothschild? A lesser financial light came to him with a sad story and a request for a loan. Said the great baron: "I will not make the loan. But I will do something better than that for you. I will walk arm-in-arm with you across the floor of the Exchange."

So make it your business to walk arm-in-arm with the great writers. Tangle with Schopenhauer over the horrors of womankind. Have a go at the *Transcendental Dialectic:* see how your mental muscle-tone freshens after a go in those murky passages, whether you can or you Kant. Read *War and Peace* and then cast an eye over your own plots. Try Hemingway for clarity and power. Walter Pater for an elegance of style. Joseph Conrad for a relationship of pure story-telling with themes that hark back to Milton.

Read Shaw's glittering prefaces to his plays, distillations of wit and thought that are astonishing in their richness. Go over Boswell's papers again to discover the importance of the trivial. Read the speeches of Winston Churchill, and don't deprive yourself of the great experience of seeing English history through his eyes—his *History of the English-Speaking Peoples* is enough to make any writer of fiction despair over the romance of fact.—Frederic A. Birmingham in *The Writer's Craft.*

Lesson twenty

Principles of good writing

Reading for writing

Besides reading for facts—the essence of research—most writers read more of everything than non-writers because they are naturally attracted to words. Indeed, one of the trade secrets of professional writers is simply this: *read, read, read!*

Some writers, it is true, show little curiosity about anything written by someone else. This sort of writer may even restrict his conversation and thoughts to his own writing, subjects and success: what other writers have put into words apparently has no significance for him. This limited writer won't go far.

A famous novelist wrote several excellent stories about writers and in one of them his hero contracted tuberculosis and was put to bed for several months. Very quickly the hospital ran out of things for the writer to read, so he began devouring technical books on medicine, nursing, gardening, construction—anything he could lay hands on. This astonished the hospital staff.

The point that he was making is quite familiar to most professional writers. All writers should be prolific readers. In fact, a writer should be the most diligent of readers. There is simply no substitute for the rule: *read, read, read!* And why not?

In the first place, no one can personally visit the endlessly varied scenes where events take place in fiction or non-fiction. Therefore, some substitute must be found to bring these localities to the writer through his imagination. Words are the wings that transport him.

In the second place, no one can experience all the endlessly varied tragic or thrilling situations of life. Reading shows you how such circumstances affect others. Sensitive reading can spark your logical or emotional reactions to problems you've never met during your own living.

Words are the wings
that transport you

In my early years I was hell-bent on becoming a humorist and so I read the humorists—read them and studied them. I knew every word of Lardner, Benchley, Perelman, Thurber, Ade, Twain and all the rest.

This is an approach to reading which I could recommend to the student writer. Find the people who write as you would like to and study them. Today my style, such as it is, is formed and I no longer have to read for instruction—I can read for pleasure.

The authors I enjoy most now are Dostoevski and Shakespeare. These are two more writers I would recommend to a beginning writer because they illuminate every corner of the human soul.—Max Shulman

---

The daily newspaper is the best of sources. In its columns range all the subjects and locales a writer could possibly wish for. Here are heartbreak, elation, victory, disaster, small talk and profound thinking—side by side. Here are the struggles of mankind placed under a microscope and delivered to a writer's door for a few cents a day. There is simply no better source of writing ideas, for fiction or non-fiction.

James A. Farley, former Postmaster General and political engineer of Franklin Roosevelt's first two Presidential victories, once said: "If I had a son who wanted to go into politics, I'd tell him first to get a job on a newspaper. After five years he'd know more about the mechanics of the world around him than he could learn from any other business or profession, and he'd know it better. There's nothing like a newspaper for teaching a young man how other people live and what they think."

Newspapers aren't the only key to gaining vicarious experience through reading. Weekly newsmagazines are excellent. Magazines of general circulation are *must* reading for any writer; their non-fiction coverage is so great today that almost no subject is uninteresting to their editors and readers.

As the modern world shrinks through air travel and rapid communication, the field of non-fiction expands because audience and subject matter are expanding. When the first rockets were sent into orbit around the earth, to the moon, the sun and the vastness beyond, a whole new field of non-fiction opened up to the writer. The widening scope of industry and business offers uncountable careers for non-fiction writers who must know, as never before, about the remotest parts of the earth.

Anyone interested in writing regards every book as a specimen, not merely a means of amusement. Writers soon find themselves reading critically, watching for styles, techniques, situations, plots or other professional aids. Through reading, writers learn how they can improve their own work. They learn ways of handling sentences and paragraphs, new meanings for words, techniques with clauses and phrases they hadn't thought of before, errors to avoid making themselves.

Writers look upon
books as specimens

Most professional writers become aware of the mechanics of writing the first time they read a piece. But student writers might better read everything twice, the first time for the story or the facts; the second time for the mechanics, the way things were done with characters and plot, style and organization, and the reasons why.

There are rhythms in writing, places where the author accelerates or slows down for emphasis. There are mannerisms and favorite words, some of them oddly used. So as he reads, a writer asks himself questions like this:

1. How does this other writer get such marked contrast?
2. How does he move his characters from one scene to another?
3. Do vocabulary and emphasis change when this author is writing about different characters?
4. How does he make them talk differently?
5. Does this author appear to be all-knowing when he's handling situations and characters, or does he allow the story and the characterization to dawn slowly on the reader through enlightenment of the people in the story?
6. How quickly does this author suggest the story's basic philosophy, its central theme, and how does he accomplish his purpose?

7. Why did he use this word in this particular spot? Why did he suddenly and perceptibly lengthen his sentences? Why did he give it this kind of ending?

A writer doesn't read other writers merely to copy them. But what you learn from other writers you can adapt to your own style and technique. When you've found a passage which seems to you to be far better than anything you are yet able to do, sit and ponder it. Just how is it better? What did this writer do that you have been unable to do with the same idea? Technical excellence can be imitated with great profit to a student writer, and many a famous professional will tell you that he or she constantly learns techniques from reading others.

Going back to fundamentals

Contemporary reading is highly useful to today's writers, yet unless a writer has read his share of the literary classics he won't understand writing technique in depth. Teachers of music often go back to Beethoven, Bach and Mozart because a musician, in whatever field, cannot wholly understand and appreciate Stravinsky without knowing where Stravinsky's music came from. In painting, an art student absorbs Michelangelo's pencil sketches of the human hand, arm, shoulder and torso before comprehending the great imagination of Picasso. There are no specific books that every writer has to read, but there are directions he may profitably take, if he has the time and the desire. Bergen Evans makes these suggestions:

If he is interested in literature, he should know such works as Homer's *Odyssey,* Sophocles' *Oedipus Rex,* the Bible, Virgil's *Aeneid,* Dante's *Divine Comedy,* Shakespeare's *Hamlet, Lear, Macbeth, Othello* and the great comedies and histories. He should know Milton's *Paradise Lost.* He should have at least looked into Gibbon's *Decline and Fall of Rome,* if only for an hour or two to see whether or not he likes sonorous, rhythmic prose (judging from the popularity of Winston Churchill's utterances in our time, most people do). He should read Goethe's *Faust,* Dostoevski's *The Brothers Karamazov,* Flaubert's *Madame Bovary.* If he is interested in politics, he should know such works as Plato's *Republic* and Machiavelli's *The Prince.*

There has been a tendency in recent years to scorn the established classics as training for a writer. But it might be well to consider a hint from the most influential of all modern writers, a man whose work seems to be drawn exclusively from his own observation and experience: Ernest Hemingway. His titles alone reveal the vast reading that his style absorbs but conceals:

For Whom the Bell Tolls is drawn from the poetry of John Donne, a 17th-Century clergyman. Scholars were pleased to be able to spot that one when it appeared. *A Farewell to Arms* is from a minor Elizabethan poet. *The Sun Also Rises* is from the *Book of Ecclesiastes. Across the River and Into the Trees,* an echo of the words of Stonewall Jackson as he lay dying, shows a knowledge of American history. For all his occasional scorn of literary pretensions, Hemingway is a learned man, widely read in great literature.

What sort of classical reading should *you* do? This depends largely on how much time you have each day. For instance, it takes about five hours to read every word of news in an average issue of the *New York Times.* Many newspapermen do it every day of their lives, plus all sorts of other topical reading. They have to, to stay in business. They don't have as much time for classical reading as, say, a professor of English. He can afford to spend more time going back to the classics, since they're part of his professional thought and expression.

Both professor and newspaperman probably read extensively in the classics long before they began to practice their professions. It was second nature to them. Curiosity was a factor—a thirst for reading as natural as breathing. Many professional writers will tell you they were reading even before they went to school and that they preferred books to tinkering with auto engines. The written word fascinated them from the day they became aware of it. In short, they didn't have to be forced to read. They were intrigued by the printed page—and early in life wanted to express themselves on it.

Tie your reading to your schedule

Classic or transient, reading can be about every subject that could possibly interest man or woman. In *Fundamentals of Good Writing* by Brooks and Warren, reading is described as a great mine of material for our thinking.

Reading gets us out of our own time and place, out of ourselves, but it can in the end return us to ourselves and help us define ourselves. It places us in relation to human history and human effort. It locates us on a map, as it were, of human experience, and sets up points of reference by which we can inspect ourselves. Reading ends by giving us ourselves as material for thinking.

How many times, while reading something that stirred you deeply, have you felt how true it was, how completely you understood it in your own terms? This sort of reading can help you express your own thoughts. Everything you read tells you, sometimes without your knowing it, something of the process of getting your thoughts down on paper.

Things you read either impress or fail to impress you, and you're personally aware of this success or failure. And thus you learn by reading. Every book is a sample, a silent lesson from one writer to another, sometimes over a magic span of thousands of years.

In *Writer's Workshop Companion,* Gorham Munson says:

Some people read
to study writing

> Reading is a task that the eyes have to learn, although in learning it the child is not aware of what his eyes are doing. There are rows of black symbols on white paper, and the child learns to follow the row left to right, and then down to the left of the next row and over to the right . . . A literary work is the result of this joint effort of writer and reader.

This writer-reader relationship shows that each person is necessary to the other. Yet the layman and the writer read for different purposes. The layman is, in the words of Walter S. Campbell in *Professional Writing,* "a consumer merely, and reads only those things which will delight, instruct or stir him; the professional writer hardly ever reads merely for such purpose."

Some people read
to uncover ideas

Campbell once heard a well-known writer say that, after a severe illness, he had read during his convalescence merely for fun, and it was for him, the professional, a strange experience, one which he had not enjoyed for years. He was a little apologetic about it: it had been part of his plan for getting well. To him, it seemed unprofessional slackness to read for the mere pleasure of reading.

In *Article Writing and Marketing* by George L. Bird, the author states that writers have three purposes in reading articles written by other professional writers:

1. They read to study the techniques of writing.
2. They read to uncover ideas for new articles.
3. They read for pleasure.

"These motives," says Bird, "are presented in order of importance, though if the article writer does much reading of articles for pleasure, he is wasting time." The most serious goal the free-lance writer seeks in reading, Bird concludes, is "to improve his mastery of the writing craft."

Different styles and viewpoints

To illustrate why reading is good for a writer, let's observe a single historical event from several points of view—read what different human beings had to say about essentially the same facts.

The event we have chosen is that portion of the fighting at Lexington and Concord which set off the American Revolution. The date is April 19, 1775, and the focal point of all these pieces, old or new, is the small bridge over the Concord River.

Some people read for pure pleasure

The first quote is from Minuteman Amos Barrett, whose house was believed to contain Colonial rebel arms—the reason the British General Gage left Boston in the first place. Note that Minuteman Barrett was, if not illiterate, certainly no trained writer. The spelling (see italicizing) and punctuation are his own:

We *marchd* before them [the redcoats] with our *Droms* and fifes agoing and also the B[ritish] we had a grand *musick*. It was *straing their warnt* no more killed but they *fird to* high.

Following is a literate and more comprehensive piece of writing about the same event in the collections of the Massachusetts Historical Society for the year 1793. This excerpt comes from *An Historical Journal of the American War,* written not more than 18 years after the Concord incident:

Hostilities were commenced by a detachment of the British troops, ordered from Boston by Governour, General Gage, who, having advanced to Lexington, about twelve miles from the capital, on seeing a company of militia parading there, fired on them while they were dispersing, killing eight and wounded many more. Then they proceeded to Concord to destroy some provincial military stores: but being opposed by the country militia, they returned to Boston with much difficulty, and not without the loss of 273 killed, wounded & missing. At this time the American war commenced.

This is more formal writing and, of course, more literate. The spelling is now normal for the period, not simply from the pen of an uneducated writer.

More than a century after the skirmish at Concord Bridge, John Fiske published *The American Revolution,* from which the following description of the same incident is taken. By now, some of the details have been pieced together, although the writing is formal rather than conversational:

This man has uncommon historical sense and sources.

Some precious minutes had been lost by the British at Lexington, and it soon became clear that the day was to be one in which minutes could ill be spared. By the time they reached Concord, about 7 o'clock, the greater part of the stores had been effectually hidden, and minute-men were rapidly gathering from all quarters. After posting small forces to guard the bridge, the troops set fire to the courthouse, cut down the liberty pole, disabled a few cannon, staved in a few barrels of flour and hunted unsuccessfully for arms and ammunition, until an unexpected incident put a stop to their proceedings.

Although this is American history done a century later, the writing is still fairly heavy and formal. Victorian living did little to improve the stiff quality of writing, which was actually freer in the Golden Age of Greece and in Chaucer's England.

When the force of minute-men, watching events from the hill beyond the river, had become increased to more than 400, they suddenly advanced upon the North Bridge, which was held by 200 regulars. After receiving and returning the British fire, the militia, led by Major Buttrick, charged across the narrow bridge, overcame the regulars through weight and numbers, and drove them back into the village. They did not follow up the attack, but rested on their arms, wondering, perhaps, at what they had already accomplished, while their numbers were from moment to moment increased by the minute-men from neighboring villages.

A little before noon, though none of the objects of the expedition had been accomplished, Col. Smith (British) began to realize the danger of his position, and started on his retreat to Boston. His men were in no mood for fight. They had marched eighteen miles, and had eaten little or nothing for fourteen hours.

Each writer sees the story from his own side—which makes reading such an interesting aid to better writing. It's the old, old tale of the blind men and the elephant—whichever part each blind man touched gave him the idea of the whole animal.

But now, while companies of militia hovered upon both their flanks, every clump of trees and every bit of rising ground by the road side gave shelter to hostile yeomen, whose aim was true and deadly. Straggling combats ensued from time to time, and the retreating British left nothing undone which brave men could do; but the incessant, galling fire at length threw them into hopeless confusion. Leaving their wounded scattered along the road, they had already passed by the village green of Lexington in disorderly flight, when they were saved by Lord Percy, who had marched out through Brookline & Cambridge to their assistance with 1,200 men and two fieldpieces.

In 1955 novelist Bruce Lancaster wrote a history, *From Lexington to Liberty,* for the "Mainstream of America" series. Here is how he related the same facts with different words:

At the North Bridge, the Light Infantry Guard took solid station. The 43rd Oxfordshires stayed on the Concord side. The 10th Lincolnshires and the 4th Royal North Lancashires, also known as the

King's Own, spread out over the hillside across the bridge . . . There was little for the bridge guard to do. On the skyline they could see a few militiamen, observers from the main body massed on the hidden Muster Field, but these watchers seemed content to keep their distance . . .

There was a sudden stir on the skyline. Cocked hats, bayonetless muskets showed. In column of twos the militiamen topped the crest and began a steady march down the steep fields, heading straight for the bridge. Captain Laurie had to think fast. His whole force numbered less than 120 men. As the militia came on, it seemed to him, standing on the sandy planks with the slow rustle of the little river below him, that their numbers had increased notably since the brief meeting beyond the prow of Concord Ridge.

He called the Lincolnshires and the North Lancashires and took up a formation designed for street fighting . . .

These were good troops, none better. The bridge and its approaches were narrow. They should have been able to shatter innumerable attacking waves . . .

Yet something was wrong. There was an inexplicable uneasiness in the tightformed ranks. Perhaps morale factors played their part. Good officers were present. But many of them were strangers . . .

The militia columns came on, headed by Captain Isaac Davis, the gunsmith, with his Acton men. Little Abner Hosmer was close by him, thumping manfully at his drum. The column was long, but it should not have seriously concerned troops like the light infantry there on the Concord side . . . There was silence, nothing but the ripple of the slow Concord River, the rustling of the budding trees, and a steady drub-drub-drub of the militia boots . . .

There was no question who fired the first shot. A volley blanketed the leading infantry in smoke. Isaac Davis was down. Abner Hosmer rolled dead on the soft grass, his clumsy drum bumping along and his now useless drumsticks slithering out of his hands. The militia formation, two abreast, made any real volume of answering fire impossible. Whether by instinct or by order, men broke ranks, fanned out right and left and returned the blast.

A few men dropped on the Concord side . . . Then, inexplicably, unless all blame is laid on morale, Laurie's men broke. It was not a retreat but a rout, a racing scarlet column that poured back to the bend in the road that led on into the town, incredibly abandoning their dead and severely wounded comrades. Their flight—and it can be called nothing else—continued along present Monument Street until the fugitives met a body of grenadiers sent out in reply to an earlier request from Laurie.

Had the grenadiers kept on, they might have changed the whole aspect of the 19th of April and of the days and years ahead. They were tough, well-trained men and they could have taken badly dis-

It's apparent by now that the writer of 1955 has benefited in two ways from previous writing—by accumulation of his facts and by ease of expression, a move toward conversational words.

We, the readers, are privileged to visit the fields of Concord and Lexington— thanks to Bruce Lancaster. Where else could he have found the facts for his book?

Having read a great deal about the bridge incident, Lancaster is explaining what must have been in the minds of the troops at the time.

Logically, he tells his re-created tale. The details gathered from wide reading give his book authenticity.

Pictured in the novelist's mind from other writing.

Speculation, but based on sound research.

organized militia in the flank. Instead, they opened their ranks, let the light infantry through, wheeled, and went back to the Common and Wright's Tavern.

If panic struck the British, a sort of premature battle shock seems to have fallen over the American militia. They had seen the best troops in the world in sudden flight. They had only two men killed. The North Bridge was theirs. But they made no attempt to follow up their stroke . . .

So events were given, for the moment, into the hands of time. It is quite possible that had nothing else occurred, the British command would have been taken back to Boston with little damage to the Colonial cause to report—if one forgot the handful of dead on Lexington Green. But . . . someone on the Muster Field, saw smoke well up from Concord. The quite understandable inference was drawn that the town was burning. There was an end to hesitation, and the whole militia body marched off to save Concord from a fate that did not threaten it.

Directly ahead of them . . . the North Bridge lay quiet in the sun with its freight of British dead. Later the villagers would bury the dead to the left of the bridge where a plain solid stone marks the grave . . .

Up to this very instant the rest of the day might have passed without further event. But the last of the grenadiers turned at the bridge and fired. It must have been a gesture of exasperation and defiance, for there was no target within musket range. It triggered off the real, the irretrievable results of the day. Militiamen closed in on the rear and flanks of the column . . .

For miles, the British were to march in a funnel of musketry and with each mile more militia closed at the head. Men who had been out since the first call dropped out, bullets or rations or courage exhausted, but always new minute-men took their places. Rarely if ever did the militia fight as units. They sighted the road, broke ranks, fired, moved on, fired again . . .

Finally, let's look at Ralph Waldo Emerson's famous *Concord Hymn*, used at the dedication of the battle monument at the bridge on July 4, 1837. These four lines of poetry offer another and very powerful way of telling the same story:

> By the rude bridge that arched the flood,
> Their flag to April's breeze unfurled,
> Here once the embattled farmers stood,
> And fired the shot heard round the world.

Thus we see the action at Concord Bridge from several viewpoints—those of the contemporary soldier, the Colonial report,

---

Again, surmise only, since he couldn't have been present. But on the basis of his reading for writing, the author knows this is how the sudden panic of the "best troops in the world" must have affected the Colonials.

The pieces and bits of research are placed into the whole mosaic.

Conjecture again, but sound, logical reasoning on the basis of a man's reading.

The author isn't absolutely certain of all these details, but they are summoned up by points in what he has read.

What it all meant—worth reading after having read the details of the battle.

the historians and the memorializing poet. So we discover that reading can be, among many things, armchair adventure. Through reading we can go anywhere, know any scene or climate, be part of any era or civilization. It doesn't matter how far from home we wish to travel—the printed word is the magic carpet.

Armchair visit to the South Seas

Not many of us have ever been, or shall ever go, to the South Pacific. Yet scores of writers have written about Tahiti and other tiny dots on South Seas maps so glamorous to the traveler. From reading we are able to picture Tahiti from a great many points of view, the sum total of which gives us a fairly clear idea of one of the earth's most picturesque spots.

The first quotation is from Captain James Cook, the British explorer whose *A Voyage to the Pacific Ocean* was the first published account of life in that vast area. Cook sees Tahiti in August, 1777, from the viewpoint of the trading which goes on between his crew and the natives:

The important news, of red feathers being on board our ships, having been conveyed on shore by Omai's friends, day had no sooner begun to break next morning than we were surrounded by a multitude of canoes crowded with people, bringing hogs and fruits to market. At first, a quantity of feathers, not greater than what might be got from a tom-tit, would purchase a hog of 40 to 50 pounds weight. But, as almost everybody on the ships was possessed of some of this precious article of trade, it fell in value, above 500 per cent before night. However, even then, the balance was much in our favour; and red feathers continued to preserve their superiority over every other commodity.

This report of the way the trading went is a fascinating observation of human nature. It gives the reader a sense of absolute truth.

Some of the natives did not part with a hog unless they received an axe in exchange; but nails and beads and other trinkets, which, during our former voyages, had so great a run at the island, were now so much despised that few would deign so much as to look at them.

Not a very glamorous picture, this one. Yet a man who was with Captain Cook, one William Bligh, later came back to the South Pacific on a ship called the *Bounty* where a famous mutiny occurred. In one of the most incredible voyages in the history of seafaring, Captain Bligh guided a small open boat, in which the mutineers had set 18 men adrift, almost 4,000 miles across the trackless South Pacific. In the famous best-seller of 1933, *Men Against the Sea,* by Charles Nordhoff and James Norman Hall, the gaunt, thirsty sailors see a Pacific island in terms of life-giving food and water:

This is seen wholly from the viewpoint of men on sea-level for many weeks but now looking down from heights which must have been miraculous to them after their long ordeal.

The island upon which we had landed was of a considerable height. While foraging parties were out, Mr. Bligh, Nelson and myself walked inland to the highest part of it for a better view of our surroundings; but we could see little more of the main than appeared from below. In our weakened condition the climb had been a fatiguing one, and we took shelter in the shade of a great rock to recover our breath.

The lagoons were miracles of vivid coloring in the clear morning light. We could plainly see the figures of foraging parties as they made their way slowly along the shallows, searching for shellfish. Almost directly below us was the launch, looking smaller than a child's toy in the bight where she lay.

"There she lies," said Bligh, gazing fondly at the tiny craft. "I love every strake of planking, every nail in her. Mr. Nelson, could you have believed that she could have carried eighteen men such a voyage? Could you, Mr. Ledward?"

Naturally, to famished men, food is the most important part of the view and the description.

It was high noon when we joined the others. Peckover's party had just come in with a supply of clams and oysters almost equal in amount to that in the pot. They had also found, on the smooth side of the island, an abundance of fresh water in the hollows of the rocks—more than enough to fill our vessels. The sun shone in a cloudless sky, so that Captain Bligh was able, with his magnifying glass, to kindle a fire at once. The oysters and clams were now dumped into the pot together with a quart and a half of native beans. The requisite amount of water was added, and to make our stew yet more tasty, each man's usual amount of bread was added to it.

You feel very grateful that at last these human beings are fed after such a harrowing voyage.

Smith and Hall, our cooks, had whittled out long wooden spoons with which they stirred the stew as it came to a boil, sending up a savory steam that made the walls of our empty bellies quiver with anticipation. When the stew had cooked for a good twenty minutes—the time had seemed hours to most of us—the pot was set off the fire; and we gathered round with our half-coconut shells, while the cooks ladled onto each man's shell all that it could hold of clams, oysters, beans and delicious broth; and when all had been served, there was still enough in the pot for a half-pint more, all around. After our meal we rested . . .

Having rested and eaten well, the men find new vistas opening themselves.

All through the night we heard the cries of innumerable sea fowl, and daylight showed us that we were on the westernmost of four small islands, surrounded by a reef of rocks and connected with sand banks whose surface was barely above high tide. Within them lay a mirrorlike lagoon. The cays were little more than heaps of rock and sand covered with coarse grass and a sparse growth of bush and stunted trees.

Sixty years after the remarkable exploit of Captain Bligh, Tahiti was visited by Charles Darwin, whose *Origin of Species* revolutionized the scientific world. Darwin told of his trip around the globe in *Voyage of a Naturalist,* sometimes known as the voyage of *H.M.S. Beagle,* a ship furnished Darwin by the British Navy. Unlike the two accounts above, Darwin sees the South Pacific islands from the botanist's point of view:

The land capable of cultivation is scarcely in any part more than a fringe of low alluvial soil, accumulated round the base of the mountains, and protected from the waves of the sea by a coral reef, which encircles the entire line of coast. Within the reef there is an expanse of smooth water, like that of a lake, where the canoes of the natives can ply with safety and where ships anchor. The low land which comes down to the beach of coral sand is covered by the most beautiful production of the intertropical regions.

In the midst of banana, orange, cocoanut and breadfruit trees, spots are cleared where yams, sweet potatoes, the sugarcane and pineapples are cultivated. Even the brushwood is an imported fruit-tree, namely, the guava, which from its abundance has become as noxious as a weed.

Darwin's details are technical, scientific and undoubtedly accurate. They don't appeal to the senses, as the next view of Tahiti will. They are factual, not emotional.

While traveling in Brazil I have often admired the varied beauty of the bananas, palms and orange-trees contrasted together; and here we also have the breadfruit, conspicuous from its large, glossy and deeply digitated leaf. It is admirable to behold groves of a tree, sending forth its branches with the vigour of an English oak, loaded with large and most nutritious fruit.

However seldom the usefulness of an object can account for the pleasure of beholding it, in the case of these beautiful little woods the knowledge of their high productiveness no doubt enters largely into the feeling of admiration.

From 1845 we jump to 1919, when Somerset Maugham published a novel called *The Moon and Sixpence,* based on the life of the artist Paul Gauguin, who fled to Tahiti to fulfill himself as a painter. Here is how Tahiti looked to the storyteller on first seeing that South Pacific island, this time from the viewpoint of one more sensitive to color than to trade, salvation or science:

The Pacific is more desolate than other seas; its spaces seem more vast, and the most ordinary journey upon it has somehow the feeling of an adventure. The air you breathe is an elixir which prepares you for the unexpected. Nor is it vouchsafed to man in the flesh to know

Here's a new and entirely different piece of writing: this one full of the beauties of the senses.

aught that more nearly suggests the approach to the golden realms of fancy than the approach to Tahiti.

This is an especially fine sentence.

Murea, the sister isle, comes into view in rocky splendour, rising from the desert sea mysteriously, like the unsubstantial fabric of a magic wand . . . You may imagine that there, Polynesian knights guard with strange rites mysteries unholy for men to know. The beauty of the island is unveiled as diminishing distance shows you in distinct shape its lovely peaks, but it keeps its secret as you sail by, and, darkly inviolable, seems to fold itself together in a stony, inaccessible grimness . . .

Reading this, we now know a few of the emotional reactions all the rest must have had but didn't express. So we get a fresh dimension of Tahiti and the South Seas.

Tahiti is a lofty green island, with deep folds of a darker green, in which you divine silent valleys; there is mystery in their sombre depths, down which murmur and plash cool streams, and you feel that in those umbrageous places life from immemorial times has been led according to immemorial ways. Even here is something sad and terrible. But the impression is fleeting, and serves only to give a greater acuteness to the enjoyment of the moment. It is like the sadness which you may see in the jester's eyes when a merry company is laughing at his sallies; his lips smile and his jokes are gayer because in the communion of laughter, he finds himself more intolerably alone.

For Tahiti is smiling and friendly; it is like a lovely woman graciously prodigal of her charm and beauty; and nothing can be more conciliatory than the entrance into the harbour of Papeete. The schooners moored to the quai are trim and neat, and the little town along the bay is white and urbane, and the flamboyants, scarlet against the blue sky, flaunt their colour like a cry of passion. They are sensual with an unashamed violence that leaves you breathless.

Colors affected Maugham always. It shows here in his use of colorful words.

And the crowd that throngs the wharf as the steamer draws alongside is gay and debonair; it is a noisy, cheerful, gesticulating crowd. It is a sea of brown faces. You have an impression of a coloured movement against the flaming blue of the sky. Everything is done with a great deal of bustle, the unloading of the baggage, the examination of the customs; and everyone seems to smile at you. It is very hot. The colour dazzles you.

The last two sentences, brief but powerful, are highly dramatic.

The South Pacific was also the locale for a postwar book in 1947 by James Michener—a book which became the source of the famous musical by Rodgers and Hammerstein. Michener's point of view is the war correspondent's. He finds the scene hard to describe in civilian terms:

Broken sentences to give the reader a quick descriptive picture.

I wish I could tell you about the South Pacific. The way it actually was. The endless ocean. The infinite specks of coral we called islands. The coconut palms nodding gracefully toward the ocean. Reefs upon which waves broke into spray and inner lagoons, lovely beyond description. I wish I could tell you about the sweating jungle, the full moon rising behind the volcanoes, and the waiting. The waiting. The timeless, repetitive waiting.

But when I start to talk about the South Pacific, people intervene. I try to tell somebody what the steaming Hebrides were like, and the first thing you know, I'm telling about the old Tonkinese woman who used to sell human heads. As souvenirs. For fifty dollars!

For the first time we have a modern view of the South Pacific as an area where flesh-and-blood people currently live.

Or somebody asks me, "What was Guadalcanal actually like?" And before I can describe that godforsaken backwash of the world, I'm rambling on about the Remittance Man, who lived among the Japs and sent us radio news of their movements. That is, he sent us the news until one day.

This aside gives us as readers a new South Seas dimension. The "unfinished" final sentence of this paragraph is very powerful.

The people intervene. The old savage who wanted more than anything else in the world to jump from an airplane and float down to earth in a parachute. "Alla same big fella bird!" he used to shout ecstatically, until one day we took him up and shoved him out. Ever afterward he walked in silence among black men, a soul apart . . .

Breathing, living characters in our setting give us, the readers, a new concept of life on this journey.

When we read Michener's *Tales of the South Pacific,* we realize that each writer sees a scene with different eyes. In 1950, after 101 days on a raft which had floated westward from Peru, Thor Heyerdahl wrote *Kon-Tiki,* a title derived from the Sun King of the South Pacific. Here is his description of Tahiti as first seen from water-level—the level of his raft:

Four days later Tahiti rose out of the sea. Not like a string of pearls with palm tufts. As wild jagged blue mountains flying skyward, with wisps of cloudlike wreaths round the peaks.

We see Tahiti as wanderers from the flat raft saw it— from the level of the Pacific Ocean.

As we gradually approached, the blue mountains showed green slopes. Green upon green, the lush vegetation rolled down over rust-red hills and cliffs, till it plunged down into the deep ravines and valleys running out toward the sea. When the coast came near, we saw slender palms standing close packed up all the valleys and all along the coast behind a golden beach.

The phrase about the palm trees "close packed up all the valleys" is especially good.

Tahiti was built by old volcanoes. They were dead now and the coral polyps had slung their protecting reef about the island so that the sea could not erode it away . . . We headed through an opening in the reef into the harbor of Papeete. Before us lay church spires and red roofs half-hidden by the foliage of giant trees and palm tops.

Papeete was the capital of Tahiti, the only town in French Oceania. It was a city of pleasure, the seat of government, and the center of all traffic in the eastern Pacific. When we came into the harbor, the population of Tahiti stood waiting, packed tight like a gaily colored living wall.

The population of Papeete that comes down in force to see the raft arrive is wonderfully described as a "living wall."

We have just had another armchair adventure. We've seen the

South Pacific, Tahiti especially, from the viewpoints of an early British explorer, a sea captain in a famous mutiny, a world-renowned naturalist, a character in a noted novel, a war correspondent, and a man who drifted across the Pacific on a raft.

Each writer saw Tahiti and the South Seas differently. Therefore, each wrote in his own particular way, not simply in different words and styles but from radically varied points of view. Some used long sentences, some short. Some were aware of the colors and smells and sounds of the South Sea islands; to others they were a geological or botanical phenomenon; to another a matter of trading with the natives; and to some they spelled safety at last.

Writer and reader are in partnership

But by reading all *six* versions (and there are scores of descriptions of Tahiti and the South Seas in print), we travel vicariously on the magic wings of words. For people who want to write, this sort of armchair experience is essential because it gives them limitless knowledge of the world in which they live and shows them how it is mirrored in the ever-varying viewpoints of those who write.

A professional's viewpoint on reading

Mignon Eberhart is an ardent believer in reading for the writer. Based upon her own experience, she calls the writer and the reader "an indissoluble partnership." Then she adds:

My own early reading was widely scattered. I read literally everything I could get my hands on and still do. I'd have read the telephone book if there'd been nothing else. But it did happen that a good solid backbone of the classics in literature was available to me.

Naturally I gobbled the easy reading, sheer romance, sheer adventure, whenever I could; there were some forbidden books in the attic which drew me like a magnet. These were not forbidden on the score of being improper but on the score of being "trashy" (my mother's word for them). This was a challenge no child could resist; I remember the tiptoe to the attic, supplied with apples—and the hours of enchantment, unaware of a few lazy wasps, the smell of mothballs and the heat, lost in perhaps brightly colored but certainly exciting worlds.

However, because better reading was at hand (or perhaps the attic books gave out) I dove into the classics, too. A child is often a ravenous and rapid reader and if or when he can wangle himself out of guiding hands, he'll tackle anything. Much of a young person's reading is far beyond his years and understanding; it is only later, when the same books are read in maturity, that their contents reveal their true significance.

I wonder how many hundreds of books I gulped down. Certainly, to this day, D'Artagnan, Porthos, Athos and Aramis are people to me. Becky Sharp is as real as she was the first time I read about her—and I am still bored with Amelia. Because plays were always at hand I read Ibsen and Shaw at too early an age and still loathe Major Barbara. But Sheridan's *School for Scandal* sticks in my mind.

I do remember when Dostoevski, Turgenev, Tolstoy (I waded through *War and Peace* for the first time at about eighteen, Heaven help me), Arnold Bennett, Willa Cather, Edith Wharton, Balzac, Scott Fitzgerald came vividly into my reading life. At least a nodding acquaintance with the Greek dramatists, and Shakespeare and Molière, with Gibbon and Taine, with English and American poets—many of the greats of literature come about either by way of introduction in school or the reader's own discovery. Even if a young reader reads too greedily, something of the use of words, something of narrative values may reveal themselves to him. It is only important to let the habit of reading start itself.

Exposure to the immortals of literature is, regrettably, not catching, but like measles the reader may get a spot or two of enlightenment about what *can* be done with words. With a writer this habit of reading later becomes a serious study. He asks himself, how did this writer accomplish this moving effect? Why does this line make me pause and think, why does this paragraph leave me unaffected? I cannot truthfully say that any one writer or any one book has influenced me more than another; perhaps I am mistaken and this has taken place without my knowledge. But I do know this: a writer reads all his life in a kind of dual role, that of the reader lost in the story, and that of the writer, alert, watching, studying all the time.

Reading is like a rich and varied feast spread before the eyes of the reader. Desserts have their place. Salads and sauces may be stimulating. But good meat gives nourishment.

Reading for writing is a splendid idea—but a word of warning. *You'll never be a writer if you do nothing but read.* You must *use* what you read and you must also *write* to be a writer. John Caples, a strong advocate of reading, says:

> I know three very well educated people who wanted to write, but they read so many books that they never got around to writing.

Reading can be a narcotic depriving a writer of the time he should spend at his typewriter. When you find yourself reading as an excuse for not working, for postponing that short story or magazine article, that business report or advertising copy due tomorrow morning, you're violating the very title of this Lesson: "Reading *for* writing."

Summing up

Besides reading for facts—the essence of research—all writers need to read more of everything than non-writers do. The writer is naturally attracted to words, as a musician loves to listen to music, or a mechanic likes to tinker with a car—any car. Indeed, one of the top trade techniques of professional writers is simply this: they *read, read, read!* Most of them set aside an allotment of hours each day for just this purpose, just as a pianist sets aside certain daily hours for practicing scales or simply listening to recordings.

Since no writer has traveled everywhere, all writers supplement travel with reading. Through reading, any writer can visit endlessly varied scenes and be aware of the fabulous events of any century. Words are the wings that transport him.

The newspaper offers a mine of ideas

The daily newspaper is a fantastic mine for writers' ideas, factual information and vicarious travel. So are magazines and books. All good writers read them constantly. But when reading, the writer regards everything he reads as a specimen, not merely as a source of pleasure. The writer soon finds himself reading with one eye to the story and the other watching for techniques and styles he can use in his own composition.

Reading is essential for all contemporary writers, yet unless a writer is constantly aware of the way a piece is written, aside from its content, he's losing valuable time and instruction. When a writer reads, he needs to notice paragraphs which please him and seem to come off well, possibly even to underline or copy them. He will say to himself, "Why does this do what I tried to do and failed?" Because of his profession, a writer's purpose in reading is unique.

What sort of classical reading should you do? This depends on how much you've read up to now, how much time you have each day, and why you're learning to write. Not every part-time writer can spend limitless hours over the printed word. Not every writing student has to, because he may not aim to become a professional writer. He may be a businessman whose reading needs are specialized and far less demanding than, say, those of a full-time magazine article writer.

All the same, the principle of reading for writing is elemental. Natural-born writers read voraciously. Their native curiosity and wonder never leave them. The world they are writing about is a continuously fascinating place and they learn much of it simply through armchair experience. All full-time students of writing should follow their example.

Yet reading alone won't do, for reading can also be used as an excuse for not working and become a narcotic which keeps potential writers from putting their own words on paper. Remember: the title of this Lesson was deliberately written this way: "Reading *for* writing."

Reading helps your writing

There is an intimate relationship between the communicative skills of reading and writing. Through reading we enrich our experiences and thinking; through writing we enrich the experience and thinking of others. Reading is nothing more than writing in reverse. And it follows that mastery of one can lead to mastery of the other.–Delwyn G. Schubert in *Creative Wisconsin.*

Read everything you like

Never stop the habit
of reading widely

I don't feel strongly about the importance of formal schooling (except for professional specialists like doctors, lawyers and engineers) but I do deeply believe that voracious reading is indispensable to anybody who's going to try to work with words. The reading should be wide in range and it's preferable that it be undirected by a teacher. It's perfectly natural for the untrained palate to prefer Edgar A. Guest to Keats, and *Jack Harkaway, Afloat and Ashore* to *Vanity Fair.* As tastes develop and mature, the change will be natural and real, not merely the result of teacher saying, "This is better than that."–Red Smith

Lesson twenty-one

Principles of good writing

Some final pointers

In this closing Lesson of *Principles of good writing,* we are including material which further emphasizes certain points of importance to every beginning writer. Some of these points have been touched on or discussed in previous Lessons: others are presented here for the first time in the form of an appendix.

Most of the items are taken from books written by professional writers or teachers, or both. You will find the passages helpful to read and to keep always in mind, because only by accepting pointers from successful writers can you hope to achieve success in your own work.

The most useful tool for a writer is a good dictionary. Nowhere else can he find so much information about words and their use, and nowhere else, if he is really interested in his language, can he find so much curious, incidental, and even amusing information about words.

But dictionaries are primarily for reference. They answer questions about the meaning of words so that the student can read with more understanding. They settle doubts (or arguments) about single words. And they help a writer decide on the most accurate and effective word or phrase to use. A writer will use his dictionary most in revision and should get the habit of turning to it frequently while revising a paper and preparing the final copy.

Obviously, to get the most out of a dictionary you need to know what various matters it includes. You should look through its table of contents to see what units of material there are besides the main alphabetical list of words. You should see if it contains a supplement of new words. You should read a page or two consecutively to see how words and phrases are handled, and try pronouncing some familiar words to see how the pronunciation key works.

1. *Spelling.* A word is entered in a dictionary under its usual spelling. As a rule a writer can come close enough to this so that he can find a word he is in doubt about, but sometimes he has to keep in mind other common spellings of a sound— so that if he fails to find *gibe* he will look under *jibe.* When usage in spelling is divided, two spellings are given for the word. The one the editors believe is more common is put first: *hemoglobin, haemoglobin; although, altho.* Ordinarily a writer will take the first of the two forms unless the second for some reason is more appropriate to other traits of his writing.

The spelling entries in a dictionary give the division of a word into syllables and so show where it should be divided at the end of lines, as in *mor·ti·fi·ca·tion, dis·par·ag·ing·ly.* They also give the spelling of compound words, showing whether the editors have found them most often as two words, as one word, or with hyphen. Most dictionaries recommend the use of more hyphens than are necessary, certainly for informal writing. The introductions to most dictionaries contain general discussions of English spelling.

2. *Pronunciation.* Dictionaries respell words in specially marked letters to show their pronunciation. The exact sounds represented by the symbols are usually shown at the bottom of the page and are further explained in a discussion of pronunciation in the preface. Here are examples from *Webster's New Collegiate Dictionary,* copyright 1949 by G. & G. Merriam Co.

ac·cli'mate (ă·klī'mĭt; ăk'lĭ·māt), *v. t. & i.* [F. *acclimater,* fr. *à* to + *climat* climate.] To habituate, or become habituated, to a climate not native; to acclimatize. — **Syn.** Inure, season, harden. — **ac·cli'mat·a·ble** (ă·klī'mĭt·å·b'l), *adj.* — **ac'cli·ma'tion** (ăk'lĭ·mā'shŭn; ăk'lĭ-), *n.*

cer′ti·o·ra′ri (sûr′shĭ·ō·rā′rī; -rär′ī), *n.* [From *certiorari* to be certified; — a term in the Latin form of the writ.] *Law.* A writ from a superior court to call up for review the records of an inferior court or a body acting in a quasi-judicial capacity.

phi·lat′e·ly (fĭ·lăt′ĕ·lĭ), *n.* [F. *philatélie*, fr. Gr. *philos* loving + *ateleia* exemption from tax (*telos*).] The collection and study of postage stamps, stamped envelopes, etc., of various issues; stamp collecting. — **phil′a·tel′ic** (fĭl′*a*·tĕl′ĭk), **phil′a·tel′i·cal** (-ĭ·k*a*l), *adj.* — **phil′a·tel′i·cal·ly,** *adv.* — **phi·lat′e·list** (fĭ·lăt′ĕ·lĭst), *n.*

quay (kē; kwā), *n.* [OF. *kai, cay* (F. *quai*).] A stretch of paved bank or a solid artificial landing place beside navigable water, for convenience in loading and unloading ships.

Dictionaries show divided usage in the pronunciation of many words, as in the Webster examples of *acclimate* shown opposite. As a rule a person should use the pronunciation most common among the educated people of his community.

3. *Definition.* The definitions of words of course take up the bulk of the space in a dictionary. The definitions of unusual words help the reader get the full and actual sense of a passage that treats material new to him. Dictionaries carry many dialect, obsolete, and archaic words to help in reading writers such as Burns and Shakespeare. Scientific, technical, slang and provincial words are generously included, although by no means all words of these classes are given.

For a writer the dictionary definitions are most useful in checking the meaning of words he is almost sure of, but not quite. When he is revising a paper, he needs to make sure that some words mean what he thought they meant when he put them in the first draft, and he wants to make sure that they stand a good chance of meaning to his reader what he intends them to. Very often he will need more information for this purpose than a dictionary can give because of its limited space and must go to an encyclopedia or other work.

Be sure what
your words mean

It is not so much the meanings of uncommon words, like *hackbut, pyrognostics,* or *zymurgy,* that a writer needs as the meanings of those near but not quite in his active vocabulary. Almost any series of dictionary entries will illustrate these words and the scope and method of dictionary definition, as shown here from *The American College Dictionary,* copyright 1949, by Random House.

check·row (chĕk'rō'), *Agric.* —*n.* **1.** one of a number of rows of trees or plants, esp. corn, in which the distance between adjacent trees or plants is equal to that between adjacent rows. —*v.t.* **2.** to plant in checkrows.

check·up (chĕk'ŭp'), *n.* **1.** an examination or close scrutiny for purposes of verification as to accuracy, comparison, etc. **2.** a comprehensive physical examination.

Ched·dar cheese (chĕd'ər), American cheese. Also, **ched'dar.**

chedd·ite (chĕd'īt, shĕd'īt), *n.* an explosive used for blasting made up of a chlorate or perchlorate mixture with a fatty substance, such as castor oil. [t. F : f. *Chedde* place name (of Savoy) + *-ite* -ITE]

cheek (chēk), *n.* **1.** either side of the face below eye level. **2.** the side wall of the mouth between the upper and lower jaws. **3.** something resembling the human cheek in form or position, as either of two parts forming corresponding sides of a thing. **4.** *Colloq.* impudence or effrontery. —*v.t.* **5.** *Brit. Colloq.* to address or confront with impudence or effrontery. [ME *cheke,* OE *cēce,* c. D *kaak*]

cheek·bone (chēk'bōn'), *n.* the bone or bony prominence below the outer angle of the eye.

cheek by jowl, side by side; in close intimacy.

cheek pouch, a bag in the cheek of certain animals, as squirrels, for carrying food.

cheek·y (chē'kĭ), *adj.,* **cheekier, cheekiest.** *Colloq.* impudent; insolent: *a cheeky fellow, cheeky behavior.* — **cheek'i·ly,** *adv.* —**cheek'i·ness,** *n.*

The great need for saving space in a dictionary makes some definitions cryptic, requiring anyone but a specialist to look up words used in the definition. Drawings are a help in leading to an understanding of objects, and illustrative phrases or sentences in which the word is used are a help in showing its meaning and construction with other words.

Dictionaries show the way to usage

There are three points to remember in using dictionary definitions. (a) A dictionary does not *require* or *forbid* a particular meaning of a word but *records* the uses that have been found for it. Now and then a word is in the process of acquiring a new meaning or somewhat altering its usual sense. (b) The dictionary definition is for the most part a record of the denotation of a word and often cannot give its connotation. For this reason it is safest not to use a word unless you have heard or read it and so know it in part from experience, at least what suggestion it carries if it is not a simple factual word. (c) Finally and most important, the words of the definition are not the meaning of the word, but they, and perhaps an illustration, are to help let you see what in the world of objects or ideas the word refers to.

4. *Levels of usage.* Words that are unlabeled in a diction-

ary are supposed to belong to the general vocabulary; other words are labeled *dialect, obsolete, archaic, foreign, colloquial, slang, British, United States,* or are referred to some field of activity—*medicine, law, astronomy, baseball, manufacturing, electricity, philosophy.*

These labels are rough guides to levels of usage, but a writer should bring his own observation and judgment to bear on individual words. Many that carry no label are rarely used (*curtilage, moot*) and would mar most writing. In general the editors' point of view is rather conservative, and many words marked *Dial.* or *Colloq.* would fit perfectly well into informal writing. It must be clearly understood that these labels are intended to be descriptive terms and are not intended to prohibit or even to discourage the use of the words so labeled. *Colloq.* means that the word is characteristic of cultivated conversation rather than of formal writing; *U.S.,* that the word is in good use in the United States but not necessarily in other parts of the English-speaking world.

Use your own
judgment on words

5. *Synonyms.* Most dictionaries gather words of similar meanings into a group and show in what ways they are alike and in what ways different, as in the following entries which appear after the words *argue* and *argument* in *The American College Dictionary:*

> —**Syn.** 1. ARGUE, DEBATE, DISCUSS imply using reasons or proofs to support or refute an assertion, proposition, or principle. ARGUE implies reasoning or trying to understand; it does not necessarily imply opposition: *to argue with oneself.* To DISCUSS is to present varied opinions and views: *to discuss ways and means.* To DEBATE is to interchange formal (usually opposing) arguments, esp. on public questions: *to debate a proposed amendment.*

> —**Syn.** 1. ARGUMENT, CONTROVERSY, DISPUTE imply the expression of opinions for and against some idea. An ARGUMENT usually arises from a disagreement between two persons, each of whom advances facts supporting his own point of view. A CONTROVERSY or a DISPUTE may involve two or more persons. A DISPUTE is an oral contention, usually brief, and often of a heated, angry, or undignified character *a violent dispute over a purchase.* A CONTROVERSY is an oral or written expression of contrary opinions, and may be dignified and of some duration: *a political controversy.*

6. *Linguistic information.* The dictionary usually indicates the part of speech in which a word is generally used; whether a verb is used transitively or intransitively; the principal parts

of verbs, plurals of nouns; and any other distinctive form a word may assume. The origin of the word, how it got into English, is usually given. Sometimes this is merely a statement of the language from which the word came into English (Italian, Latin, Japanese), and sometimes it is a more complicated chain of origin and change of form, as in the *Webster New Collegiate* statement on *course,* tracing it from Latin, through Italian and French, to English:

> **course** (kōrs; 70), *n.* [From F. *cours* (OF. *cors, curs*), fr. L. *cursus,* and fr. F. *course,* fr. It. *corsa,* fr. *correre* to run; both fr. L. *currere, cursum,* to run.]

7. *Miscellaneous information.* Most dictionaries contain some reference material not strictly needed in a book of definitions, such as lists of places and prominent historical figures, abbreviations, foreign words and phrases. Formerly these items were run in lists in the back of the volume, but the tendency in recent dictionaries has been to put them in the main alphabet.—From *Writer's Guide and Index to English* (revised edition) by Porter G. Perrin, published by Scott, Foresman and Co., copyright 1950.

Words to sharpen
your meaning

Most writing people use a wider vocabulary than non-writing people. This is quite natural, since writers work with words day after day. They realize that many common English words are seldom if ever used by the average person to express shades of meaning. Non-writers are likely to fall back on the same old clichés, feeling no daily need for sharper substitutes.

Following are a couple of hundred long and short words which will sharpen your writing. There are thousands of others. All of them are common English words, but few are used regularly by the average person either in conversation or composition.

Take the simple word *towering.* It's a more telling, a sharper word than *high;* it has more punch for the writer. Used occasionally, *towering* can sharpen your style, as can *beguiling, saucy, sparkling, singular, bungling, coy, arbiter, callow, tenuous, artless, crusty, radiance* or any word in the list below.

Some of the words are offered not in their usual sense but as neglected synonyms with less common meanings. For example, *spring* or *fountain* can make excellent synonyms for *source; covey* can be used nicely for something besides a flight of quail; *princely* doesn't always have to mean *royal* in the literal sense; *armor* isn't a word that must always refer to something military; and *singular* has useful meanings other than grammatical.

Writers work with words every day

Used slightly offbeat, these and many other words in the dictionary will raise the level of your prose by making it just a little different and just a little better.

abate	artless	carnage	crave
aberration	astute	cashier	credulity
absolve	authorized	caste	crotchety
absurd	autocratic	caustic	crusty
acumen		chagrin	culpable
adage	baneful	chaste	
addicted	banter	chasten	defame
admirable	becoming	chattering	defile
admissible	beguiling	checkmate	demure
adroit	beset	cheerless	depart
affectionate	bewitch	cherish	deportment
affinity	biting	chide	depravity
agile	bitter	chronicle	derange
alacrity	bleak	citadel	desist
allay	blessed	clemency	dexterity
alleviate	blow	clownish	direful
amalgam	bluff	compact	discernment
ambiguous	blustering	compel	disciple
annex	bold	composure	disinclined
aperture	boundless	conceit	displeasure
append	brisk	conclude	disquieting
appetite	bungling	confront	docile
applaud	butchery	consign	dodge
arbiter		consternation	duplicity
ardent	calamity	consummate	
armor	callow	contrivance	edict
arrest	candor	countenance	epitome
arrogant	canon	covey	equivocal
artifice	caress	coy	error

essay	indigenous	palpable	rustic
eternal	indisposed	parody	
evident	indistinct	paroxysm	salutary
exacting	indolent	patent	sanitary
exemplary	inelegant	pedantic	satiate
exquisite	inequity	perceived	saucy
	inflexible	pernicious	scurried
facsimile	ingenuous	persuasive	searching
fashion	inhibition	petition	sedulous
fastidious	inquisitive	petulance	seeming
felicitous	insolvent	pique	shackle
fellowship	intercede	predilection	shrieking
fiction	interminable	prevailing	shudder
fluid	intrepid	prevalent	singe
foul		press	singular
fountain	jaded	princely	skirmish
forsake	just	proclivity	slackness
foretaste		propinquity	snappish
fretful	ken	prudence	snug
furtive	kindle	prying	solicit
	knave	purposeless	sour
garb			sparkling
given	latent	quicksand	splendor
glistening	lofty	quiver	spring
glow	luster		spry
graceful		radiance	still
gratification	majestic	rancor	stipulation
guileless	maladroit	rank	straightway
guiltless	manageable	recant	stratagem
	mandate	receipt	strive
harbor	manifest	recondite	stupor
hasten	maudlin	reduce	subsisting
havoc	meddlesome	refute	suitable
hazard	meet	refractory	supple
heed	merited	relegate	surly
hostile	mischief	relish	surmise
	mitigate	reluctant	
ill-matched	morose	remains	taint
impairment		rend	tarnish
impel	neglected	renegade	tart
impending	nimble	repugnant	taunt
imperfection		reprove	teem
imperturbable	obscure	repudiate	tenuous
implore	obviate	reticent	terminate
inadvertence	ostentation	rude	terrified
incandescent	overbearing	ruse	testy

token	uncivil	unwholesome	vicissitude
towering	underling	upshot	vigilant
trenchant	unfailing		
trespass	unsheltered	vacate	wile
tyrannical	unspotted	veer	wit
	untoward	vernacular	
unceasing	urgency	vestige	zest

Short words
for long ones

The following list will help you find short words or phrases to replace long ones. The list is not meant to do the job of either a dictionary or a thesaurus. Often the suggested substitutes will not fit the longer meaning precisely but may lead you to fresher terms.

You'll find the list helpful if your writing begins to become heavy with polysyllables. In some instances, two or more words or phrases are offered as substitutes. This is to give you another expression for an overworked word.

abandon: give up, desert
abbreviate: shorten
abdicate: give up, resign
abduct: kidnap
abhorrent: disgusting, hateful
ability: skill
abjure: renounce
abolish: do away with
abridge: shorten
abrogate: cancel, do away with
abscond: go off and hide
absolutely: wholly
accede: give in
accelerate: hasten
acceptable: welcome
accessible: easy to reach
accidental: chance
accommodating: obliging
accompany: go with
accomplish: carry out
accurate: correct

accusation: charge
acknowledge: admit, express
    thanks for
acquiesce: agree, accept
acquire: gain
acquit: set free
acrimonious: sharp, bitter
actuate: put in action, move
adamant: hard, inflexible
adapt: make fit
additional: added
adhere: stick fast
adjacent: next to
adjustment: settlement
administer: manage
admonish: warn
adroit: skillful
adverse: harmful
adversity: distress
advocate: speak for
affable: pleasant

affectionate: loving
affluent: rich
aggravate: provoke
aggregate: total
agitate: shake, stir, excite
alacrity: speed
alienate: turn against
allegation: assertion
allegiance: loyalty
alleviate: make easier
allotment: share
allude: refer
alteration: change
altercation: dispute
alternate: take turns
alternative: choice
amalgamate: combine, blend, unite
ambiguous: not clear
amendment: change
amicable: friendly
amplify: make greater
amputate: cut off
animation: life
animosity: hatred
annihilate: destroy
annually: yearly
anonymous: nameless
anticipate: expect
antiquated: out-of-date
apathetic: indifferent
apparent: clear, plain
appease: calm
append: add
appliance: device
apply: put on, use, ask
appoint: name
apportion: divide
apprehend: seize
apprehensive: uneasy
approval: praise, consent
approximately: about
arduous: hard
ascend: climb
ascertain: find out
aspiration: longing

assemble: gather
assembly: meeting
assent: agree
assimilate: absorb, digest
assistance: help
assuredly: surely
astute: shrewd
attain: gain
attempt: try
attractive: pleasing
austere: harsh, stern
authentic: real
authorize: give power
autonomous: independent
available: ready
avaricious: greedy
aversion: dislike

banal: trite
barbarous: coarse, brutal
bargain: deal
bashful: shy
becoming: fitting
belligerent: warlike
beneficial: helpful
benevolent: kindly
bereavement: loss
biannual: twice a year
biennial: every second year
bilateral: two-sided
bizarre: odd, queer

capacity: ability, power, position
captivate: charm
catalogue: list
catechism: set of questions
categorical: positive
censure: blame
certainly: surely
character: nature
characterize: describe
chicanery: trickery
chivalrous: gallant
circuitous: roundabout
circumspect: careful

circumvent: get around
clarify: make clear
collaborate: work together
collection: mass, heap
comical: funny
commence: begin
commencement: start
commiseration: pity
commitment: pledge
commodious: roomy
compassion: pity
compensate: pay
competent: able
component: part
compose: make up
composed: calm, quiet
composition: make-up
compunction: regret
concealment: hiding
conceive: think up
conciliate: win over, soothe
conclude: end
conclusive: final
concrete: real
condescend: stoop to
conformity: likeness
confront: meet
confuse: mix up
conjecture: guess
connoisseur: expert
conscious: aware
consequence: result
considerable: much
consolation: comfort
consolidate: unite, combine
constant: fixed
consternation: dismay
constitute: make up, form
construct: build
constructive: helpful
consume: use up
contaminate: taint
contemplate: think about
contempt: scorn
contemptible: mean
contemptuous: scornful

contingency: chance
continue: keep on
contort: twist, bend
contradict: deny
contribution: gift
convenient: handy
conversation: talk
conversion: change
cooperate: work together
correct: true, right
correspond: agree
corroborate: confirm
counteract: hinder
countermand: cancel, recall
counterpart: copy
courteous: polite
criterion: rule, test
criticize: blame
cryptic: secret
curriculum: course of study
custody: care, keeping
customary: usual

decentralize: scatter
decline: go down, refuse
dedicate: devote
deduct: take away
defective: faulty
deficiency: lack
deficit: shortage
definitive: final
delectable: pleasing
delete: strike out
demonstrate: show
depart: go
deplete: empty
depreciate: lessen
depress: lower
description: kind
designate: name
determine: settle
detest: hate
detrimental: harmful
development: growth
deviate: turn aside
difficult: hard

digress: turn aside
diplomacy: tact
disagreeable: cross
disarrange: disturb
disburse: pay out
discerning: keen
disconnected: undone
discontented: uneasy
discontinue: give up
discount: take off
discordant: harsh
discredit: doubt
discussion: talk
disdain: scorn
disengage: free
disguise: hide
disintegrate: break up
dispatch: send
dispel: drive away
dispense: give out
disperse: scatter
display: show
dispossess: put out
disregard: ignore
disrespectful: rude
disrupt: split
disseminate: scatter
dissimilar: unlike
dissipate: scatter, waste
dissolute: evil
distend: stretch out
distinguish: tell apart
distort: twist
distribute: spread
disturbance: trouble
divert: turn aside
divest: strip off
divulge: tell
doctrine: belief
domesticate: tame
dominant: ruling
dominate: control
domineer: rule over
donation: gift
dubious: doubtful
duplicate: copy

eccentric: odd
economical: thrifty
educate: teach
effect: bring about
effective: getting results
effervescent: bubbling, gay
effusive: pouring out
elect: choose
elevate: raise, lift up
eliminate: throw out
elongate: stretch
elucidate: make clear
elude: slip away
emaciated: thin
emanate: go out from
emancipate: free
emerge: come out
eminent: high
emphasize: stress
employ: hire
employment: work
encounter: meet
encumbrance: burden
endeavor: try
endorsement: support
endowment: gift
engrave: carve
enigma: riddle
enigmatic: puzzling
enmity: hate
entirely: wholly, fully
entirety: whole
equitable: fair
equivalent: equal
erratic: uncertain
erroneous: wrong
erudite: learned
evident: plain
exaggerate: stretch
excessive: too much
execute: carry out
exhausted: worn out, used up
exhibit: show
existence: being
exorbitant: much too high
expand: spread out

expedience: fitness
expedite: make easy, hurry
   along
expenditure: spending, expense
expensive: costly
explicit: clear
extemporaneous: offhand
exterior: outside
exterminate: destroy
external: outer

fabricate: build, make
facilitate: make easy
fallacious: misleading
fallacy: error
fantastic: odd, unreal
fascinate: charm
fatuous: silly
feasible: can be done
felonious: wicked
ferocious: fierce
fictitious: made-up
fluctuate: rise and fall
formulate: draw up
fortunate: lucky
fracture: break
fragile: frail
fragment: piece
frequently: often
frivolous: silly
frustration: defeat
fundamental: basic

generate: produce
genuine: real
germinate: sprout
gigantic: huge
gratify: please
gratuity: gift, tip
gravitate: settle
guarantee: backing, promise

hazardous: risky
humorous: funny

identical: same

illustration: picture
imitate: copy, mimic
imitation: copy
immaculate: pure, spotless
immediately: at once
immense: huge, vast
imminent: near
immoral: evil, wicked
immovable: firm, fixed
impair: harm
impartial: fair, just
imperative: urgent
imperceptible: very slight
imperfection: fault, defect
impertinent: rude, saucy
impetuous: rash
impolite: rude
impostor: cheat, fraud
impotent: helpless
imprudent: rash
inaccuracy: mistake
inactive: idle
inadvertent: careless
inadvisable: unwise
inanimate: lifeless
inattentive: careless
inaugurate: begin
inauspicious: unlucky
incipient: beginning
incisive: cutting
incite: rouse
incoherent: confused
incompetent: unfit
inconsiderate: thoughtless
inconstant: fickle
inconvenience: bother
incorrect: wrong
increase: gain, grow
incredulity: doubt
increment: growth, increase
incumbrance: burden
indebtedness: debts
indefatigable: tireless
indefinite: vague
indemnify: repay
independent: free

indeterminate: vague
indicate: show
indication: sign
indigent: poor, needy
indiscriminate: confused
individual: person
indolent: lazy
indorsement: support
indubitable: certain
ineffectual: useless
inelegant: crude, vulgar
inexhaustible: tireless
inexpedient: unwise
inflexible: stiff, rigid
information: news
infrequent: rare
infuriate: enrage
ingenious: clever
ingenuous: frank, open
inhibition: restraint
inimitable: matchless
initial: first
initiate: begin
injudicious: unwise
injunction: order
innocuous: harmless
innovation: change
inoperative: not working
inquire: ask
inquisitive: curious, prying
insecure: unsafe
insensible: unaware
insidious: wily, sly, tricky
insinuation: hint
insolvent: bankrupt
instruct: teach
instrument: tool
insubstantial: flimsy
insufficient: not enough
intention: aim
interminable: endless
intermission: pause
interrogate: question
interrupt: hinder, stop
intersection: corner
intimate: hint

intimidate: frighten
intrigue: plot
invaluable: priceless
inviting: tempting
irrelevant: off the subject
isolate: set apart

judicious: wise

lenient: mild, gentle
lethargic: dull
liberate: free
liquidate: pay
liveliness: vigor
locality: place
lucid: clear
luminous: bright

magnificent: grand
manifest: clear, plain
manufacture: make
meditate: reflect
melancholy: sad
mentality: mind
mercurial: quick, fickle
meritorious: worthy
meticulous: very careful
minimal: smallest
misapprehension: wrong idea
miserable: wretched
mitigate: make mild, soften
modification: change
morbid: sickly
moribund: dying
municipality: city

narrative: story
nebulous: hazy, vague
negation: denial
neglectful: careless
negotiate: talk business
neutralize: offset
nonsensical: foolish, absurd
notification: notice
notify: let know
numerate: count

objective: aim, goal
obligate: pledge
obligation: duty
oblige: compel, force
oblique: slanting
obliterate: blot out
oblivious: forgetful
obscure: dim
observation: remark
observe: note
obsolete: out-of-date
obstinate: stubborn
obstruction: block, hurdle
obtuse: dull, blunt
obviate: wipe out
obvious, plain
occasion: event, cause
occasionally: now and then
occupy: take up, fill, live in
occurrence: event
officious: meddling
operate: work, run
opportunity: chance
oppose: be against, fight
oppressive: harsh, unjust,
    severe
option: choice
ordinance: rule, law
original: first
originate: invent
ostracize: banish
outrageous: shocking

pacify: make calm
palatable: pleasing
paralyze: cripple
paramount: top, chief,
    supreme
partially: partly
participate: take part
particularize: state in detail
peculiar: odd, strange
pendulous: hanging, swinging
penetrate: pierce
penitent: sorry
peremptory: positive

perforation: hole
permanent: lasting
permission: consent, leave
perpendicular: upright
perpetrate: commit
persevere: persist
persuade: win over
pertain: refer
pertinence: fitness
pharmacist: druggist
phlegmatic: sluggish
pinnacle: peak
placate: soothe
plaintive: sad
poignant: sharp
possess: own
postpone: put off, delay
powerful: strong
practicable: can be done
preclude: shut out
predilection: liking
predominant: superior
preeminent: top
preparedness: readiness
preponderant: chief
preposterous: senseless
presumptuous: forward
principal: main, chief
probability: chance
problematical: doubtful
procedure: way, method
proffer: offer
proficiency: skill
proficient: expert
profound: deep
project: plan
promulgate: proclaim
propensity: bent
prophesy: foretell
proposal: plan
propriety: fitness
provoke: vex, stir up
proximity: nearness
punctilious: exact
punctual: prompt
pungent: sharp

pursue: chase

qualified: fitted
querulous: fretful
quiescent: still, quiet

radiant: bright
radiate: give out
recapitulate: sum up
reciprocal: mutual
recognize: know, accept
recollection: memory
recommendation: praise
reconciliation: settlement
reconstruct: make over
recover: get back
rectify: make right
recuperate: get well
redeem: buy back
redundant: extra, not needed
refrigerate: cool
regulation: rule, law
rehabilitate: restore
reimburse: pay back
reinforce: strengthen
rejoinder: reply
related: akin
reliance: trust
relinquish: give up
remainder: the rest
remedy: cure
remonstrate: protest
remorseless: cruel
repentance: regret
replica: copy
reproduction: copy
repudiate: reject, disown
requisite: needed
rescind: repeal, cancel
resemblance: likeness
residence: house, home
resilience: bounce
resolute: firm
restrain: check
resuscitate: revive
reticent: silent

retrench: cut down
retrieve: bring back
reversion: return
ridiculous: absurd
righteousness: virtue
rigidity: stiffness
rigorous: harsh, strict

sagacious: wise
salacious: lewd
salient: striking, main
sanitary: healthful
saturate: soak, fill
scandalous: shocking
scepticism: doubt
scintillate: sparkle
scrutinize: inspect
segment: part
segregate: set apart, separate
selection: choice
semblance: likeness
shortcoming: fault
similar: like
similarity: likeness
simulate: pretend, feign
sincere: frank
sinecure: easy job
situated: placed
slovenly: untidy
solicit: ask for
solicitous: anxious, eager
solitary: alone
speculate: reflect
stimulate: excite
stringent: strict, tight
stupendous: immense
subsequently: later
subservient: servile
substantial: real, strong,
   large
substantiate: prove
sufficient: enough, ample
suffocate: smother
suitability: fitness
supercilious: proud
superlative: top

supersede: replace
surreptitious: secret

tabulation: table
tantalize: tease
technicality: detail
tempestuous: stormy
tenuous: thin
terminate: end
tortuous: twisting
tranquillity: quiet
transcendent: superior
transcription: copy
transpire: take place
transpose: shift
trepidation: fear
tribulation: trouble
triplicate: triple
triviality: trifle
tumultuous: noisy

ulterior: hidden
ultimate: last, final
unassuming: modest
unavailability: lack
uncertainty: doubt

uncivilized: savage
uncommonly: rarely
uncompromising: firm
uncultivated: wild
undisguised: frank
undulations: curves, waves
unequivocal: clear
unfaltering: firm, steadfast
unfavorable: bad, adverse
unfounded: baseless
ungovernable: unruly
uniformity: sameness
unmistakable: plain, evident
unnecessary: needless
utilize: use

vacillate: waver
validity: truth
variation: change
vehement: eager, forceful
venomous: spiteful
ventilate: air
vigilance: caution
vindicate: defend, justify
visualize: picture
voluminous: bulky

How's your spelling?

Following is a list of 100 words commonly misspelled by all kinds of people. We suggest that you study the list and try to memorize the correct spellings. If you succeed, your memory will be the best spelling teacher you ever had.

hygiene	professor	recede	balloon
kimono	finesse	siege	prairie
appraisal	hindrance	nickel	contemptible
bachelor	inseparable	yeoman	discernible
remittance	concede	occult	dissipated
compatible	negligible	embarrass	conceit
dilapidated	rhythm	accommodate	grammar
misspell	renovate	arraignment	inherent

irreducible	exaggerate	tomato	anomalous
parallel	disappoint	fulfill	canoeing
pavilion	gantlet	accumulate	irrevocable
violoncello	inoculate	dismissal	carrot
reverent	consensus	excerpt	indefensible
proceed	buoy	exhilarate	dissent
seize	permissible	ingenious	irrelevant
tonsillitis	raisin	misstep	exorbitant
gauge	hemorrhage	commitment	oculist
plagiarism	tragedy	personnel	naphtha
ecstasy	separate	recalcitrant	psychology
aberration	unnecessary	saloon	liaison
ascertain	deceive	hypocrisy	receive
coliseum	weird	supersede	secede
precede	harass	villain	sergeant
corroborate	sacrilegious	occurrence	suppress
innocuous	symmetry	propeller	already

One idea
to a sentence

Competition is fierce
for readers' time

Readers these days have less and less time for their newspapers. The competition for their non-working time grows constantly. Television, of course, is the latest competitor and a strong one.

What conclusions should the press draw from this? Well, first, that newspapers should resist further inroads into the time devoted to them by making themselves more attractive and more indispensable. Second, that newspapers should find ways of getting information across to readers more easily, more quickly.

The way to do this is to frame stories so that everything is immediately clear. The reader must never have to go back and reread a sentence to grasp its meaning. He must be able to comprehend at once.

How can this be done? A few years ago a researcher applied himself to the problem. He noticed that one daily columnist-commentator had the reputation of being more understandable than his competitors. He examined the man's writings to find out why. He found that the only major factor that appeared consistently was a shorter average sentence. By "sentence" he meant the number of words between two periods. He did not mean the number between the first word and a semicolon, or between the first word and an "and" or between the first word and a "who" or a "which." He was talking only about the number of words from point to point.

Let's leave aside for the moment whether the diagnosis was completely accurate. The question was whether it would stand up under testing.

Tests were made and continued. The procedure was to submit a news story to a group of college students—not to newspapermen nor even to journalism students, who might have specialized interests, but to ordinary English majors. The students were allowed to read the story only once, but without time limit. Then they were asked a few questions about it to test the information they had derived.

Next, a rewritten version of the story with reduced average sentence length was submitted to a different group of students and the same questions were asked.

Here is an actual story from a trade journal that was tested:

Total word count in this story	271
Total number of sentences	5
Average words per sentence	54

American London Shrinkers Corp. has spent a year and a half experimenting and compiling data on the shrinking and finishing of man-made fibers used in combination with woolen and worsted yarns and is now equipped to handle all types of blends, it is made known by Theodore Trilling, president.

The trend toward blends in suiting and coating woolens and worsteds brought with it the need for a variety of alterations in the shrinking and sponging operation, Mr. Trilling adds, pointing out, for example, that the orlon content in a fabric turned yellow, the rayon and acetate content tended to moiré and the 15 to 20 per cent of nylon now often used to give added strength tended to shine.

No new machinery is involved, just alterations in the processing, such as a change in the action or the weight of the apron of the leader, but it took a lot of trial and error observations, testing to make sure that further shrinkage would not take place, and tabulation of the data before the "we are now in a position" statement could be made, it was added.

Special reports of the tests and their results have been passed along to the mills and selling agents of these blends, and in some cases they have served as a guide in the correction and improvement of these fabrics, Mr. Trilling states.

He adds that his firm has been offering its 100 per cent woolen and worsted finishing and shrinking service to the industry for the past 55 years and that with the alterations to handle blends now completed, an important step has been made.

Questions asked students	Percentage of correct answers
Who is making the statement?	26
What firm is doing the work?	18
How long were experiments under way?	30
What kinds of materials are involved?	11
What, briefly, is the story about?	9

The really significant question is the final one. This is the one, it was decided, that tests reader comprehension. To be rated *correct* an answer did not need to be elaborate. Almost any relevant one- or two-word reply was so rated.

Following is the shorter-sentence version of the same story:

Total word count in this story 265
Total number of sentences 21
Average words per sentence 13

American London Shrinkers Corp. has come to the end of an 18-month search.

One year and a half ago that firm set out to find a safe way to shrink, sponge and handle blended materials without damage. Much experimentation was required. Many volumes of data were gathered. The trial and error method was given a thorough test.

And now—success.

Theodore Trilling, president of American London Shrinkers, has announced that the problem has been solved.

Exactly what was the problem?

The trend toward blends in suiting and coating woolens and worsteds created the necessity for developing some alterations in shrinking and sponging operation.

Mr. Trilling mentioned the color change problem. He pointed out that the orlon content in a fabric turned yellow. The rayon and acetate content tended to moiré. The 15 to 20 per cent of nylon, used to give strength, tended to shine. These color changes do not occur in the new process.

No new machinery is needed, Mr. Trilling said. He made clear that only alterations in the processing are necessary. He referred to alterations such as a change in the action, the weight of the apron or the leader.

The firm's president emphasized that many tests were required to make sure no further shrinking would occur.

Reports of the tests and results have been passed on to the mills and selling agents of these blends, Mr. Trilling said. In some cases the new information has served as a guide in the correction and improvement of fabrics, he added.

This is an important step in the industry, according to Mr. Trilling.

Questions asked students	Percentage of correct answers
Who is making the statement?	68
What firm is doing the work?	55
How long were experiments under way?	71
What kinds of materials are involved?	29
What, briefly, is the story about?	64

Let it be said at once that neither story would win a Pulitzer Prize. Yet, note the 64 per cent comprehension of the second version as against the nine per cent of the original.

When the objection was raised that the story was a technical one and that people in the trade would do better with it, the story was shown to executives and other workers in a mill town. Sure enough, their comprehension of the original piece was higher than that of the students. But—and this is an important but—the rewritten version raised the percentages of correct answers proportionately as much as it had in the case of the students.—From *Watch Your Language* by Theodore M. Bernstein, published by Channel Press, Great Neck, L.I., N.Y., copyright 1958.

Brevity can be the secret of success

Fifty short story classics

Following are the titles of fifty short story classics which every writer should have read but which many haven't. If you haven't read all of them, or if you've forgotten how good some of them were (and still are) take time off to find them in collections or anthologies:

Conrad Aiken:	"Silent Snow, Secret Snow"
Sherwood Anderson:	"I'm a Fool"
Stephen Vincent Benét:	"The Devil and Daniel Webster"
Ambrose Bierce:	"An Occurrence at Owl Creek Bridge"
	"The Damned Thing"
	"The Horseman in the Sky"
Dorothy Canfield:	"The Murder on Jefferson Street"
Anton Chekhov:	"The Bet"
Richard Connell:	"The Most Dangerous Game"
Joseph Conrad:	"Typhoon"
Stephen Crane:	"The Open Boat"
Richard Harding Davis:	"Gallagher"
A. Conan Doyle:	"The Red-Headed League"
	"The Speckled Band"
Lord Dunsany:	"Two Bottles of Relish"
William Faulkner:	"A Rose for Emily"
F. Scott Fitzgerald:	"The Rich Boy"
Anatole France:	"The Procurator of Judea"
Edward Everett Hale:	"The Man Without a Country"
Ernest Hemingway:	"The Killers"
	"The Snows of Kilimanjaro"
	"The Undefeated"
O. Henry:	"The Gift of the Magi"
	"The Third Ingredient"
Washington Irving:	"The Legend of Sleepy Hollow"
	"Rip Van Winkle"
W. W. Jacobs:	"The Monkey's Paw"
Jerome K. Jerome:	"The Passing of the Third Floor Back"
James Joyce:	"Boarding House"
Rudyard Kipling:	"Rikki-Tikki-Tavi"
Ring Lardner:	"Champion"
	"Golden Honeymoon"
	"Haircut"
D. H. Lawrence:	"The Rocking-Horse Winner"
Katherine Mansfield:	"The Garden Party"
W. Somerset Maugham:	"Rain"
Guy de Maupassant:	"The Necklace"
	"A Piece of String"
Dorothy Parker:	"Big Blonde"

Edgar Allan Poe:	"The Gold-Bug"
	"The Murders in the Rue Morgue"
	"The Pit and the Pendulum"
William Saroyan:	"The Daring Young Man on the Flying Trapeze"
Irwin Shaw:	"The Girls in Their Summer Dresses"
John Steinbeck:	"The Red Pony"
Frank R. Stockton:	"The Lady, or the Tiger?"
James Thurber:	"The Secret Life of Walter Mitty"
Mark Twain:	"The Man That Corrupted Hadleyburg"
Henry Van Dyke:	"The Other Wise Man"
Stewart Edward White:	"The Weight of Obligation"

This Lesson, "Some final pointers," concludes Volume II of *Principles of good writing*—the two-volume preliminary Course which must be taken by every student of the Famous Writers School. As we said earlier, it's a Course we have made obligatory because we believe it serves a twofold purpose:

1. To orient the beginning student in what the School and its Faculty feel are the useful fundamentals of writing;

2. To refresh the more advanced student in his recollections of work previously undertaken in school or college.

Now that you have finished Volumes I and II, along with the Home Projects and Assignments accompanying them, you are ready to take up the special field of writing you chose when you enrolled as a student. Whether your field is fiction, non-fiction, advertising or business writing, what you have learned in *Principles of good writing* will guide you in all your future work.

As we have pointed out many times, the Famous Writers School *cannot create talent in any field of writing*. All we can do is teach you by the methods we have designed—teach you to express yourself as clearly and effectively as your capabilities permit. However, Volumes I and II have been designed to increase these capabilities by exposing you to the methods used by professional writers. If you have profited from this simple and direct method of teaching, then you are well equipped to achieve even greater success with the Lessons we offer you in the two final Volumes to come.

	Proof marking	Explanation	Corrected proof
⊙	The proof∧	Insert period	The proof.
(:)	The proof∧	Insert colon	The proof:
;	The proof∧	Insert semicolon	The proof;
ॳ	The boys proof	Insert apostrophe	The boy's proof
ॳ	The proof∧	Insert comma	The proof,
ॳ/ॳ	Mark it ∧proof∧	Insert quotation marks	Mark it "proof"
ॳ/ॳ	Mark it ∧proof∧	Insert single quotation marks	Mark it 'proof'
(/)	The proof∧1∧	Insert parentheses	The proof (1)
[/]	The ∧Jones∧boy	Insert brackets	The [Jones] boy
!	Prove it∧	Insert exclamation mark	Prove it!
?	Is it good∧	Insert question mark	Is it good?
=	A by∧line	Insert hyphen	A by-line
$\frac{1}{en}$	January∧June	Insert 1-en dash	January – June
$\frac{1}{em}$	He ∧John ∧said	Insert 1-em dash	He — John — said
$\frac{2}{em}$	Mr. A∧	Insert 2-em dash	Mr. A ——
ॳ	$A^2+B^2=C$∧	Insert superior figure	$A^2+B^2=C^2$
ॳ	Water, H∧O	Insert inferior figure	Water, H_2O
⊐	[The proof	Move right	The proof
⊏	[The proof	Move left	The proof
‖	‖Three women Two men	Align type	Three women Two men
⊓	T∧h∧e proof	Move up	The proof
⊔	T∧h∧e proof	Move down	The proof
=	The pr∧oof	Straighten line	The proof
⊓	The proof	Indent 1 em	The proof

Proof marking	Explanation	Corrected proof
The proof	Indent 2 ems	The proof
The proof	Indent 3 ems	The proof
The proof	Delete	The proof
The proof	Delete and close up	The proof
less # The proof	Less space	The proof
The proof	No space	The proof
# The proof	Insert space	The proof
# → The proof was read by Jones	Insert space between lines	The proof was read by Jones
even # A good proof	Even space	A good proof
tr. A proof good	Transpose	A good proof
l.c. The proof	Lower case	The proof
s.c. The proof	Small caps	THE PROOF
c.s.c. The proof	Caps and small caps	THE PROOF
caps The Proof	Caps	THE PROOF
ital. The proof	Set in Italic	*The* proof
rom. The proof	Set in Roman	The proof
b.f. The proof	Set in boldface	**The** proof
stet. The proof	Let it stand	The proof
¶ read. The	Start new paragraph	read. The
no ¶ marked. Three men	No paragraph: run in	marked. Three men
sp. King Geo.	Spell out	King George
figs. twenty-five	Use figures	25
(t/?) Carker	Spelling questioned	Carter
(?) Proof ∧ read by	Is this right?	Proof was read by

Principles of good writing

Acknowledgments

The Famous Writers School thanks these writers, publishers and literary agents for permission to use the materials listed below:

American Medical Association: passages from "Why Men Don't Talk to Their Wives" by Marjorie Holmes, *Today's Health*, August 1958, and *Reader's Digest*, February 1959, by permission of Ruth Aley, literary agent.

American Philosophical Society: passages from "Our Widening Culture" by Frederick Lewis Allen, condensed in *Reader's Digest*, August 1940.

Associated Press: passage from newspaper item, *New York Herald Tribune*, August 7, 1958.

Author & Journalist: passages from "Book Reviewing, Anyone?" by Robert Averett, June 1958.

Channel Press, Inc.: passages from *Watch Your Language* by Theodore M. Bernstein, © 1958.

Curtis Publishing Company: passages from: "We Pooled Our Resources" by Betty Coe Spicer, *Ladies' Home Journal*, © June 1957; "New England Boiled Dinner," *Ladies' Home Journal*, © January 1958; "Fashion Separates—Night and Day" by Nora O'Leary, *Ladies' Home Journal*, © November 1957; *The Saturday Evening Post*, editorial, May 1958, permission of J. C. Furnas.

J. M. Dent & Son, Ltd.: passages from "Typhoon" by Joseph Conrad, © 1927.

Dodd, Mead & Company, Inc.: passage from *South Wind* by Norman Douglas, © 1925.

Doubleday & Co., Inc.: passages from: *The Glory Road* by Bruce Catton, © 1952; *From Lexington to Liberty* by Bruce Lancaster, © 1955; *The Moon and Sixpence* by W. Somerset Maugham, © 1919; *Something of Value* by Robert Ruark, © 1955 by Robert Ruark; *I Wanted to Write* by Kenneth Roberts, © by Anna M. Roberts and the Canal National Bank of Portland, Maine, executor of the estate of Kenneth and Anna M. Roberts.

Ford Times: "Horse Farms of the Bluegrass Country" by Mary Jane Gallaher, © June 1959 by Ford Motor Company.

John Hancock Mutual Life Insurance Co.: advertisement in *The Saturday Evening Post,* February 11, 1950.

Harcourt, Brace and Co.: passage from *Fundamentals of Good Writing* by Cleanth Brooks and Robert Penn Warren, © 1950.

Harper & Brothers: passages from: *The Way to Write* by Rudolf Flesch and A. H. Lass, © 1947, 1949; *A New Way to Better English* by Rudolf Flesch, © 1958; *Inside U.S.A.* by John Gunther, © 1947 by the author, © 1947 by Curtis Publishing Co.; *Writing and Rewriting* by Harry L. Shaw, © 1946; *The Art of Readable Writing* by Rudolf Flesch, © 1949; *Reading for Pleasure* by Bennett Cerf, © 1957 by Bennett Cerf; *Making Ads Pay* by John Caples, © 1957; "Calamophobia or Hints Toward a Writer's Discipline" by Jacques Barzun from *The Writer's Book,* edited by Helen Hull, © 1950.

Hawthorn Books, Inc.: *The Writer's Craft* by Frederic Birmingham, © 1958: passages by Richard Gehman in the chapter "The Personality Piece"; by Ben Hibbs in the chapter "Jungle Lore."

Hearst Corporation: passage from "Quilt Making" from *Good Housekeeping,* October 1958.

Henry Holt and Company, Inc.: passages from: *A Guide to Creative Writing* by Roger Garrison, © 1951; *Brave Men* by Ernie Pyle, © 1944.

Houghton Mifflin Co.: passage from *Song of the Lark* by Willa Cather, © 1943.

Alfred A. Knopf, Inc.: passages from: *The Spoor of Spooks* by Bergen Evans, © 1954; "Gold Spurs" from *Swords and Roses* by Joseph Hergesheimer, © 1928–29 by Joseph Hergesheimer; "The Sculptor's Funeral" from *Youth and the Bright Medusa* by Willa Cather, © 1920; "The Strongest Lady" from *Out of the Red* by Red Smith, © 1950; *Galatea* by James M. Cain, © 1953; *The Spirit of Liberty* by Judge Learned Hand, © 1953; "The Feel" from *Farewell to Sport* by Paul Gallico, © 1938.

Little, Brown & Co.: passages from: *History of the U. S. Operations in World War II,* volume IV, by Samuel Eliot Morison, © 1949 by the author; *Men Against the Sea* by Charles Nordhoff and James Norman Hall, © 1934; "Yellow Girl" from *Jackpot* by Erskine Caldwell, © 1940 by the author.

The Macmillan Co.: passages from: *Writing and Revising* by William S. Morgan, © 1957; *Magazine Article Writing* by Ernest Brennecke, Jr., and Donald Lemen Clark, © 1946; *Tales of the South Pacific* by James Michener, © 1946, 1947, 1954.

G. & G. Merriam Co. Definitions from *Webster's New Collegiate Dictionary,* © 1949.

Otto Nathan, Esq., trustee for the estate of Albert Einstein: passages from "Science and Life," subtitle "Ten Fateful Years," from *Out of My Later Years* by Albert Einstein, © 1950.

New York Times: passages from news item, London dateline, December 8, 1958; column by Charles Poore, London dateline, June 14, 1958; "The Art of Letter Writing by an Expert" by Robert Moses from *New York Times Magazine,* March 2, 1958.

Newsweek, Inc.: passage from "Uncaged," *Newsweek,* February 23, 1959.

Oxford University Press: passage from *A Study of History* by Arnold J. Toynbee, abridgment by D. C. Somervell, vol. II, © 1957.

A. D. Peters, London: passage from *Midnight on the Desert* by J. B. Priestley, *Reader's Digest,* February 1959, permission of Harper & Brothers in U.S.A. and William Heinemann and Company, Ltd., in England.

Post Publishing Company: passage from item in *The Bridgeport* (Conn.) *Post.*

Rand McNally & Co.: passage from *Kon Tiki: Across the Pacific by Raft,* by Thor Heyerdahl, © 1950 by the author.

Random House, Inc.: passages from: *Between the Thunder and the Sun* by Vincent Sheean, © 1943; *Postmark Murder* by Mignon G. Eberhart, © 1955; "Love in Wartime" from *The Young Lions* by Irwin Shaw, © 1948; *The Desperate Hours* by Joseph Hayes, © 1954 by Marijane and Joseph Hayes; "No Mistakes" from *Selected Short Stories of John O'Hara,* published by Modern Library, Inc., courtesy of Random House, © 1956; *The American College Dictionary,* © 1949.

Rath Packing Company: advertisement for "Chop-ettes."

Reader's Digest: "He Invented a New Kind of Goodness" by Donald Culross Peattie, © 1941 by the author, permission of *Reader's Digest* and James Brown Associates, Inc.; "Frozen Sleep: New Frontier in Surgery" by J. D. Ratcliff, *Reader's Digest,* September 1958; "The Truth About Hawks" by Peter Farb, *Reader's Digest,* June 1958; "Advertising: Its Contribution to the American Way of Life" by Bruce Barton, *Reader's Digest,* April 1955; *Reader's Digest* Tappan Company ad as it appeared in *Time,* May 11, 1959.

Reynal & Co.: passages from *The Reporter's Trade* by Joseph and Stewart Alsop, © 1958.

Rinehart & Co., Inc.: passages from: *American Family* by Faith Baldwin, © 1935; *Blockade* by Robert Carse, © 1958; *Forests of the Night* by Jack Denton Scott, © 1959.

Rolls-Royce, Inc.: advertisement as it appeared in *The New Yorker,* March 7, 1959.

Science Service: passages from "Don'ts for Would-Be Writers of Science" by Edwin E. Slosson from *Science News Letter.*

Scott, Foresman & Co.: passages from *Writer's Guide and Index to English* (revised edition) by Porter G. Perrin, © 1950.

Charles Scribner's Sons: passages from: "The Killers" from *Men Without Women* by Ernest Hemingway, © 1927; *Ethan Frome* by Edith Wharton, © 1911 and 1922, Modern Student Library edition.

Max Shulman: "A Connecticut Yankee in Queen Elizabeth's Court," © 1952.

Simon and Schuster, Inc.: passages from *Patterns* by Rod Serling, © 1957.

Street & Smith Publications: passage from "Summer Jobs" by Joan Alleman Rubin, *Mademoiselle*, March 1958, © 1958.

Time, Inc.: passages from: "Garden Addict Kicks the Habit" by Phyllis McGinley, *Life,* May 12, 1958; "The Death of Calvin Coolidge," *Time,* January 16, 1933; "Pope John XXIII's First Papal Mass," *Time,* November 10, 1958; "The Weather—January Thaw," *Time,* February 2, 1959.

United Feature Syndicate, Inc.: passage from "I Hate Hats" by Robert Ruark. Column by Inez Robb.

United Newspapers Magazine Corp.: passage from "Dizzy—but Scientific" from *This Week* magazine, May 26, 1957, © 1957.

U.S. News Publishing Corp.: passage from *U.S. News and World Report.*

Viking Press: passage from *Of Mice and Men* by John Steinbeck from *The Short Novels of John Steinbeck,* © 1953.

Warner-Lambert Pharmaceutical Co.: Listerine advertisement.

The Writer, Inc.: passages from: "Literary Discipline" by Mignon G. Eberhart from *The Writer's Handbook,* edited by A. S. Burack; "Busting the Block" by Willard Marsh, *The Writer,* June 1958.

The School would like to tender special thanks to the staffs of the Public Library of Westport, Connecticut, and the Pequot Library of Southport, Connecticut, for their help in identifying research and reference sources.

Principles of good writing

Index

A

This volume of
Principles of Good Writing
is set in Times New Roman type.

The format and binding were designed by
Bradbury Thompson.

The illustrations are by
Ric Estrada.

It was composed, printed and bound by
H. Wolff Book Manufacturing Company
of New York City.

The text paper is
Perkins & Squier Antique made by
P. H. Glatfelter Paper Company.